Where Past Meets Present

THE AMAZING PEOPLE, PLACES & STORIES OF SOUTHERN OREGON

DENNIS M. POWERS

HELLGATE PRESS   ASHLAND, OREGON

WHERE PAST MEETS PRESENT

Published by Hellgate Press

(An imprint of L&R Publishing, LLC)

Hellgate Press
PO Box 3531
Ashland, OR 97520
email: sales@hellgatepress.com

Cover & Interior Design: L. Redding

Library of Congress Cataloging-in-Publication Data available from the publisher on request

ISBN: 978-1-55571-870-1

Printed and bound in the United States of America
First edition 10 9 8 7 6 5 4 3 2 1

After numerous books published, I have dedicated previous ones to my parents, my so supportive wife (Judy), and other important people in my life. This time, I dedicate to my son (Denny M.), my daughter and her husband (Kimberly and Pascal), and my granddaughter (Aela). I add my long-time agent and friend, Jeanne Fredericks. And all of you who have been friends over time.

Advanced Praise for *Where Past Meets Present*:

"There are many surprises in *Where Past Meets Present*, from interesting people and strange places to little known facts and milestone events. A must for anyone who wants a better understanding of what makes Southern Oregon unique."

—Ron Brown, Retired KDRV-TV Anchor/Reporter

"A well-researched and entertaining history of Southern Oregon and its people, places, and institutions. Complete with photos from the Southern Oregon Historical Society archives…a must-have book for anyone interested in local history."

—Ed Battistella, SOU Professor of Humanities and Culture, Oregon Book Award Finalist, Linguistic and Historical Researcher/Writer

"…a wonderful collection of historical nuggets from our region. It will be read (and re-read, again and again) by newcomers and long-time residents alike."

—Jeff LaLande, Co-Editor-in-Chief of the *Oregon Encyclopedia of History and Culture*

"…a delightful and engaging romp through the history of Southern Oregon! Its stories are a perfect entree into the people, places and events of this area's rich and interesting past."

—George Kramer, Kramer & Company, Historic Preservation Consultants

"As an avid history buff and longtime fan of Dennis Powers' stellar prose, I looked forward to *Where Past Meets Present* with great expectations. It did not disappoint… this talented author informs and entertains. It is a fun, enlightening read."

—Paul Fattig, Journalist and Author of *Up Sterling Creek Without a Paddle*

"*Where Past Meets Present* is a meticulous and remarkable history of the Southern Oregon area (which includes the most northern parts of California). It's a massive work—astonishing in its depth and breadth—that will serve not only as a reference book but offers a lucid, engaging narrative."

—Chris Honore, Journalist

CONTENTS

Where Past Meets Present

THE AMAZING PEOPLE, PLACES & STORIES OF SOUTHERN OREGON

AUTHOR'S NOTE

THIS BOOK IS A COMPILATION OF DIFFERENT TOPICS discussed on the "Past and Present" radio show aired on KMED-AM, 1440, in Medford, Oregon, hosted by Bill Meyer. These weekly shows started in mid-2013 and are still going strong after four years — past this publication date. I thank, again, Bill Meyer and Bill Ashenden (Bi-Coastal Media's General Manager in Medford) for their support.

Relying on over 200 stories I wrote for another favorite radio show of mine, "As It Was," (aired on Jefferson Public Radio with its long-time editor, Kernan Turner), a 175-storied CD produced with Ryan Mallory ("Past and Present: What You Might Not Know (But Want To) About Southern Oregon History"), and different sources, I looked for articles in this book that would include our region's standout stories.

I have always believed that history should be entertaining, as well as informative, and that we can see the past in our present lives. When I first arrived here over twenty years ago, I remember wondering what was the "State of Jefferson," the "flood" (being the 1964 Rogue River flood), who was Ben Hur Lampman (as well as his poetry), or how different towns became named. Why is "Sasquatch" part of our lore, and what about this mystical Vortex, the House of Mystery? A race track inside our first airport?

Not every subject or topic (another volume, perhaps?) could be included. And although every effort has been made to be accurate, this is not intended to be a historical reference book. It is also impossible to list all of the references that went into any particular article, as this would create an unwieldy, thirty-five page bibliography.

Anyone who wants to learn more or update any subject can start with the "Partial Bibliography" and their favorite search engine. An Internet search of your local newspaper — whether the *Grants Pass Daily Courier,*

Ashland Daily Tidings or the *Medford Mail Tribune* — may also be useful. Other sources are named as well.

I hope that you enjoy reading these stories: history that's informative, entertaining, and that you can see, enjoy, or touch today. Cheers!

—Dennis Powers

PART I

Buildings, Roads, and Institutions

The Early Days of Cars in the Valley

*A*S BACKGROUND, THE 1901 CURVED DASH OLDSMOBILE was the first automobile to be mass produced in the U.S.; Henry Ford in 1908 introduced the Model T, and this was very successful. After installing the first conveyor belt-based assembly line in 1913, Ford became the world's largest car manufacturer. By 1927, fifteen million Model T's had been built.

It took time for cars to be accepted, as roads, service stations, and transportation networks needed to be constructed. In the early 1900s, horses, buggies, and wagons predominated. Elmer Elwood, a jeweler and later optometrist, is credited with owning the first car in the Valley; in fact, it was the first privately owned automobile south of Salem. In 1903, he pushed his car from the Medford train station to his home; unfortunately, it wouldn't start and he needed a new engine installed before being drivable. When Elwood's family moved to Northern California, the car caught fire and was destroyed.

In early 1905, the Orchard Boom was starting. A rich orchardist, Albert Allen, then owned two Oldsmobiles and these were the only two in Jackson County. William Hodson left Roseburg in late 1906 for Medford to open a garage and buy a "carload" of automobiles from the factory. Although he is credited with starting and owning Medford's first car dealership, he became bankrupt in late 1910 and lost the business.

Despite Hodson's woes, the automobile's acceptance over time brought about streets (dirt roads, however, were tough during the rains), gasoline stations (where before, gasoline was only available at hardware stores), more garages (livery stables were converted), and legal changes. In Grants

Ford touring car with not a service station in sight. (Southern Oregon Historical Society (SOHS) #12082)

Pass, for example, one law required that pedestrians and horse-drawn carriages had the right-of-way; despite this, the noisy, erratic automobiles scared horses and caused accidents.

Model Ts were shipped with the frame and body needing to be assembled—five to a railcar—so the owner had to put his car together before it could be driven. After a ship brought one owner's new White Steamer to Crescent City, he had to have it hauled over the mountains on a lumber wagon since passable roads didn't exist.

Before better roads and the Collier Tunnel, driving to the ocean was an adventure in itself. Although the need to continually rest tired horses that pulled wagons—especially up passes—had ended, the trip to Crescent City was risky. One newspaper reported: "The modern vehicle travels up the steep grade at ten miles an hour, or more, and coasts downward at a speed only limited by the driver's nerve and ability to turn sharp corners, where one skid of a foot would plunge the whole party down the mountainside to instant death on the rocks below."

The Orchard Boom accelerated the need for cars in the Valley to such an extent that a *Medford Mail Tribune* article on November 28, 1909, reported that the city led the world that year in the number of automobiles per capita. It noted that Medford had one automobile for every thirty people when nationally there was one car for every 500 people. The reason was the wealth and numbers living in town who needed to travel daily to the orchards located away. This is now known as the modern commute.

An example of the development required was Highway 199 from Southern Oregon to Crescent City. The Redwood Highway was a "mean" trail until the Oregon Mountain Tunnel came to the rescue. This passage started as a wagon route in the late 1850s to connect Jacksonville with Crescent City and its port. Although the route was improved numerous

Scene on a road near Prospect, OR, 1915. (SOHS #20863)

times, for decades this trip was dangerous, especially with the "jeep path" through Hazel View Mountain's timber and brush summit. The tunnel construction through the mountain began in 1960, cost over $30 million dollars, and took three years.

When Randolph Collier—the California state senator who rammed the project through and the tunnel is named after—cut the ribbon, the tunnel and its twenty-three miles of roadway eliminated 128 turns and five, tortuous switchbacks over the steep pass. From twenty-five miles-per-hour over a dangerous summit to the present sixty miles-per-hour drive, we motor from the Valley to and from Crescent City in the comfort we now take for granted.

Sources: Powers, "As It Was," 2011; Miller, *Medford Mail Tribune*, 2010; Miller, *Medford Mail Tribune*, 2013.

Note: For any particular cite search in the Partial Bibliography, the following newspaper names have been shortened: *Medford Mail Tribune* (*Mail Tribune*), *Ashland Daily Tidings* (*Daily Tidings*), *Grants Pass Daily Courier* (*Daily Courier*) and the *Eugene Register Guard* (*Register Guard*).

Interstate 5 (I-5)

W E SOMETIMES TAKE INTERSTATE 5 (I-5) FOR GRANTED, but building this fast, vital connection through Oregon took time, money, and politics to accomplish. This transportation network connected the small towns in Southern Oregon—from Ashland to beyond Grants Pass—with the same advantages as the much larger cities of Portland and San Francisco.

The interstate is 308 miles long from the California state line to the Columbia River, was established by the Federal-Aid Highway Act of 1956 (FAHA) under President Dwight D. Eisenhower, and was part of the overall 41,000 mile network of roadways built throughout the nation. When completed through Oregon in 1966, this state became the first one west of the Mississippi to finish its interstate connection.

Like many other rural states, pre I-5 highways were usually two lanes with roadside businesses, stoplights, crossroads, and twisting curves over mountain passes. Under the interstate design criteria, on- and off-ramps controlled how cars intersected, businesses were located away from the freeway, and cross streets placed over or under the freeway.

By 1953, the State of Oregon had started on its limited-access and grade-separated (or cross streets that didn't directly intersect) roadways. These avoided existing roads and included the Portland-Salem Expressway (later named the Baldock Freeway) and Banfield Freeway (east of Portland). Underneath the FAHA's provisions, the federal government subsidized 90% of expenses of the to-be-built interstate network.

The Oregon Highway Department decided that the freeway construction would be in sections which allowed parts to be started and finished at different times. Delayed completions of politically-charged sections (as with the viaduct over Medford) and difficult ones (the Siskiyou Pass and Summit), therefore, wouldn't delay completion of less-complicated segments.

Siskiyou switchback before I-5 was built. (SOHS #197057112)

In Medford, businesses did not want the proposed I-5 to bypass them in favor of an alternate route along Hillcrest Road. These commercial interests strongly believed if the thoroughfare didn't follow the downtown route of Bear Creek, that they would lose significant business. The strongest opposition was largely from the orchardists, who didn't want the freeway going through their pear lands to the east and the west of downtown.

They made their case to Glenn Jackson, who later would be appointed to the Oregon Highway Commission, and Earl Miller, Medford's Mayor, who agreed with their arguments. Although the central route brought important traffic closer, this would cut the town in half, had no place for on-ramps, and was expensive. Although the decision was controversial, the powers-to-be decided in 1956 to put I-5 over Medford, and the I-5 Central Point to Barnett Road off-ramps opened in 1962; the Barnett-to-Ashland section was completed in late-July 1963.

The Siskiyou Summit is not only the highest of any I-5 pass (at 4,310 feet), but it handles the most traffic with the steepest grade. Its course over the Siskiyou Mountains came from political pressure by those who wanted the new freeway to run parallel to U.S. Highway 99 through the Rogue Valley, not parallel to U.S. 97 through central Oregon. As with all freeway construction, homes and businesses in the right-of-way had to relocate. Callahan's Siskiyou Lodge was no different. The owners used the condemnation money to buy a larger piece of land a short distance up Old Highway 99, below the Siskiyou summit and just off Exit 6 from I-5. When this portion was completed in 1964, Callahan's reopened in July 1965 where it's now located. Old Highway 99 was deactivated upon the freeway's completion; despite that this four-lane, modern freeway over the summit is better designed than the previous two-lane, twisting course, winter storms still can close it down for a day or two.

The California-Oregon border at the Siskiyou Summit does not have an exit and is designated the "0" mileage point. Heading north towards

Two women posing on the Siskiyou Summit at the Oregon-California state line, 1925. (SOHS #18356)

Ashland and eventually Portland, approximately one mile away is Exit 1 at the Siskiyou Summit. Each exit number from that point is the number of rounded miles traveled from the border. Accordingly, Exit 19 is 19 miles away at the Valley View turnoff; and one has driven 30 miles once at Medford's Exit 30 for Highway 62 and Crater Lake.

When the last link through Oregon was completed in October 1966, I-5 was ready for the public's transit through this state. It still is as valuable now as it was then.

Sources: Kramer (George), *Oregon Encyclopedia*; *Medford Mail Tribune*, April 22, 2007 (two articles); Kramer (George), "The Interstate Highway System in Oregon."

The Orchard
Boom and Bust

WITH THE RAILROAD CONNECTING Southern Oregon to Portland, other cities in the state and country, as well as international markets, the orchard industry took hold and flourished. Countless acres were planted with fruit trees, especially apples at first and then pears. The Medford Commercial Club—now the Chamber of Commerce—promoted a long advertising campaign in the early 1900s about the great advantages of the area's orchard industry: Anyone could plant fruit trees and make enough money to retire on. The Southern Pacific railroad and real estate industry joined the chorus of advertising promotions in moving this along.

Real estate agents met the out-of-towners arriving at the Medford railroad station and hawked the orchards. Although the speculation eventually led to a terrible bust, Medford was cemented as Jackson County's commercial center. Newspapers reported that newcomers were jamming the hotels, and even Southern Pacific Railroad bedded down up to 200 potential investors nightly at its station; an independent venture even set up a tent city. With this background, wealthy Easterners and Mid-Westerners flocked to the Valley.

Whether wealthy Easterners or poorer farmers, newcomers joined residents in buying, managing, and selling orchards. From 1905, the boom continued to where two years later, a carload of Comice pears from Bear Creek Orchards sold at an auction in New York City for $4,600, the highest ever. The 1909 real estate sales in the area totaled $5 million with a record $2,300 paid per orchard acre.

From bringing about the city's main water supply and Sacred Heart Hospital (later Providence Medical Hospital) to building Medford's historic downtown, residents and the wealthy out-of-towners contributed.

Smudge Pots in Central Point orchard. (SOHS #13301)

By 1909, numerous Medford buildings were under construction or in the planning stages. Buildings with the names of Sparta, the Carnegie library, Woolworth building, and four-story Liberty building were built or under construction. By 1912, Medford had a high school, four banks, three elementary schools, a city park, new passenger depot, Carnegie library, indoor swimming pool, several movie theatres, and an opera house. Streets were paved and electricity with telephone service stretched to outlying areas.

Along with the hype and inexperienced buyers, the con men were also busy. North of Medford in the Agate Desert (where White City now is), promoters planted more than 400 acres in the desert-like area. Although the land was not suitable for fruit trees as apples and pears due to the numerous rocks, the swindlers answered that this was the best point: Since the rocks kept the heat from the day's sun, smudge pots weren't needed at night. Although the successful orchards were planted elsewhere, the gullible forked over their money.

A Chicago promoter bought land on Roxy Ann Butte, covered the rocks with layers of dirt, and planted fruit trees. Promoting out-of-state by telephone, he sold plots for $15 dollars down and $15 a month so that the investors could retire later to a "little place." The trees died, the buyers lost everything, and the promoters disappeared.

In 1910, valley nurseries reported that one-million trees were contracted to be planted. The inevitable bust occurred when the hype couldn't match the fruit oversupply and overzealous real estate speculation—with even the hustlers going broke. Owing to World War I, the blockades had ended the pear (and other fruits) international markets; insect blight, frost, drought, and forced sales didn't help either. Medford's population by 1920 had dropped by twenty-eight percent, all due to the orchard bust, and it took years to recover.

Nearly one hundred years later the same type of boom-to-bust economic cycle occurred again in real estate speculation as well as the lumber and building construction industries.

Sources: Truwe, *"Southern Oregon History, Revised*: The Orchard Boom and Bust"; Dunn, *Land in Common*, 1993; Atwood, *Oregon History Project*: "Orchard Boom and Bust"; Powers, JPR: "As It Was," September 7, 2009; Fattig, *Medford Mail Tribune*, November 1, 2009.

Rogue Community College

$\mathcal{R}$OGUE COMMUNITY COLLEGE (RCC) dates back to when Jackson County in 1970 voted "no" to a ballot measure creating a two-county district for a two-year community college. Josephine County passed a $330,000 levy at the same time to start its college. RCC began at the original campus — known as the Redwood Campus — located five miles west of Grants Pass off Highway 199 where the Fort Vannoy Job Corps Training Center operated in the late 1960s.

By 1971, the startup Josephine County college had 1,000 students. The problem was that Jackson County students needed to drive past Grants Pass to attend and then pay a high tuition. Into the early 1980s, RCC grew steadily but without a Medford presence.

In 1984, Dr. Harvey Bennett left Eastern Oregon State College in La Grande to serve as RCC's Dean of Instruction. The following year, the college opened a Medford Center in the former KOBI-TV building and began its search for a new college president; it named Dr. Bennett as its president in 1986 from eighty candidates. When the search committee asked Bennett if he was willing to get "down in the trenches," he replied that this "depends on what's in the trenches."

During the critical annexation period whereby Jackson County could join RCC, Dr. Bennett knew he had a hard task ahead. The counties mistrusted one another, Southern Oregon College (now SOU) feared that it would lose enrollment, and uncertainty existed over what a community college's role was with a four-year institution. Overcoming these obstacles wouldn't be easy and would take time.

Along the way, Dr. Bennett had the Redwood campus upgraded from its "shabby collection of old Job Corps buildings" when he first arrived. RCC and SOU also signed a contract that allowed SOU to bring upper division classes to Josephine County and RCC's Medford Center. Working closely with the state legislature, SOU leaders, and community officials, Bennett continued to lobby and press with humor for the annexation.

The long-worked-for annexation was passed in 1996 by over 80% of the voters in both Jackson and Josephine Counties. Moneys were set aside by the state, and RCC with SOU partnered to plan courses and tuition costs. Bennett worked closely with SOU President Steve Reno on this accord: RCC would offer basically the same first two years of undergraduate curriculum as SOU, so students could take their pick. In return, SOU agreed on procedures allowing more RCC students to transfer to SOU for their junior and senior years.

In 1997, RCC leased three downtown Medford buildings and hired twenty-seven instructors for its new Riverside campus. Quickly expanding to seven buildings, by 1998 RCC's Medford enrollment passed Josephine County's by 1,000 students (4,000 to 3,000). The Oregon Community College Association in 1998 awarded Dr. Bennett its "Pacesetter of the Year" award. With RCC's strong presence in Medford, he announced his retirement one year later.

RCC continued to expand. In 2005, it established the Table Rock campus at White City that offers, among other courses, technical programs including diesel technology, electronics, landscaping, and commercial truck driving. Three years later, a joint Higher Education Center opened in a brand new building.

Owned and operated jointly with SOU, this 68,700-sq. ft. center serves both RCC and SOU students in a partnership designed to ease their transition into higher education. Both schools offer multiple classes at the center, including math, art and biology through RCC with business, psychology, education, and other classes from SOU. RCC-Medford also consolidated operations into the new center.

In addition to the RCC/SOU Higher Education Center and the RCC campuses in Grants Pass, Medford, and White City, other facilities now include the Illinois Valley Business Entrepreneurial Center in Kerby and the Small Business Development Center in downtown Grants Pass, among others.

In 2016, Jackson County voters overwhelmingly approved RCC's $20 million bond to pay for new buildings in both Jackson and Josephine counties. The funds include a new facility or remodel of existing

RCC Medford campus, circa 2005 (*top*) and today.

buildings at the White City, Medford, and Grants Pass campuses—all to increase the courses and classes offered.

RCC offers numerous two-year degree programs, over 80 career and technical training programs, and community education classes. One of seventeen community colleges in Oregon, RCC employs over 100 full-time and 650 part-time faculty with 20,000 students in total. The Medford campus still leads in enrollment as to the three main campuses.

Sources: Jay, *Medford Mail Tribune*, 1999; Landers, *Medford Mail Tribune*, 2007. Varble, *Medford Mail Tribune*, 2013. See generally, "Rogue Community College," at its website.

Rogue Valley International-
Medford Airport

*L*OCATED AT THE FORMER FAIRGROUNDS ON Medford's south end — and bought for use by the U.S. Forest Service — the City of Medford and Jackson County in 1922 purchased the Medford field known as Newell-Barber field. This was the first field in Oregon bought to be used as a municipal airport, and its gravel runway was 1500 ft. long and 25 ft. wide. Pacific Air Transport Company was granted an initial four-year lease for one dollar and built its hangars and administration building; Standard Oil Company received the exclusive contract to sell gasoline and oil.

Granted a U.S. Post Office air-mail contract in 1926 to carry mail from Los Angeles to Seattle, Medford was the only stop between San Francisco and Portland on the first airmail route over the Pacific Coast. This contract meant financial stability for a new venture such as Pacific Air, but it also meant regular deliveries through all weather, good or bad.

A passenger waiting list was in use since the open-cockpit airplanes only had room for the pilot and one passenger, who sat on the mailbag in the front seat while wearing goggles and a helmet. As these planes didn't have radios, all flying was done visually. The airport radio operator kept track as the planes landed or took off and relayed these times along with the weather conditions.

But Barber Field was so small that aviation officials threatened to close it if the adjoining fairgrounds continued running its auto racetrack. Passenger service was in the planning stage, and a larger field at least one mile long with a rotating beacon for night-time flying was needed. In the

SOHS 00962

Medford Fairgrounds and racetrack inside Barber Airport, 1926. (SOHS #00962)

largest bond issue at the time, residents passed a $120,000 measure to buy 288 acres of land three miles north of the town's center on Biddle Road and construct runways, a terminal, and hanger building. Located on the present site and opened in late 1929, it featured a 2.5-million candlepower beacon, new radio station, weather bureau, pilot quarters, a restaurant, and the headquarters of the Rogue Valley Gun Club. (Barber field has been replaced by buildings that now house the Rogue Credit Union and Walmart Supercenter structures on Highway 99.)

Charles Lindbergh visited Medford as part of his cross-country tour the year after his famous solo flight to Paris; photos show him examining his plane and then leaving Medford Airport on August 29, 1928. In 1931, Pacific Air Transport merged with three other pioneer airlines to form United Airlines. And over time, nearly every major or smaller airline served Medford.

The City of Medford approved bond issues and accepted grants that increased the acreage, landing field, and improvements so that by 1940 the runway was 6,700 feet long and 75 feet wide. During World War II, the War Department took control of the airport and its acreage increased to 550-plus acres. In August 1944, fruit, flowers, and fish from Medford flew on a United Air Lines cargo-liner to New York City, the first full cargo of perishables flown coast to coast.

In January 1971, the voters approved transferring ownership of the airport from the City of Medford to Jackson County, which accepted all bond issues and liabilities, relieving the city from these obligations. As the years passed, the airport added more acreage and facilities to reach its

Medford Airport, Nov. 1929. (SOHS #09604)

present 925 acre size. In January 1995, the U.S. Department of Commerce designated Jackson County as a foreign-trade zone. This allowed it to be a legally secured area outside the United States for customs entry procedures, duties, and quotas — thus becoming an international airport.

The runway was extended in 2000 to allow larger jets; a new passenger terminal and air traffic control tower were constructed during 2009. Serving the Rogue Valley and seven counties, it is now the third largest commercial airport in Oregon. The grooved asphalt runway is now 8,800 ft. long and 150 ft. wide with nearly sixty flights which arrive and depart daily — a far cry from Barber Field all those years ago.

Source: Hattie B. Becker, *The History of Rogue Valley International-Medford Airport*, Gandee Printing Company: Medford, Oregon, 1995.

The Architects Who Changed the Towns

*I*N THE LATE NINETEENTH CENTURY, OUR TOWNS were comprised mainly of saloons, churches, stables, dirt streets, and perhaps three-story buildings, but nothing resembling what we see today. Plans weren't really needed, and an experienced "tradesman" could construct structures simply by drawing down ideas. Over time, professional architects relocated here and drew the detailed plans that became residences, theatres, and buildings that still stand today.

One such person was a Canadian expatriate, Arthur Weeks. An experienced architect in Portland, Weeks moved to the Valley in 1882, to start an orchard that eventually became Bear Creek Orchards. Although he didn't design buildings for a period, he had created the design plans for a few of Medford's earliest structures, such as the Joseph Stewart mansion and Medford Bank Building, still existing on the northwest corner of East Main and Bartlett.

William J. Bennet (pronounced "Ben-Nay") had a major impact and moved to Medford in January 1895, but only after working in Roseburg for a short one and a half years. Bennett generally designed residences, and one of his design—named now the Curry Manor Residential Care Facility on Quail Lane—was accepted on the National Register of Historic Places. When given the contract to design the Hotel Medford, Bennett decided to set up his office in Medford.

Quickly making important contacts, he began drawing plans to build residences and more buildings. That year, Bennet was one of several architects asked to submit plans to construct the state capitol at St. Paul, Minnesota, but didn't win the bid. With steep-pitched roofs, high ceilings,

Frank Clark. (SOHS # 02134)

dormers and windows, gables, and Queen Anne or Swiss-chalet looks, his residences became widely known. Ones as the Sophenia Ish-Baker House at Jackson and McAndrews — and the Shone-Charley House at Fourth and Grape — were later placed on the National Register of Historic Places.

In the spring of 1896, Bennet was the architect for a new courthouse for Siskiyou County in Yreka. Bennett moved his offices there and again started up. By 1898, he moved to La Grande, creating plans throughout that eastern region. Owing to financial failures, W.J. Bennett died from an alcohol and morphine overdose in 1898. In a very short time, however, his accomplishments here and throughout Oregon were legendary.

Frank C. Clark, however, is the most prominent architect of our times. After learning his drafting trade back East and practicing architecture in Los Angeles and Arizona, the thirty-year-old Clark gained the contract to design two new buildings in 1902 for the Ashland Academy (now SOU). He moved to Ashland and for forty years was a major architect in Jackson and Josephine counties.

While in Ashland, he designed residences, the Elk's Building, and the Enders Building. When the Orchard Boom of the early 1900s arrived, he was well positioned and moved to Medford. Clark designed stylish orchard homes, colonial-style residences, and major buildings as St. Mark's Episcopal Church, the Sparta Building, Medford Elk's Club, Newell-Barber Field, the Swedenburg House (at the entrance to SOU), and many others.

After World War I and into the early 1930s, a second phase of his long career started. During these years, prominent Medford residents commissioned his sought-after residences in styles ranging from Craftsman and Period Colonial to English Tudor; buildings as Medford Senior High School, Washington School, the Holly Theatre, and Hillcrest Orchard buildings were designed in different styles and constructed.

Clark continued on with an associate, Robert Keeney, in 1931. Six

Frank Clark designed building for the Elks Club, North Central and 5th Avenue in Medford, circa 1915. (SOHS # 08631)

years later, the firm became known as Clark and Keeney. After World War II with Kenney returning from service, Clark turned over the bulk of his design work to his partner. Continuing with his design work, Clark's career spanned over sixty years as he worked past his 80th birthday. He died in 1957 at age eighty-four.

Frank C. Clark arrived in Ashland well over a century ago, and he was responsible for designing and creating several hundred structures. From 1910 Craftsman bungalows to the exquisite 1930 Holly Theatre and 1937 Art Deco "Harry and David" Packing House, numerous structures that he designed are still standing—a testimonial to the times that continue into our present.

Sources: Miller, *Medford Mail Tribune*, 2013; Truwe, "Southern Oregon History, Revised (W.J. Bennett)"; Atwood, *Oregon Encyclopedia* (Frank Clark).

The Cyclical Life of SOU

SOUTHERN OREGON UNIVERSITY (SOU) DATES BACK to 1869 when a cadre of locals met to create a college or academy. Calling themselves the Rogue River Valley Educational Society, the group raised money and began constructing a building in Ashland. However, the money ran out. The Reverend Joseph Skidmore of Oregon's Methodist Episcopal Church took over, raised more funds, completed the construction, and in 1872, the Ashland Academy opened that November. Six years later, the Methodist Episcopal Church took over the academy, again owing to financial difficulties.

One year after the academy graduated its first three students, the Oregon legislature in 1882 authorized the creation of state normal schools to train future teachers and prepare students to enter a university: Ashland Academy then became the Ashland College and Normal School. Since the legislature didn't authorize funding, different groups operated the school over the next several years, including the Methodist Episcopal Church and different individuals or groups that included Ashland citizens.

In 1899 the State of Oregon bought the school when the legislature approved funding, and in four years, the Ashland Academy became Oregon's largest normal school with 270 students. But the legislature stopped funding in 1909, so it closed after local citizens donated enough money to enable its students to finish out the year. After fifteen years of lobbying, the legislature finally reauthorized the normal school — renamed the Southern Oregon State Normal School ("SONS") — with funds to construct a new building on a site donated by the town. With 22 faculty members and 173 students, it reopened in the fall of 1926 to train teachers and was headquartered in Churchill Hall (now an administrative building).

Southern Oregon Normal School (predecessor of Southern Oregon University).
(SOHS #09722)

The legislature in 1939 eliminated the normal schools in Oregon, but with accreditation from the American Association of Teachers Colleges, its name was changed to the Southern Oregon College of Education, the fifth name change with two closures and re-openings to that time. World War II's demands brought another crisis and exacerbated enrollment declines to where a mere forty-five students were studying there in 1945-46.

A new president, Elmo Stevenson, was hired in 1946 to close the campus (then named the "Southern Oregon State Normal School") if he couldn't increase enrollment. After arriving, he believed it to be a unique college; instead of closing it, Dr. Stevenson traveled throughout the region and Oregon, speaking to service and other clubs to promote its importance, rekindle interest, and build enrollment. He was very successful.

Stevenson is credited with not only saving the college, but also putting in place changes that continued for decades. During his twenty-three years as president, the longest by far of any leader of this campus, he brought about the construction of a dozen buildings, including the Cascade dormitories and the McNeal athletic complex.

Three more name changes next occurred: to Southern Oregon College (SOC) to reflect its different degree options (1956); from SOC to Southern Oregon State College (SOSC) in 1975; and finally in 1997, SOSC became Southern Oregon University after it successfully withstood a drive to change it to the University of Oregon — Ashland campus.

After its 2005 expansion, SOU's Hannon Library is now nearly 125,000 square feet; the renovated student union building, Stevenson Union (named after Elmo Stevenson) has over 100,000 square feet of usable space. Joining other improvements since 2000 (i.e., the Center for Visual Arts, the Madrone dorms, Medford Campus, and more), two residence halls totaling 200,000 square feet and a separate 28,000 square-foot dining hall were constructed to replace the Cascade Complex, one of the largest projects in Ashland's history and opened for fall term, 2013. Upgrades to its Science Building were completed, and currently the old McNeal athletic facilities is being replaced by a $30 million reconstruction (anticipated to be done in 2017). Since 2010, more than $130 million in capital improvements at SOU has been completed.

Oregon has passed laws mandating independent governing boards, or a board of trustees, to run each of its seven public universities. On July 1, 2015, SOU's Board of Trustees became its governing board with broad authority to supervise and manage its affairs, subject to the supervision of a state agency — the Higher Education Coordinating Commission (HECC) — that generally approves such policies. The governor appoints fourteen members that are approved by the state Senate to typically serve four-year terms. The board includes an SOU faculty member, non-faculty staff member and a student who serve two- instead of four-year terms. SOU's President holds the fifteenth seat as an ex-officio, nonvoting member.

SOU is now a regional university with 6,200 students, 750 faculty and staff/administrators, and well in excess of 100 programs, all spread over 175 acres with numerous complexes — one would think that even Elmo Stevenson would have been amazed.

Sources: Montgomery, *Oregon Encyclopedia*: "Southern Oregon University"; Ristow, *Medford Mail Tribune*, April 14, 2013 (Elmo Stevenson); Wheeler, *Mail Tribune*, March 17, 2015; Paulson, *EugeneWeekly.com*, July 9, 2015; Darling, *Mail Tribune*, April 24, 2016.

The Rebuilding of
Medford's Downtown

*L*ESS THAN HALF THE SIZE OF THE ORIGINAL ten-story tower proposed a decade ago (scaled down owing to the economy and city), Lithia Motors' new headquarters—built on land it already owned (basically, the old location of its car lots)—was completed in August 2012. The four-stories high, 70,000 square-foot structure brought together eight different departments of the now $8 billion-dollar-annual-sales-volume car company.

Layers of glass—from the entryway to the rooftop—allow light to shower the structure from 360 degrees. Meeting rooms have different automotive names, from Cadillac to Tucker. The first floor contains retail space, including Lithia's franchised Starbucks, with the next three floors utilized by Lithia. From the top executive floor, Wagner and Anderson buttes and Roxy Ann Peak seem close. Passenger airlines pass by at eye level, and cars on I-5 seem to be floating through the trees.

Mark DeBoer (Lithia's Vice President of Real Estate), along with father Sid, oversaw the construction of Lithia's headquarters, and Mark played a key role in the development of the Commons, the two-block-long park next to Lithia, planning this to be an anchor for downtown development. Lithia partnered with the Medford Urban Renewal Agency (MURA) to create the Commons. Both the headquarters and park were completed at the same time and were public-private partnerships with some $14.1 million in MURA dollars invested in the two projects—and matched by Lithia.

Next was the Red Lion Inn, immediately across Riverside Avenue. A complicated deal involving MURA, the City of Medford, and DHD, LLC

Downtown Medford, OR, circa 1910. (Courtesy, Ben Truwe)

(set up by Sid and Mark DeBoer), were involved. DHD bought the entire 8-acre Red Lion property for $2.8 million with the intention of selling the hotel back to hotel developers, Doug and Becky Neuman, and another part to the city. The couple had already completed a major renovation of the Lithia Springs Resort (north of Ashland), along with the Windmill Inn (on Ashland's south side), not to mention the Ashland Springs Hotel and other developments.

DHD arranged the financing so that the Neumans could own the hotel, and the couple invested some $1.5 million in its renovation. The new name: The Inn at the Commons. The city of Medford purchased a 3.29-acre portion of the Red Lion property for $1.6 million from urban renewal funds. The hotel featured 185 rooms, but that number dropped to 118 when the city took over its portion of the property to demolish those rooms to make way for a public parking lot.

Carnegie Library, downtown Medford.

Although not adjacent to this development, One West Main is another piece of this revitalization. Three local companies financed the cost of all but $2 million of the $9 million project, which opened in 2014. MURA paid the rest. The 116,600-square-foot, four-story building in the heart of downtown serves as the headquarters for Pacific Retirement Services (owner/operators of nationwide retirement communities, including the Manor), Rogue Disposal & Recycling, and Procare Software (a developer of accounting software for daycare and childcare facilities). The lower floor is for retail tenants.

Not surprisingly, more development has occurred around the Commons. In October 2014, Neil Clooney (owner of Smithfields Restaurant in Ashland) opened the Bohemian Club in the restored brick building at 123 W. Main St. Behind the historic sign, the space still includes a restaurant (a Southern inspired menu) and bar downstairs with a nightclub upstairs, as well as an outside patio. Ashland developer Allan Sandler won the city's approval to build twenty-six units of downtown housing (named "The Sky Box") that's a few blocks from Lithia's headquarters. Plus a major renovation of Hawthorne Park ($1.65 million)—just across I-5 from Lithia and the Inn at the Commons—was completed.

Meanwhile, the Sam Jennings building—a downtown Medford fixture for nearly 100 years located at the corner of Riverside Avenue and East 4th Street—had been having run-ins with city officials, dating back to 2013 over its "unsightly" equipment, among other issues. Dan Reisinger and his family own the truck and heavy equipment repair shop. All of their six properties downtown have been put up for sale for $1.8 million, and it remains to be seen what will happen.

This redevelopment is underway and, when completed, will make a big difference in the City of Medford. (Note: Owing to the fast pace of real estate development and transactions, the above will change after the date of publication.)

Sources: Stiles, *Medford Mail Tribune,* August 9, 2012; Mann, *Medford Mail Tribune,* August 22, 2013; Cook, *Oregon Business*, February 2015; Mann, *Medford Mail Tribune*, May 11, 2016.

The Redwood Highway

B Y 1854, CRESCENT CITY WITH ITS SEAPORT had a population of 800 with 300 houses and buildings. As the primary maritime stopover between San Francisco and Portland, its merchants wanted a wagon trail to connect the thriving town with the gold-rich Illinois River area in the Oregon Territory. Although a stock company was organized to build a "plank and turnpike road," or the Crescent City Plank Road, actual construction didn't start until three years later due to a severe economic recession.

With a $50,000 stock offering (and a later assessment), the wagon road to Sailors Creek in what's now Josephine County was completed in May 1858. The tri-weekly stage from Crescent City stopped at Sailors Creek (later at Waldo) to connect with the stage line for Jacksonville and then over the Siskiyou Pass to Yreka. Where pack mules once hauled supplies to the mining camps, wagon trains could carry much heavier loads over the planked road. This was a toll road with the toll house at the Smith River ferry. A two-horse team paid five dollars, for example, and a four-horse team paid eight dollars.

The wagons forded the river when it was low, and the teams could travel from April until the fall rainy season began. A four-horse team could pull one-and-a half tons of freight uphill to Oregon, and often two wagons were hitched together with six or eight horses pulling the load. Over time, the road passed up Elk Valley, crossed Howland Hill (one-half mile south of where U.S. 199 does now), turned to the northeast, and crossed the Smith River. Climbing the high ridge dividing watersheds (Smith River and Myrtle Creek to High Divide and Altaville), the rough path continued on for Jacksonville.

With the advent of the automobile age in the mid-1910s, a rough, risky trail from Medford was possible though Grants Pass to Eureka, and then

Old Redwood Highway 199. Note the planked road. (SOHS #34188)

through the Smith River Redwoods to Crescent City. The road from Grants Pass southwest to Wilderville, and then along the Crescent City Plank Road to the state line was named in 1917 as the "Grants Pass-Crescent City Highway No. 25."

With long grades and a plank road still in California, this was a narrow, winding unpaved mountain path. Although travelers no longer had to rest their tired horses periodically on the long haul over the mountains, this was still a risky adventure even by car. The steep grades and rapid coasting downward was limited only by the driver's nerve and ability to turn sharp corners with frightening or deadly accidents occurring all too frequently.

Oregon changed its Highway No. 25 designation in 1924 to the Redwood Highway. The two states completed a paved way between Gasquet (near Crescent City) and Kerby (near Grants Pass) in September 1926, and the newly constructed Hiouchi Bridge over the Smith River was completed in 1929, linking Medford with Crescent City through Grants Pass. Although the route was improved upon at different times, any road trip was risky, especially when navigating the mean "jeep path" through Hazel View Mountain's forested and brush-ridden summit.

At the 1960 groundbreaking of the new tunnel through this mountain, 1,000 people gathered on the California side of the Redwood Highway (Highway 199). With an unexpected appearance by the Grants Pass Cavemen—wearing their animal skins and waving clubs—the ceremonies could start after receiving their blessings. Named for the California state senator who was responsible for the project's completion, the Randolph Collier Tunnel opened three years later. The tunnel and twenty-three miles of new road eliminated the numerous tortuous turns, removed switchbacks, and allowed a reasonable speed of sixty miles per hour from its once twenty-five mph.

Over time, major road repairs on Highway 199 have been necessary due to calamities from truck collisions and forest fires to heavy rains and mud slides. Despite this, the Redwood Highway is a comfortable trip now through unsurpassed beauty and rural settings with even movies, such as "Redwood Highway," filmed in making it a central character. What was once a hard wagon ride measured in days is now a two-hour trip to the coast—and that is real progress.

Sources: U.S. National Park Service, *Redwood National Park*, 1969; Miller, *Medford Mail Tribune*, 2010; Powers, "As It Was," 2011.

The Water Systems of Medford (and Other Towns)

WHETHER FOR DRINKING, WASHING, OR CLEANING, having sufficient potable water is vital to living regardless of era. Fed by the snow melt and watershed rain runoff from Mount Ashland, Ashland relies on Ashland Creek. Cities such as Grants Pass rely on the Rogue River; living in an unincorporated area usually means depending on a well. Mt. McLoughlin is the water source for nearly 150,000 people today in Medford, Central Point, Eagle Point, Jacksonville, Phoenix, Talent, White City, and four rural water districts—all served by the Medford Water Commission and its contracts.

Area residents first relied on wells for their needs; Medford in 1888 caused a ditch to be excavated from Bear Creek and built a storage tower for its first water system. Although a pumping station was added four years later, it became clear that Bear Creek water wasn't clean enough for use. This water was so dirty, foul, and unusable—owing also to dumped sewage from Ashland to Phoenix—that some residents preferred whiskey and forgetting about baths.

The question was whether Fish Lake or Big Butte water would be better. Unfortunately, the thirty-one-mile pipeline from the Big Butte watershed would cost $400,000. Since the twenty-two-mile, gravity-fed system from Fish Lake would be considerably less expensive, this alternative won out. In 1910, the wooden-stave pipeline was constructed for $254,000; but after the orchard-boom building frenzy of the 1910s and system inadequacies causing algae and near-putrid water (flowing in open flumes without filters or settling tanks), it became clear that Fish Lake was not working out. The city purchased the water rights at Big

Butte Springs in 1915 for $15,000 after enduring water shortages and contaminated supplies.

In 1922, the voters approved the five-member Medford Water Commission as a city charter amendment. Three years later, the Oregon Legislature granted Medford the rights to all of the unappropriated waters from Big Butte Creek and its tributaries. Given this, the city's voters approved a $975,000 bond measure to build the thirty-one-mile pipeline from Big Butte Springs to Medford's 10,000 residents. Instead of the unreliable wooden pipeline and flumes, the Commission decided to use high-quality steel that was coated inside and out with a thin layer of hot asphalt to prevent rust, On July 1, 1927, the two-foot diameter pipeline began carrying water to the city by gravity flow.

The snowmelt on Mt. McLoughlin (9,494-foot elevation) percolates through the porous, volcanic soils to emerge again at Big Butte Springs (2,700-foot elevation) near the town of Butte Falls. The watershed consists of 56,000 acres of private and publicly-managed land with 75 % managed by the U.S. Forest Service. The springs discharge high quality water that is consistently cold, clear, and low in mineral content. Collected underground, the spring flows required only minimal treatment for disinfection in meeting water-quality standards. Consequently, the slogan of "A mountain spring in every home" came about to note the purity of the city's water.

The Medford Water Commission (MWC) in 1952 completed a second pipeline and a fifty-two-foot high, earth-fill dam of the Big Butte Springs water. This created Willow Lake that stores the waters of Willow Creek, a tributary of the South Fork of Big Butte Creek. On land owned by the county, Jackson County developed the Willow Lake Recreation Area. Facilities were built for camping, overnight stays, picnicking, and fishing with a paved boat ramp and a small, private resort located on the shore. Covering some 925 acres, the lake has nearly four and one-half miles of lake frontage.

In 1962, chlorine began to be added to the water when bacteria traces were discovered. It also obtained water rights to the Rogue River to supplement the needs required during the high-use months of May to September. Built in 1968, the Robert A. Duff treatment plant near TouVelle State Park draws the Rogue River water. Over the years, the MWC then signed agreements with the surrounding cities mentioned above to provide their water needs.

Hauling water mains from the depot in Eagle Point to bring water to Medford, 1909. (SOHS #12811)

The two original pipelines still carry this important water, and the commission maintains the entire pipeline, including repairing small sections when needed. The question is still out as to when this eighty-five-year-old-plus system will need to be replaced. For now, when the great majority of Jackson County residents turn on their faucets, they are drinking Big Butte Springs water from Mt. McLoughlin.

Sources: *Medford Mail Tribune*, April 22, 2007; Miller, *Medford Mail Tribune*, May 31, 2009; Mann, *Medford Mail Tribune*, March 12, 2013; Mann, *Medford Mail Tribune*, April 14, 2013.

U.S. Fish and Wildlife
Service Forensics Lab

*P*RIOR TO THE CREATION OF THE U.S. Fish and Wildlife Service (USFWS) Forensics Laboratory, it was difficult to prosecute wildlife lawbreakers for violations. Needing to prove an individual's guilt "beyond a reasonable doubt" was difficult, as eye-witness testimony (if present) is questionable and linking any physical evidence required corroborating expert testimony. Prior to 1988, wildlife law enforcement officers were at a real disadvantage due to their limited access to wildlife-related forensic services.

In 1979, Terry Grosz at the USFW had persisted in his belief on this need, and the agency hired Ken Goddard, a police crime lab director from Southern California, to set up a wildlife forensics program. In six months he drafted the forensic wildlife protocols and manual chapters. Six years later, the initial funding for the laboratory was approved. This took the help of numerous people, including Dr. Ralph Wehinger of Eagle Point, who had listened to a lecture on illicit falconry in Portland, and Oregon Senators Hatfield and Packwood (enlisted by Dr. Wehinger).

Due to Wehinger's efforts again, the USFW selected Ashland for the lab's location. When the 23,000 square-foot building was completed in 1988 on the Southern Oregon State College campus (now SOU), Goddard hired the initial team of ten forensic scientists and support staff plus purchased the first equipment. Crimes against wildlife include illegal hunting, trafficking in endangered species, and producing and selling products made from endangered or threatened species; thus, the situations being faced vary greatly.

The lab handled investigations ranging from the nailing of a spotted owl to a park sign to whether fish eggs sold as caviar were from a sturgeon (okay) or a protected paddlefish (not okay). A particularly unusual case occurred when 300 headless walruses washed up on Alaska's Seward Peninsula (later determined to be tribal tusk hunters). These cases involved investigating the Hells Angels in Alaska for illegally trafficking in walrus ivory, as well as whether ivory tusks were from modern elephants (illegal) or Ice Age mammoths (legal).

In 1991, the facility was rededicated as the Clark R. Bavin National FWS in memory of its late, Law Enforcement Chief. Although the lab was assisting in investigations outside the U.S. that involved this country, treaties were signed in 1998 at Interpol's headquarters in Lyon, France, that designated the facility as the official lab of Interpol's Wildlife Working Group.

The investigations centered into multi-billion-dollar, black-market international criminal enterprises that traded in skins, eggs, organs, hides, and other wildlife specimens. As the world's only specialized wildlife police laboratory, a sizeable portion of its caseload involved Caviar samples; in one three-year period, federal agents seized $180 million worth of caviar that inundated the lab with sample testing. From tiger penises to ground rhino horns, the world abounds in different cultural beliefs to increase virility—and these investigations determined if they were from a protected species or simply ground chalk.

In 2007, the lab's new 17,000 square-foot addition was completed. To protect the federal building, the facility heads opted for creative landscaping such as berms, contours, and "security" landscaping—not concrete and barbed wire—to prevent would-be car bombers. Technology plays its ever-increasing role: a laser surface scanner creates three-dimensional "pixel-skin" images of bones and skulls; DNA analysis is used to connect the fibers on a person's clothing with a protected species; electron microscopy is employed, for example, to distinguish between modern elephant ivory and an ancient mammoth.

The laboratory works with federal agents, the fifty state fish-and-game commissions, and over 175 countries that are signatories to the convention prohibiting international trading in endangered species. Headed since its inception by Ken Goddard (even into 2017)—also a very successful writer of crime novels—staffing has more than tripled from its original levels. Called wildlife's "Scotland Yard" with scientists

The U.S. Fish & Wildlife Service Forensics Lab in Ashland, OR, before protective berms, contours and "security" landscaping were installed in 2007.

who are "animal detectives," this facility continues in its fight to protect wildlife as the laws intended — and nature requires.

Sources: U.S. Fish & Wildlife Service: Our Lab's History; Pahl, *National Geographic Today*, April 2, 2003; Denson, the *Oregonian*, June 7, 2009.

When Electricity First Came to the Region

*I*N JANUARY 1889, A MR. TUTTLE PRESENTED AN electrical show to a crowd at Ashland's Plaza. Hooking up a two-horsepower dynamo to a drive belt powered by an Ashland Flour Mill drive motor, the carbon light glowed in the dark to everyone's amazement. The privately-owned Ashland Electric Power & Light company soon built a hydroelectric plant on Ashland Creek (in what's now Lithia Park) and that summer generated electric power.

The Grants Pass Water, Light & Power Company started up its operations in that December for its residents. Edward Brown oversaw the building of the Grants Pass Diversion Dam across the Rogue River, south of the bridge, and electricity became available. As with Ashland's initial power delivery, there were conditions. Its hydroelectric power was only for daily use from 6 p.m. to 10 p.m., and then Grants Pass folks needed to use their whale-oil lamps or candles. The hours of service increased over time, including adding an "ironing hour" that gave homemakers electricity on Tuesday mornings from 9 a.m. to 10 a.m.

Other towns followed, such as Roseburg in the following year, and Yreka and Dunsmuir in 1891. Medford came later. Mr. R.A. Proudfoot in 1894 constructed a small wood-burning plant on Bear Creek that used steam to turn its generators. The city bought this facility six years later.

It took the Ray brothers to bring dependable electricity to the entire region. Colonel Frank H. Ray had convinced his brother, Dr. C.R. Ray, to inspect the Braden mine near Gold Hill as a potential purchase. With his positive report, they bought it, along with the rights to a power site to be constructed on the Rogue River, all to supply electricity to the mine for around-the-clock operations.

Gold Ray Dam provided most of the region's early electrical needs. (SOHS #16066)

As the Colonel was wealthy and a vice-president of the American Tobacco Company, there were little problems in raising the money to build the large hydroelectric complex at Tolo, four miles above Gold Hill. When completed, the dam was 350-feet long and 17-feet tall; the impounded river was diverted through a powerhouse, first generating electricity in 1904. The Ray brothers' Condor Water and Power Company soon furnished power from Grants Pass, Gold Hill, and Medford to Jacksonville, Central Point, and Ashland.

This relatively cheap electricity drove the region's development, as mines, flour mills, machine shops — and all businesses from restaurants to retail stores — including private residences now had the power to function by. Southern Oregon could join the rest of the country in its growth.

During this time, Yreka's Jerome P. and Jesse W. Churchill had developed similar hydroelectric power from the Shasta River and were distributing this to communities in Northern California, including over the Siskiyous to Ashland. The Rays' company (now named Rogue River Electric) by later agreement took over supplying Ashland's needs, while the Churchills continued developing power through Northern California.

The twenty-four light and power companies controlled by the Churchills and Rays consolidated in 1912 under the name of the California-Oregon Power Company (COPCO). This holding company controlled power plants throughout Southern Oregon and Northern California with distribution lines from Klamath Falls to Yreka and Grants Pass to Dunsmuir. COPCO then over time absorbed smaller power companies, constructed numbers of substations, and increased or added distribution systems. The large utility, Pacific Power Co., bought all of COPCO's operations in 1961 and brought about a generating and transmitting power giant that operated throughout six Pacific Northwest states.

As to Gold Ray dam, less expensive power grids and cheaper land-generation systems caused those operations in 1972 to shut down. Pacific Power transferred the dam, powerhouse, and twenty-seven acres to Jackson County. Forty years later, Gold Ray dam was demolished.

The story of delivering vital electric power to this region is one based on taking risks, individualism, and persistence. Without this, what everyone takes now for granted would be completely different.

Sources: Powers, *Oregon Encyclopedia* (Gold Ray Dam); *Medford Mail Tribune*, April 22, 2007; Powers, JPR: "As It Was," October 11, 2011; Powers, JPR: "As It Was," July 6, 2012.

PART II

Gold, Stagecoaches, and Railroads

Where Past Meets Present

Mattie's Nugget and the Currency of Gold

*T*HROUGHOUT THE COUNTRY—AND ESPECIALLY in Southern Oregon— gold nuggets, bars, and even dust were used as currency until the 1930s. During the Great Depression, President Roosevelt made the private ownership and use of gold as a currency to be illegal. Before then, gold was used to pay debts and anyone, whether a resident or not, could buy gold nuggets at any local bank, from Grants Pass to Ashland.

In 1859, a small, nervous Irishman—one Mattie Collins—was working through the tailings around Althouse Creek in Josephine County's Illinois Valley. Althouse Creek winds its way from the Siskiyou Mountains and flows over fifteen miles into the Illinois River. The area had been a fine place for placer gold discoveries. Although the great finds were largely over, Mattie was ever hopeful. On one of the tributaries, he looked up the bank and spotted a large stump with exposed roots. Hoping he might find something, he began pulling out rocks—and came across a huge nugget.

It weighed seventeen pounds, the largest gold nugget reportedly discovered in Southern Oregon. Terrified that someone would rob him, or con him, if they heard about his good fortune, Mattie hired a fellow Irishman by the name of Dorsey to help him bring the nugget to a San Francisco bank. Collins and Dorsey jumped at every noise or strange shadow; they checked every side trail to avoid an ambush. They were able to arrive safely in San Francisco, and he sold the nugget for $3,500, which would be worth some $500,000 today. When word was out about his find, miners flooded into the area—but didn't find anything that came close to this.

Miner with gold pan. (SOHS 00375.1)

Mattie kept the money in the San Francisco bank and worked for wages, first in California, and then in Nevada, Idaho, and Montana. The frugal man deposited his earnings into the same bank. The years passed by and at age sixty-five, however, Mattie Collins fell in love with a younger woman. She succeeded where everyone else had failed:

skimming the money away and then leaving him. Collins died near penniless, despite his good fortune and years of hard work.

Although the great majority of prospectors never came close to Mattie's good fortune, gold for all those years was a currency — and preferred. Banks weighed the gold nuggets, accepted them, and gave gold coins in return. The coins were in five-dollar, ten-dollar, and twenty-dollar denominations. One problem was that the five-dollar gold coin was nearly the size of and appearance of a penny. Mistakes were made when passing out a five-dollar gold coin as change for a penny, the loss not equal to ones chagrin when later discovering this.

Whether Gold Hill or Jacksonville, prospectors came to town and exchanged their gold or nuggets for whiskey, women, clothing, food, or whatever provisions that were needed. When they needed more money, the miners trudged back into the hills. Disdainful of banks, they carried or hid their nuggets. If big enough or armed, some held them in public, including one who would set his quart glass jar of gold nuggets on the counter when ordering his meal.

The ones who owned the general stores and sold provisions to the miners were usually the ones who became prosperous. One local prospector, Lester Foley, wrote in 1931: "After seventeen years, I'm a little weary, hungry. I'm reduced to Spartan austerity. Have a depressed feeling. Am on a diet of beans. After 17 years, my pocket averaged $2.30 a year, excluding expenses — but included frost-bite, fly-bite, and rattlesnake bite, with bleeding fingers, an aching back, a frosted lung, and pain."

His experience was typical of many of the old-time prospectors; but their courage and conviction continues as a valued tradition in different ways today.

Sources: Truwe, "William Mackey: Althouse Creek in the Early Days"; see also, Jackson, OregonGold.Net: "Great Gobs of Gold Abound in Southern Oregon"; Powers, *Gold Hill: Images of America* ("Mattie's Nugget").

Stagecoaches and
Their Drivers

BEFORE THE RAILROADS OPENED UP Southern Oregon in the mid-1880s, stagecoaches and their drivers ruled — but this was a hard way to travel. For example, Henry Williams and his family were traveling in 1873 from Portland, Oregon, to their San Francisco residence. They left Portland by train in the early morning and arrived in Roseburg that evening. Taking the stagecoach the following day, they endured a "jolting, 23-hour ride" to the Rock Point station near Gold Hill. The stop now is a wine-tasting, hospitality room for Del Rio Vineyards.

Williams penned in his diary: "Not having slept...we at once went to bed and got about four hours sleep. We breakfasted at 10:00 A.M. and had a very good meal. We have spent a very quiet day, and I found a number of San Francisco newspapers of much later date than any I had seen and was much interested in reading them. My wife and Miss Isabella slept most of the day. Late this afternoon we took a long walk in the edge of the woods near the banks of the [Rogue] river where we found a number of beautiful wild flowers."

From 6:00 a.m. to midnight, the party spent the next three days on a stagecoach that only stopped for meals and to change horses. Once in Redding, they went by train to San Francisco. Their travels took one full week, whereas today we can speed down I-5 from Portland and make San Francisco in one to two days, depending on how hard we push.

More than likely, the stagecoach "whip" driver for the Williams family was Norton Eddings, a well-liked and respected driver. Norton Eddings was born in 1852 and began running coaches regularly in the 1870s for the California & Oregon Stage Company. His run for numbers

Four-horse stagecoaches on the Plaza, in front of the Ashland post office, lined up for the last run over the Siskiyous. (SOHS 34329)

of years was from Rock Point across the valley, over the Siskiyous, and ending at Cole's Station, just over the California border. He lived at the Rock Point Station until he married in 1879.

Two years later, Norton was returning from California when the stagecoach abruptly overturned. Although the driver and passengers only had bruises, Eddy suffered a badly broken leg. He couldn't drive for months and had no earnings, as worker's compensation didn't exist then. His friends decided to put on a benefit with musicians during the next week to help his finances. When Norton finally healed and could "whip" again, he was the main driver again into California. When Eddings died in 1925, he was buried at the Rock Point Pioneer Cemetery, close to where his stagecoach station was.

Interestingly enough, Lytle and Jane White built the Rock Point Hotel as a stagecoach stop in the late 1850s. Jane White would have cooked the "very good meal" eaten by the Williams family. She continued running the hotel and station after her husband died in 1877 and is credited with the longest record of stagecoach service by any woman between Portland and San Francisco. When the railroad by-passed tiny Rock Point for Gold Hill, Jane moved to Ashland with over twenty-five years of running that stagecoach stop and hotel.

Sources: Mullaly (Alice), JPR: "As It Was," September 14, 2011; Powers, JPR: "As It Was," August 16, 2011; Powers, JPR: "As It Was," August 22, 2011.

Stagecoach used to carry President Hayes and party towards Southern Oregon. (SOHS 01179)

The D'Autremont Brothers
and the Old West's
Last Train Robbery

T HE COMPLETION OF TUNNEL NO. 13 underneath the Siskiyou Pass in 1887 allowed Southern Pacific to connect California and Oregon by rail. Located a short distance east of the historic pass, the grades on both sides of the Siskiyou Summit are steep. Some thirty five years later, the D'Autremont brothers saw this as the ideal location to pull off what's considered to be this country's last Old-West-style train robbery.

On October 11, 1923, the train was traveling from Seattle to San Francisco and cresting the summit after its Ashland stopover. Awaiting the lumbering train was nineteen-year-old Hugh D'Autremont and his twin, twenty-three-year-old brothers, Ray and Roy. They had heard rumors that the train was hauling nearly $500,000 in gold. They decided to stop the train at the 3,107-foot-long Tunnel 13, because it would be easy to get onboard as it slowly chugged its way up. The grade to the summit is 3.67%, the steepest on this trip.

Roy and Hugh jumped onto the train when it slowed to test its brakes, while Ray waited at the tunnel's end with dynamite. They jumped onto the baggage car and climbed over the coal tender. Leaping down into the engine cab, Hugh with his gun drawn ordered the engineer to stop, which he did at the tunnel's south end. As coal smoke began to leak into the cars, the passengers were upset, of course, but didn't know what was happening.

When the postal clerk locked himself inside the mail car, the twins packed their dynamite against one end and ignited it. Not knowing what they were doing, the immense explosion destroyed the car, ripped open one side, and killed the clerk. Hearing the explosion and choking in the dense smoke, the passengers staggered towards the end of the tunnel and away from the wrecked track and train.

The unfortunate brakeman managed to make his way out through the thick smoke, but his appearance startled the brothers. Ray with a shotgun and Hugh with a .45 semiautomatic opened fire and killed the man. Knowing that they didn't have time or any money or gold in sight, the D'Autremonts shot and killed the train engineer and fireman, the only witnesses they believed had seen them. Wiping their feet in creosote to keep the bloodhounds from their scent, the brothers fled into the woods. Despite an extensive manhunt by local posses, angry railroad workers, Oregon National Guard troops, and even federal officers, the brothers had managed to disappear.

With four men murdered and mangled car remains, it was maddening to the authorities that this crime couldn't be solved. It wouldn't have been, but for a forensic scientist by the name of "The Wizard," Edward O. Heinrich, who was pioneering in the use of forensic science to solve criminal cases. A scientist at a University of California-Berkeley laboratory, the law authorities gave him the scant evidence left behind: a single pair of coveralls and conflicting passenger testimony.

In a few weeks, Heinrich informed them that their "coverall man" was white, light complexioned, had light-brown eyebrows, a mustache, medium-brown hair, and was near 5-feet, 10-inches tall. He was a logger in the Pacific Northwest, left-handed, and very meticulous about his appearance. The man smoked and when caught, Heinrich said he would probably be wearing a new jacket and a bowler hat. When Roy D'Autremont finally was captured, he was smoking a cigarette and wearing the jacket and hat.

Wizard Heinrich, also called the "Edison of Crime Detection," concluded the discovered "dirt" on the overalls wasn't oil or grease, as the police had thought, but fir pitch from Douglas fir needles peculiar to the Northwest. The man with the coveralls was left-handed, since in swinging with his left hand, his right-side pocket would face the tree and collect wood chips, as found in that pocket. In a breast pocket, Heinrich discovered fingernail clippings, rolled-up cigarette butts, and mustache wax indicating that this man was vain.

The definitive clue found was a crumpled up, mail receipt, deep in a pencil pocket, and signed by Roy D'Autremont. The address was in "Lakewood, N.M.," where the brothers and their divorced mother in

The destroyed mail car left by the D'Autremont brothers during the great train robbery of 1923. (SOHS 06791)

1920 had lived. Although the D'Autremont brothers had left the area, assumed new identities, and started new lives, they were eventually caught. In 1927, Hugh was arrested while in the Philippines with the military; he had been fingerprinted when joining the Army. Officers soon arrested the twins in Ohio.

The brothers were tried in the Jackson County courthouse in Jacksonville, convicted, and each one sentenced to life in prison. Paroled in 1958, Hugh died from cancer a few months later. Roy had a mental breakdown in prison and was given a frontal lobotomy; he died just a few months after his 1983 parole. Ray's sentence was commuted in 1972 by Governor Tom McCall, and after working years as a part-time janitor at the University of Oregon, he died in 1984.

Sources: Miller, *Medford Mail Tribune*, August 30, 2009; Fattig, *Medford Mail Tribune*, October 11, 2012.

The Ghost Towns and
Stories of the Illinois Valley

*L*EARNING ABOUT THE JUST-DISCOVERED GOLD finds in Jacksonville, sailors deserted their ship near Crescent City in 1852; they found rich gold deposits along the way in the Illinois Valley, twenty-five miles south of what's now Grants Pass. Known as "Sailor Diggings," its large miner population made it one of the important mining center. Although later named Waldo, many of the miners left six years later, headed for British Columbia's Frazier River when the news of its gold discoveries came. Sailor Diggings became the first county seat for Josephine County, and again under the name of Waldo. After Kerbyville received a similar nod with its increased population, the railroad's entry through Grants Pass made it the county center—which it has retained to the present.

In the same year that the sailors struck it rich, the Althouse Brothers did the same at Althouse Creek, so named for their discoveries on its east fork. Althouse Creek feeds over fifteen miles from the Siskiyou Mountains before dumping into the Illinois River. Other miners raced there upon hearing this news, and the first arrivals discovered large nuggets from that creek, as well as from nearby Sucker and Bolan Creeks.

The town of Althouse became a trading post in 1852 and twenty five years later had a post office; at one time, a bawdy town of 500, Althouse over time headed into oblivion when the miners and merchants left for other finds or better ways to earn a living. Only a few decaying chimneys and fireplaces are now visible. These settlements, mining camps, and small towns in the Illinois Valley had colorful histories and few places aside from Althouse Creek in Oregon produced more placer (or surface discovered) gold. Their stories are rich, but there is very little evidence of their existence today.

Located on a flat near the mouth of Walker Gulch on Althouse Creek's east side, Browntown and its suburb of "Hogtown" quickly became the largest town and mining center by 1853. Named for an early miner and storekeeper, "Webfoot" Brown, the town quickly expanded to where it had hotels, saloons, blacksmith shops, dance halls, ten stores, and a bowling alley. The gamblers and charlatans followed the miners, and Browntown grew another notch to becoming a tough, crude, and boisterous town.

One of the fabled success stories came from a broke, ex-Willamette Valley man by the name of Vaun. Arriving in Browntown in 1853, he had to find his fortune. Not knowing any better, Vaun asked a few grizzled miners where a good place was to pick for gold. The men told him to find the "large rock pile" on the creek that was a considerable distance away, upstream from a place called Rock Hill. They told him he would soon be rich. Vaun thanked them profusely and left, not hearing the raucous, sarcastic laughter from the men who had played another sucker joke on a newcomer.

The rains soon came, as Vaun trudged to find the place. Finally digging where he thought they had told him, Vaun soon was yelling and acting like a crazy man. Miners, who had been working below, ran to his aid—only to find that he had unearthed a forty-ounce nugget, worth more than $60,000 today. Vaun bought a horse with a bridle and saddle, returned to the Willamette Valley, and was never heard from again. The location of his fortunate find was named "Slug Bar."

Farmers from the Willamette and Umpqua Valleys during the 1850s hauled vegetables, fruit, bacon, and butter to Browntown, and then sold them to the miners. Unfortunately, these hard-working men were also easy prey for the gamblers and rough men. If a drunken farmer didn't lose his money at the gambling table, he might have had his remaining produce stolen at the same time from his wagon.

One of the games played was called the "Russian Play." Picking a fight with a farmer, a gambler or miner would grab two pistols, throw one to the farmer, and challenge him to a dual. Numbers of shots would quickly ring out; not knowing that these were blank cartridges, the victim would run away. One hapless farmer in his fright stumbled into Althouse Creek at night and nearly drowned in the high waters of a fall runoff. The miners raided his wagon before the man could make shore. The next time, the farmers came to Browntown with their wagons, they waved their guns—with real bullets.

Althouse, Oregon, circa 1890s. (Courtesy, OregonGold.net)

On the East Fork of Althouse Creek in 1859, the largest gold nugget reputedly found in Oregon was discovered. A small Irish miner by the name of Mattie Collins located the seventeen-pound gold rock under a large stump in the stream bank, twelve feet above the normal waterline. This nugget by itself would have been worth some $500,000 at today's values, but its size and historical significance would put this into the millions.

These towns were mobile: When the gold ran out, the storekeepers and miners moved to where more gold could be found. Tents usually served as the dining halls, general stores, and saloons, sometimes followed by crude wooden buildings. When the gold around Brownhouse played out, for example, the town moved upstream in 1876 to the mouth of North Seven Gulch and Althouse Creek. Renamed Tigertown, finding the gold deposits there required hydraulic mining with a powerful stream of water. The undeterred miners built eighteen miles of trails to cover the fourteen miles of the stream and eight miles of ditches. Tigertown fell into oblivion when its gold deposits played out.

Other than tailing piles, perhaps a foundation or some rotten timbers, there is little left in the overgrown brush and timber that these Illinois Valley mining towns were ever there. Their mining activities, however, were the beginnings of Josephine County until the railroad came through and cemented the deal.

Sources: Truwe, "William Mackey: Althouse Creek in the Early Days" and "Wm. Mackey: Sailor Diggings—Pioneer Town of Gold Production"; Jackson, OregonGold.net: "Finding Gold in Oregon"; Jackson, OregonGold.net: "Great Gobs of Gold Abound in Southern Oregon."

Men weren't the only ones panning for gold. (SOHS 01988)

The Golden Bank and
House of C.C. Beekman

C ORNELIUS C. ("C.C.") BEEKMAN IN 1853 became a "connecting agent" for the Yreka-based, express company of Cram, Rogers & Company in the new gold-mining town of Jacksonville. The business delivered gold dust, parcels, and letters over the Siskiyou Mountains from Jacksonville to Yreka; each week the twenty-five-year-old man— unsuccessful at mining—rode over the passes carrying these important deliveries for the gold miners, settlers, and their families.

Three years later when the firm went out of business, Beekman bought their operations—primarily the Jacksonville stables and corral— for $100. Working from a one-story building that he shared with a drugstore on the southeast corner of California and Third Streets, he established "Beekman's Express" that also operated as a gold-dust depository.

One year later in 1857, his office became the first bank in Southern Oregon and second oldest one in the Pacific Northwest. Beekman was a shrewd businessman, who charged the gold depositors for his safe storing of their gold, but didn't pay any interest on those accounts. Running his bank with a personal touch, he approved every loan request. If the borrower was trustworthy and the loan sensible, C.C. even loaned his own money rather than the bank's capital. He also sold books, supplies, and stationery from the bank, as well as dealing in gold and being a Wells Fargo express agent.

Beekman constructed a new bank building in 1863 at California and Third, and this structure still stands, surviving the various city fires and with millions of dollars of gold dust passing through its doors. Along

C.C. Beekman in his Jacksonville Bank. (SOHS 01959)

with his bank, mining, insurance, and real estate interests, the very wealthy Beekman wanted a house to store the many items he had kept from the gold-rush days. Building it in 1875, C.C., his wife, and two children lived there. This one-and-a-half story Gothic Revival style home at Laurelwood and California was part of Jacksonville's late 1800's "millionaires' row," but wasn't ostentatious as was then the style. Beekman not only served as Jacksonville's mayor, but ran a close, but losing race for governor in 1878, and served on the University of Oregon's Board of Regents.

When Beekman died in 1915, the bank ceased operations and its doors closed. Now owned by the city, Historic Jacksonville manages it, but the building remains as it was when C.C. was there. Also owned by the City of Jacksonville, the Beekman house is also managed (and leased) by

Beekman House, 1926. (SOHS 10314)

Historic Jacksonville. C.C. Beekman was listed as one of Oregon's 100 outstanding leaders of the past century in the *Oregonian* Centennial Edition.

Sources: "Historic Jacksonville: Beekman Bank/Beekman House" at http://www. historicjacksonville.org/; Boom, *Medford Mail Tribune,* April 17, 2011.

The Golden Rhoten
Family of Giants

*J*OHN AND ELIZABETH RHOTEN HOMESTEADED on Kane Creek in 1860, near what would later become the town of Gold Hill. When their children were born, they grew tall—very tall—and became known as the "family of giants." Although mother Elizabeth was a mere 4'9" (but weighing 250 pounds), father John was 6'8", or one of the tallest men in the Pacific Northwest—and lean. They had ten children, five girls and five boys. All grew to be over 6' tall, ranging from the tallest, Enos Rhoten, who was 6'11-3/4" (really 7 feet), to the shortest, Cynthia Ann, who was a mere 6'1".

But the tall-giant, Rhoten brothers (Enos, Ed, and Al) were as well known in Southern Oregon for their ability to "sniff out" gold, no matter where it was located. From Sardine, Galls, Foots, Kane, and Graves Creek to entire sections of the Applegate and Rogue Rivers, they pocket-mined every river, stream, and area that was around.

Led by Enos in 1905, the brothers discovered the famous Alice Group, or Revenue Pocket, a few miles south of Gold Hill above Kane Creek. Knowing that the highly producing Braden Mine was nearby, they used pick, pan, and shovel to find "some color, dig a little hole, and then follow it up the hill 'till coming to the pocket." Looking down on Gold Hill at 2,600 feet, they found it; in less than two days, they dug out 5000 ounces of gold, worth millions at today's values. All was quickly blown away in wild spending sprees.

This wasn't all luck, however. Enos Rhoten used a system—kept secret for years—to find the pockets. After coming across a sprinkling of gold particles on (or under) a slope and knowing that the trail led from above, he'd take sample after sample on both sides as he worked his way up. Numbering where each was precisely found, Enos stored them in jars and assayed out the amount of gold that was in each one. Once he worked up the trail and ran out of particles to analyze, he headed back down. Figuring where the strike was, he would dig deep until the gold pocket "magically" appeared.

With their new-found wealth, the brothers lived extravagantly until they had spent their find. One night, they were partying in a Medford saloon. When the tired owner said he was closing down, they tossed gold nuggets onto the bar and bought it. When morning finally came, the Rhotens handed the bar back to the shocked owner. Another time while nursing a bad hangover, Enos threw all of his gold nuggets over a Gold Hill dirt street, saying that the town folks needed it more than he did: He was known as a generous man.

When a Rhoten needed money, he would head away, search for a week or two, and return with gold nuggets in his backpack. They used the gold as money—disdaining any conversion into cash or depositing at banks—and Enos carried his around in a glass jar. After another spending spree, they would leave again for the wilds and search for another find. When the surface gold became harder to find and their luck ran out, Ed and Al worked in a local cement plant and eventually on an uncle's hay fields.

Starting at age seven when he found $150 worth, Enos was the best of all at locating gold. After making and losing several fortunes by the 1910s, he tried farming on 160 acres in the Applegate and running a general store. Losing interest, in 1915 he headed back to gold hunting until the late 1920s. After lying sick in a crude bed for three years in his old Kane Creek cabin, Enos died in 1931 from a stroke at age seventy. Although his last days had been spent in poverty, he was said to have died with a smile on his face, having enjoyed the life he had lived.

Sources: *Medford Mail Tribune*, December 13, 1931; Powers, JPR: "As It Was," May 10, 2012; Gold Hill Historical Society, "Nuggets of News," December 1992.

The Story and History
of the Railroads

*T*HE RAILROAD'S PATH CHANGED HAMLETS into cities while causing others to wither or die along the way. Owing to the heavy capital requirements needed to build the tracks, bridges, stations, and infrastructure, individuals and their railroad companies went out of business, reorganized, or were bought out. Backroom politics were the norm.

The Oregon story begins in 1861 when Joseph Gaston of Jacksonville incorporated a company to raise the funds for a preliminary survey to build a railroad from the Rogue Valley to the Columbia River. Passionate about constructing an Oregon railroad that would connect with a northern one coming from California, he then was practicing law and the editor of Jacksonville's *Oregon Sentinel*.

With funding and capital requirements being a continuing problem, the U.S. Congress passed legislation in 1866 that made available large grants of public land to the company that built the railroad between Portland, Oregon, and Marysville, California. The Oregon legislature would decide who was to build the railway through the state, and the incentive of acquiring large parcels of land galvanized strong forces into action.

Two years later, Joseph Gaston was in Salem to lobby the legislature for his company. His main rival, powerful shipping mogul Ben Holladay (who owned a stagecoach empire throughout the west), however, received the legislature's blessing. Gaston accused Holladay's award as due to his having caused "judges, legislatures, and attorneys to betray their clients." As the California railroad began to build north from Marysville, Holladay took over Gaston's company and sold $10.5 million in bonds to German investors to finance the southern route.

An 1880 Baldwin locomotive of the O&C Railroad. (Gold Hill Historical Society [GHHS])

During the early 1870s, different railroad companies came and went, as reorganizations became the norm. Although Holladay was able to build his railroad tracks to reach Salem, Eugene, and then Roseburg from Portland, he ran out of money in 1872, some 145 miles north of Ashland close to the California border. If he had followed his planned route, the railroad would have run through Eagle Point—not Medford— and that city would never have existed. The venture stopped at Roseburg, and one year later Holladay couldn't meet the required interest payments on his bonds. The company went bankrupt.

Henry Villard represented the German investors and took control four years later of Holladay's Oregon and California Railroad Company (O&C). It took years to reorganize the company with new debt, and the work to extend the railroad to the California border couldn't begin again until mid-1883, due to a bad economy, the high costs, and politics remaining difficult obstacles.

Having restarted construction, Villard's O&C track was extended from Roseburg through Josephine and Jackson County, finally stopping at Ashland on May 4, 1884, a total of 310 miles south from Portland. Villard's company, however, couldn't meet its debt obligations either, and further building to meet California's track coming from the south then ended.

In 1887, the once-again, reorganized O&C was now under control of the Southern Pacific Company, and it began to connect the two states. As part of the agreement, the control and stock of the O&C passed to Southern Pacific. The completion of the railroad over the Siskiyou Summit was then completed from both sides. On December 17, 1887, Charles Crocker, the vice president of the Southern Pacific Railroad Company, drove in the golden spike in Ashland that formally connected the two tracks.

The passage of the railroad through Josephine and Jackson County created new towns and left others in the wind. Towns such as Grants Pass, Rogue River, Gold Hill, Central Point, Medford, and Ashland were made. When Thomas Chavner offered concessions to the railroad, he ended up platting and creating in 1884 the town of Gold Hill with its train station and stop. A few miles down the Rogue River, neighboring Rock Point and its stage stop was by-passed and it withered away. Landowners in the Central Point area made a right-of-way deal with the railroad to build its tracks over their land. In return, they relocated Central Point to the railroad line and that township flourished with its stop.

The story of Jacksonville took another turn. Its leaders assumed that the railroad would come through there, especially since the first surveyors came from the town. Despite its rich history and the assumptions, the cost of building one mile of track was estimated at $30,000 per mile, and a detour from the straight line through Bear Creek Valley would have been too expensive. The railway continued from Gold Hill through Tolo on the river and direct to eventually reach Ashland.

Four property owners in Jackson County, including Cornelius Beekman, had donated land to the railroad in late 1883, and this land was platted for a new town named Medford. As the railroad stopped there, dozens of businesses were created. The depot building was replaced in 1900, and in 1910, the brick station was constructed where Porters Restaurant and Bar on North Front Street is now located.

Jacksonville shriveled away until Robbie Collins and others with their vision brought about its designation in the 1960s as the first National Historic Landmark Town in the country. With the coming of the railroad, property values substantially increased and new county seats were born at Grants Pass and Medford. The fast movement of crops, freight, and goods—compared to the days and weeks taken by wagon train—brought the two counties and Southern Oregon into a new prosperity.

Source: Webber, *Railroading in Southern Oregon*, June 1985. Also, *Medford Mail Tribune*, December 23, 2012; Fattig, *Medford Mail Tribune*, December 23/25, 2012; Miller, *Medford Mail Tribune*, December 25/27, 2012.

PART III

Businesses and the Economy

Adroit Construction

O N ANY GIVEN DAY, YOU WILL PROBABLY drive by, walk into, or work in a building that Adroit Construction built. In 1979, Bob Mayers relocated from the Bay Area to join up with Steve Lawrence. Having graduated from Bradley University with a construction engineering management degree, Bob had managed large commercial construction projects in Chicago and San Francisco. Lawrence and Steve Shapiro, who had run an Illinois company also known as Adroit, started the business that Mayers joined, and two years later brought him in as a partner. Bob and Steve bought out Shapiro's interest in 1983, and what was formerly a two-man shop has grown substantially from there.

All was not "bed and roses," however, in that the primary focus then was small commercial projects and a few single-family residential construction projects. When the economy took large downturns--especially in Oregon with its basic lumber and timber industry stagnating—it was a very difficult go. The word "adroit" was picked and is defined as being "skillful and resourceful." They had to do this in order to survive.

As Southern Oregon and the country suffered through an early-1980s recession, Bob Mayers had an important asset: a California contractor's license. He took on general construction work on the Klamath River, including driving to Forest Service locations that no one else wanted to do. Adroit began to use their own field employees for concrete, carpentry, and steel work at these remote locations (such as Hornbrook and Happy Camp). But to them, this was like driving to Grants Pass and they had work.

Becoming one of the highly regarded general contractors in Southern Oregon and Northern California, the small firm grew substantially over the years—including with major projects through the "Great Recession of 2008"—to where its annual revenues are $80 million-plus and the ability to work twenty commercial projects at a time. The company has managed developments now from the northern Oregon border to south of Sacramento; from the Pacific Ocean to eastern Nevada mining towns.

From medical centers, libraries, and schools to banks, fire stations, and even airplane hangers, Ashland-based Adroit has completed some 2,000 projects. A few of the recognized projects are: Lithia Motors' headquarters (the Commons), the Jackson County Sheriff's headquarters, SOU's 200,000 square-foot North Campus Village dormitory complex, Medford Airport Terminal and Control Tower, new Medford Police Building, Ashland's Fire and Rescue Station #1, SOU/RVCC classroom building, and many other important area structures.

Showing their forward-looking focus, Lawrence and Mayers brought in two of their younger, talented employees as co-owners in 2007. The two wanted to bring along their successors and let them develop further at an executive level. Jason Stranberg and Tom Walker were not only Ashland High School graduates, but also graduates at different times from Oregon State University in construction engineering management. They had been project managers with large out-of-state construction firms. With the ten-year transition period starting after 2007, Stranberg and Walker are soon to be 50 percent partners in Adroit just as Mayers and Lawrence have been.

Additionally, Bob Mayers has shared his time with the community. Rotary International honored him as its Outstanding Business Person of the Year. He has served on the boards for the Oregon Shakespeare Festival, Ashland YMCA, and Ashland Chamber of Commerce, not to mention Peoples Bank of Commerce (Medford), the Mt. Ashland Association, and the SOU Foundation. Jason Stranberg has also served as President of the Ashland YMCA board of directors, along with other nonprofit work, and Bob Mayers has led the successful, annual "Y" Kids Scholarship drive for several years for the YMCA. Steve Lawrence has actively supported youth skiing programs in the Valley.

Adroit over time has also been awarded high placements in the "Top 100 Best Companies to Work for in Oregon" rankings. The story about Adroit is another impressive one.

Sources: See "Adroit Construction" and "Adroit—Profile" at its website; Stiles, *Medford Mail Tribune*, May 2, 2007; Stiles, *Medford Mail Tribune*, November 20, 2011.

Two of Adroit's most visible projects: *Top*: Lithia Motors headquarters at the Commons, downtown Medford. *Bottom*: Ashland's Fire and Rescue Station #1.

Dutch Brothers Coffee

*I*N 1992, THIRTY-EIGHT-YEAR-OLD DANE BOERSMA was wondering what to do. A Grants Pass dairy farmer for fifteen years, he had learned that Oregon's enacted environmental law changes mandated he spend $150,000 to protect the creek that ran through his pasture, as well as having to get rid of half of his herd. He had graduated from Grants Pass High School, attended the University of Oregon, worked on the Alaskan pipeline, operated a Dairy Queen franchise, and now was raising a family on the farm.

As he pondered his choices after the dairy's close, his then twenty-one-year-old brother, Travis, had come from attending Ashland's Southern Oregon State College. Seeing the problem that they were facing, Travis talked Dane into thinking about selling espresso. They talked to the owner of a local coffee shop, Paul Leighton, who gave them coffee, sold them a two-handled espresso machine, and spent one day in the milking shed of his dairy barn, explaining how to make the coffee.

Inside their empty milk house, they experimented in making coffee drinks for their friends. After using 100-pounds of coffee and handing out free samples of their flavored coffee, the two headed with a mobile espresso pushcart to downtown Grants Pass. Given the Dutch-derivation of their last name, the two named their venture as the "Dutch Brother's Coffee Company," or as shortened, "Dutch Bros. Coffee (DBC)."

After their first cart, they discovered that their approach and coffee was popular. Their one cart turned into five carts; standing kiosks then replaced the carts, and finally they opened a coffee house in Grants Pass. As the coffee craze for lattes, espressos, cappuccinos, mochas, and other coffee drinks swept through Grants Pass, the region, and the country,

Customers lined up at a Dutch Bros. drive-thru.

their business began to grow with more locations. As to the dairy farm, Dane converted it into the Dutcher Creek Golf Course.

From the start, the two Boersma brothers painstakingly went over every detail on how to make a fine cup of coffee. The roasted their coffee by hand, blended it similarly, and then ground it by hand. The brothers worked with local suppliers to ensure quality. They worked long, hard hours but expected only the best. The company roasted (and still does) all of its own coffee, and from the beginning, the owners focused on how best to grow their business with drive-through coffee shops.

It wasn't until ten years later that DBC emphasized franchising their operation, as it contracted for others to own their business, but operate under DBC's trade name and follow their guidelines, in exchange for a fee and continuing royalty. In 2005, DBC had opened its seventy-fifth coffee stand in Sutherlin, Oregon (Douglas County). It sells franchises only to people who have worked for the company for a minimum of three years, understanding its mission of quality, helping their community, and working together.

Dane Boersma tragically discovered that he had Lou Gehrig's disease, or Amyotrophic Lateral Sclerosis (ALS), which is a progressive neurodegenerative disease affecting nerve cells in the brain and spinal cord. Shortly afterwards, the company began raising money (nearly $2 million by now) for ALS research. After battling the disease for five and a half years, Dane died in 2009 at age fifty-five.

As DBC continued on, other coffee shops competed against it. The giant Starbucks opened up new stores nationally and in their region. Although the later tough economic times held DBC's expansion back for a few years, it picked up steam and by mid-2013, there were nearly 200 locations operating in the West and Pacific Northwest states. Two years before, CNN had ranked it as the sixth fastest growing coffee chain in the country.

Having started from humble beginnings, as a single espresso pushcart in a small town, DBC now has over 260 locations (and growing!) in Oregon, California, Washington, Idaho, Nevada, Colorado, and Arizona. Dutch Bros. Coffee serves specialty coffee drinks, smoothies, freezes, teas and even a private-label energy drink, along with other products.

The company is the country's largest privately held, drive-through coffee chain. Dutch Bros. donates 1 percent of gross sales to its communities, which generally totals over $1 million to nonprofit organizations, including local food banks, the Muscular Dystrophy Association, American Cancer Society, the Boys & Girls Clubs of America, and localized fundraising drives.

The Boersma brothers rode the coffee wave, but it was their focusing more on people than the bottom line — with a desire to transform lives rather than only conducting business — that was responsible for this success. This personal approach to their business is the reason why Dutch Bros. Coffee continues to stand out — and it is still headquartered in Grants Pass.

Sources: Hsuan, *Oregonian*, October 15, 2009; Dutch Bros. (website) "About Us"; Adams, *Forbes*, June 29, 2016.

KMED and Bill and Blanche Virgin: Southern Oregon's Radio Pioneers

WILLIAM ("BILL") JACKSON VIRGIN WAS BORN in 1886, and five years later, his father moved the family from Wisconsin to Ashland. While his father owned and operated the Ashland Mill, Bill attended Ashland schools and played football for Ashland High. After enlisting and serving in the Navy, he and a few friends built and tested an experimental radio transmitter in an Ashland garage.

With his life-long interest in electronics, he applied for a radio broadcasting license and started constructing the station. The *Medford Mail Tribune* agreed to supply him with news reports to broadcast, and in September 1922, Bill Virgin acquired a license for station KFAY in Medford; this activity came several months after KGW acquired a radio license in Portland, the first one in Oregon to do so. KGW operated until changing its call letters in 2003 to KPOJ.

On September 23, 1922, KFAY began broadcasting at 5-watts and was located at the old Jackson County Fairgrounds. Having relocated to Medford, Bill Virgin broadcasted orchestra music, which could be picked up by listeners from Santa Cruz to Salt Lake City. His later programs were: "broadcasting that suits you, music, news, sermons, addresses, daily market, weather, and crop reports."

Virgin's keen business sense in promoting radio was found in his KFAY's broadcasts from the old fairgrounds, and then later lowering equipment into the Oregon Caves to determine the depths at which he could transmit and receive. Selling radio sets by day at his Medford

KMED Studio, circa 1937. (SOHS 15241)

store, however, and broadcasting at night proved to be a problem. The well-capitalized, national radio shows broadcasted their best programs at night—and he couldn't compete. Going off the air in 1924, Virgin returned KFAY's license to the Commerce Department, which regulated radio stations until the creation of the Federal Communications Commission (FCC) in 1934.

Realizing he needed support and capital, Virgin brought in his friend, Robert Ruhl—the publisher and half-owner of the *Medford Mail Tribune*—as a partner. On December 13, 1926, Bill filed his application for a new station, KMED. Two weeks later, the license was granted (it can take years now), and the new station began broadcasting on December 28th from his newly built studios in the Sparta Building at Riverside and Main.

With state-of-the-art equipment such as a fifty-watt, Western Electric transmitter, KMED was off to a fine start. Two eighty-five-foot wooden towers (purchased from local farmers and more than likely used before as windmills) were mounted eighty-two feet apart on the building's roof, and copper wire was stretched between the two to send out its signal.

Although Ruhl had bought his interest for a reported $1,500, the newspaper then and for years referred to KMED as the "*Medford Mail Tribune* — Virgin station." Owing to its relationship with the newspaper, moreover, the station was also known as the "*Mail Tribune* station." Robert Ruhl apparently thought that radio was a passing fad and graciously gave his interest back to Bill Virgin.

From the beginning, KMED was very active in sports broadcasting. It reportedly was the first to broadcast a high school football game in November 1927, and the first to broadcast a college football game — the University of Oregon versus California — on October 15, 1927. It broadcast more football games, play by play, than any other West Coast station and was the only station to broadcast the full returns of the 1929 baseball World Series.

Suffering from Bright's disease (a severe kidney inflammation) for years, Bill died in 1928 at the young age of forty-one. His widow, Blanche, inherited the radio station, one of the first women to own and operate one in the country. In 1933, she purchased land west of Medford, had new studios built, and remodeled the old ones in downtown Medford.

KMED became part of the NBC network in 1937, broadcasting national programs such as Eddie Cantor and "Amos 'n Andy." It moved to 1440-AM in 1941 where KMED has been to date. During World War II, different programs were broadcast over the NBC network from Camp White outside Medford in what's now White City. Instrumental in continuing the development of KMED, Blanche became a strong supporter of community programs, from the arts to music.

Sensing the changes to come from television, Blanche sold KMED in June 1950 to a group of local businessmen: a doctor, dentist, mill and

KMED (now part of Bicoastal Media) today.

lumber operator, packinghouse and fruit-shipping operator, and an insurance broker, who used the name of "Radio Medford, Inc." She never returned to the station and an era in broadcasting in Southern Oregon had come to a close. She died in 1978 in Marysville, Washington.

Operating continuously since then, KMED (1440-AM; 106.7-FM) had flourished and is certainly the oldest station in the Valley — if not the oldest in Oregon — and the 5,000-watt station is now owned by Bicoastal Media as a Fox Affiliate.

Sources: Kramer (Ron), *Western States Museum of Broadcasting:* "Bill Virgin"; Kramer, *Western States Museum of Broadcasting:* "History of Radio in Southern Oregon."

Rogue Creamery

GAETANO "TOM" VELLA CAME TO Sonoma, California, in the early 1920s, and held various jobs with the Sonoma Mission Creamery; his brother, Joseph, held "considerable" stock in the creamery. In 1931, local dairymen called on Tom and asked if he would start his own cheese factory, if they guaranteed him all of the quality bulk milk that was needed. Tom agreed.

Once he started the Vella Cheese Company in Sonoma, Tom realized that another larger market existed further north. When he visited this area in the mid-1930s, the Rogue Valley was then quite different: It was a sea of small but diversified farms, pear orchards, and lumber mills, but in the grasp of the Great Depression. Despite this, he chose Central Point, halfway between San Francisco and Portland, for a new rural cheese factory and creamery.

With Kraft's assistance, he helped local farmers acquire cows and in 1935 began using their milk to make cheddar, jack cheese, cottage cheese, and butter. He kept his Sonoma dairy business, although on a reduced scale. His son, Ignazio "Ig" Vella, was learning the trade, starting in Sonoma when he delivered dairy products in his dad's Model-A truck.

Tom's Rogue River Creamery grew slowly but surely; when the U.S. entered World War II, however, and troops around the world needed food, his operations ramped up. For four consecutive years, it produced one-million pounds of cheddar that was shipped to troops in many countries. With the ending of the war, the civilian market accelerated and his creamery became the first major supplier of cottage cheese in Oregon.

The Rogue Creamery in Central Point.

Tom traveled in the 1950s to Roquefort, France, where he toured its famous blue cheese operations, from the farms and cheese factories to the curing limestone caves at Cambalou. He left with plans for a Roquefort-type cheese factory, and construction began in Central Point. Envisioning caves similar to Cambalou, he designed a building to duplicate its atmosphere: Two Quonset-shaped, half-circled rooms of cement were poured, one over the other, with space in between for insulation. The result was a true cave-like atmosphere. The Rogue Creamery began its production as the first blue cheese produced in caves west of the Missouri River. Its dairies along the Rogue River produced the whole milk used for their gourmet blues.

During this time, son Ig graduated magna cum laude from Santa Clara University and eventually took over the operations of the Vella Cheese Company in Sonoma. When Tom died in 1998 at age 100, the businesses were inherited by Tom's wife, Zolita, and his four children: Ignazio, Carmela, Moris, and Zolita. Ig soon ran the operations of the Rogue

Creamery. As the CEO of both operations, Ig believed strongly in artisan dairy products. When the American consumer grew tired of the bland, mass-produced cheeses, they returned to his handmade specialty "artisan" cheeses. For thirty years, Ig trained cheesemakers and instituted a union-recognized apprentice cheesemaker program.

For three years after his dad's death, Ig split his time between Sonoma and Central Point. Sales were suffering in the Rogue Creamery after his father died, however, as he shuttled back and forth. He also had strong Sonoma ties: Ig was a Sonoma County supervisor for three consecutive terms (four years each), manager of the Sonoma County Fair, and even President of the Association of Bay Area Governments.

In 2002, Cary Bryant and David Gremmels acquired Rogue River Valley Creamery from Ig under the condition that he stay on as the master cheesemaker and teach them all that he knew. Buying the business on a handshake on the porch at the facilities, Ig traveled from Sonoma to Central Point one week each month for a time, happy to hand over his family's local legacy to these two men. The name was changed to its present one of the Rogue Creamery.

It won the award for the World's Best Blue Cheese at the 2003 World Cheese Awards in London, a first for a U.S. creamery. Their long award's list includes four trophies and thirty medals and awards, including the coveted Best New Product Award as the world's first smokey-blue at the national trade show in 2005 and Best in Show at the 2009 American Cheese Society show.

The third and fourth generations of Tom Vella manage the Vella Cheese operation in Sonoma; it produces jack and monterey jack, habañero dry jack, cheddar cheeses, and even salami. The separate Rogue Creamery's specialties are blue cheeses, cheddars (different varieties), and TouVelle. And along with an increase in business, the companies continue to win awards every year.

Sources: Rogue Creamery: "An Historical Overview," at its website; "Vella Cheese Company: The History of Vella Cheese," at its website; Specht, *Medford Mail Tribune*, June 14, 2011.

Rogue Credit Union

*T*HE LACK OF FINANCIAL SERVICES IN THE mid-1950s brought a group of ten teachers in Southern Oregon together to find a way to help one another. By forming a non-profit, financial cooperative (or credit union) — owned and operated by a group of individuals for their mutual benefit — they ensured in 1956 to have access to fairly priced credit, a safe investment, and generally lower fees.

Members elect a volunteer board of directors to oversee the credit union, and the President/CEO reports to this board. Membership then was open to only public school employees who worked in Jackson County, employees of the Credit Union, immediate family members, and organizations to which they belonged.

During the early 1960s, Jackson County Teachers Federal Credit Union (JCTFCU), as it was known, moved from a garage into an office, started a newsletter, and hit the $1 million mark in assets. They ended the decade with a part-time operation in Ashland.

In 1972, a merger and name change to Rogue Federal Credit Union (RFCU) allowed membership to expand to city, county, state, and school employees. Rogue Credit Union in 1980 met the $20 million mark in assets and in 1984 opened its Ashland Branch. The thirtieth year was marked with the opening of an office in North Medford and the credit union hit $50 million in assets by 1986.

With the end of 1996 and forty years later, RFCU boasted $120 million in assets and over 27,000 members. During 2001, the National Credit Union Administration approved an amendment to its charter expanding membership to include Josephine and Klamath counties, as well as allowing a branch to be operated in Grants Pass (2004) and Klamath Falls (2005).

In 2012, it purchased and assumed the Oregon operations of Chetco

Rogue Credit Union headquarters' office in Medford.

Federal Credit Union from the National Credit Union Administration. This resulted in the addition of Curry, Coos and Del Norte counties to its charter area (with five full service branches from Brookings to Bandon). The membership then voted in 2013 to convert to a state charter and became Rogue Credit Union (RCU). Presently with nineteen full-service branch locations in six Oregon counties (with one California location in Del Norte county), and one drive-up location in Medford, it serves a variety of financial needs from basic financial services to mortgage loans, investment services, and business loans.

RCU has been recognized as the #1 Financial Institution in the *Medford Mail Tribune* Reader's Choice Award for numerous years, and earned the #1 place for Best Customer Service in the *Curry Coastal Pilot* Reader's Choice Award. *Oregon Business* magazine also has recognized it as the #1 Best Large Non-Profit to work for in Oregon. And more recognition has been received.

The credit union now has over 100,000 members, boasts assets in excess of $1 billion (85% of this is loaned out to members), and annually returns over $2.5 million in dividends. Any individual who lives, works, owns a business, or has an immediate family member in twenty-eight

Oregon counties (this state has thirty-six) can become a member and keeps ownership by maintaining a savings account balance of at least $5; each person is allowed only one share in the credit union.

Its growth rate is among the top five credit unions in the country — all due to continuing excellent management, every member being an owner, and the efforts of one small, insightful group in 1956.

Sources: See the Rogue Credit Union website, generally and its "history."

Sid DeBoer and Lithia Motors

*L*ITHIA MOTORS BEGAN AS A Chrysler-Plymouth-Dodge dealership in Ashland, Oregon, when Walt DeBoer started the business in 1946. Located in Ashland's downtown Plaza and named after the town's Lithia Springs, in its first year a grand total of fourteen cars were sold. When struck by a car in 1968, Walt tragically died and his twenty-five-year-old son, Sid, took over to run the operation. He then purchased it from his mother for $60,000.

Two years later, Dick Heimann joined Lithia after three years as a district manager for Chrysler Corporation. Working together, the two increased the business by the 1990s to five stores and nineteen franchises (allowing dealers to sell more than one brand at the same location) in Southern Oregon. Lithia was providing parts and maintenance, repairs, finance, and warranty-credit insurance services.

Sid DeBoer had been thinking, however, about a bigger and different strategy: He would buy car dealerships in rural communities and the smaller towns he was familiar with, and then increase their sales with the techniques he knew well. Using his existing base of five dealerships in Medford and Grants Pass, he could reach northward into Washington and southward into California, and then diversify east as opportunities arose. Sid decided he would use the proceeds of an equity offering—not unpredictable bank debt. This way, he had quick funds for expansion and could lessen the problems of economic downturns.

DeBoer headed to Wall Street in 1996 with confidence and his plan. He needed this, as no one knew him: Lithia was then about the 500th largest car dealer in the country. After tireless work, he and Dick Heimann convinced the investment banking firm of Furman Selz to underwrite a public offering. In December, Lithia Motor's offering

Ashland Plaza in 1964; note the Walt DeBoer dealership to the far right. (SOHS 12311)

raised $25 million for their expansion plans, and the stock began trading at $11 per share on NASDAQ. They started looking for dealerships to buy in small to medium markets with agricultural or rural ties— hometowns like their Medford.

Moving primarily through the West, Lithia by 1998 grew to thirty dealerships. A network of brokers, old friends, or dealers themselves brought dealerships to Lithia's attention. The management team then analyzed what the specific problems were for a particular site: for example, lack of professionalism, poor management, or store layout. If it could be fixed, then the site was a potential acquisition. Lithia's success was in its ability to bring an acquisition into sync with its other dealerships and practices, including detailed cost accounting, use of promotional pricing, and fast changing promotions.

By 2000, Lithia's dealerships had increased to forty; ten years after the public offering, the company had ninety-four car dealerships in thirteen states. Lithia was the eighth-largest car dealer in the county (out of the top U.S. ones) and closing in on $3 billion in annual sales. The wisdom of relying on equity — not debt — was key when the great recession of 2008 hit. Although Lithia needed to trim non-performing dealerships, its balance sheet and operations were safe.

With dealerships ranging from Alaska through the Pacific Northwest and California, Lithia has concentrations in Texas, along with ones from New Mexico to Idaho. The brands carried varied from Chevrolet, Chrysler, BMW, and Ford to Hyundai, Nissan, Mazda, Toyota, and Suzuki. Determining that the greater value still lies in the West, Lithia's towns are the communities within the original plan: Odessa, Texas; Anchorage, Alaska; Bend, Oregon; Great Falls, Montana; Missoula, Montana; Santa Rosa, California; Redding, California; Des Moines, Iowa; Grand Forks, North Dakota; and so on.

Sid's son, Bryan DeBoer, with years of experience at Lithia is now its CEO, while Sid presently is Chairman of the Board. In 2013, Lithia exceeded $1 billion in sales for its second quarter and headed to $4 billion in annual sales. In 2016, the company reported for the year well in excess of $8 billion in sales. Lithia continues to diversify and concentrate more into branded Internet and used-car sales. The business employs 5,000-plus employees, including 600 in this area.

Further, Lithia and the DeBoers have contributed strongly to this area. From the Lithia Motors Amphitheater at the Expo ($500,000 donation) and The Commons (see "The Rebuilding of Medford's Downtown," pg. 27), Lithia itself has made sizeable donations, including to Dogs for the Deaf, American Red Cross, Oregon Food Bank, and many others. Sid and Karen DeBoer have individually contributed through their foundation well over $1 million to SOU for different programs, as well as purchasing Camp Low Echo (the Girl Scout Camp at Lake of the Woods) and donating this to the Ashland YMCA. They followed this with a $3 million donation in 2016 to renovate the camp as a recreational site for all ages — and space limits where else they have contributed to help others.

How can you match this: starting out with five stores some twenty years ago, still headquartered in Medford, and making a difference.

Sources: Battistella, *Oregon Encyclopedia*: "Lithia Motors"; Fowlkes, *Medford Mail Tribune*, June 21, 2016; Stiles, *Medford Mail Tribune*, July 28, 2016.

Snider's Dairy: Medford's First Commercial Dairy

*I*N DECEMBER 1904, MAUDE AND JOHN SNIDER were on a train destined west for Medford and just married. One week before, John had proposed and they decided to move there to manage the Warner Ranch. Once there, they discovered their house wasn't ready, but John finished the house in 1905. He started selling milk, dairy products, and chickens as a partner of "Warner and Snyder." (By the early 1910s, the spelling of his name changed to "Snider".)

The business was the first commercially successful diary in Southern Oregon; hence, its title of being the "first" one. Before 1910, milk deliveries were by wagon with five-gallon cans to dip out the customer's milk by a ladle. Rising every morning at 2:30 a.m. to cook breakfast and prepare lunch and dinner, Maude was usually in the wagon with John when delivering the morning milk. This was hard work at best, especially with the freezing winter temperatures and the overall work.

Increasing his herds to 250 dairy cows, Snider and his Swiss workers hand-milked them while yodeling. (Later, milking machines were used.) They filtered the milk though cheesecloth to "clean" the milk before delivering it. In 1911, John Snider acquired Warner's interest and the operation became the "Medford Dairy." The first order for its milk bottles — changing the delivery mode from ladle to bottles — was made then.

Over time, they expanded their production, delivery routes, and marketing. They bought the Independence Creamery in 1918, followed three years later by acquiring a larger creamery from Eldridge Dairy on North Bartlett. They moved their operations to Medford, first to North Grape and then to North Bartlett, where it became "Snider's Dairy and Produce Co."

Snider Dairy, circa 1920. (SOHS 09696)

They added farm produce and even soda bottling under the brand of Whistle and Green River. With two children—Mary and John W.—the Sniders continued their business. They opened branches in Ashland and later Grants Pass, but closed them after finding out that their central location on Barnett was more efficient. When John Snider died in 1930, Maude with her children continued the business, and by 1935, its dairy was the largest Oregon creamery outside Portland.

By then, their enterprise was well into the bottling business. The family was bottling both Pepsi and Coke in the back room of their dairy, and as these brands grew, they had to choose between the two. They decided on Pepsi. In 1933, the first shipment of beer in Medford arrived there from Weinhard's Brewery. As part of this, the Sniders operated a major beer and wine distributorship with their flagstaff beer being Blitzweinhard, a leading Oregon beer. This distributorship was sold later to Karl Schmidt.

In 1937, the family became Medford's first Pepsi-Cola distributor that joined their existing lines of Mission Orange, root beer, Schweppes, near

Snider's Dairy transitioned into Pepsi Bottling.

beer, Whistle Soda, and Green River sodas. Product lines were dropped and added over time, however, such as replacing the orange soft drinks with Sunkist and the root beers with Mug Root Beer.

Their dairy continued to prosper, as well. It bottled milk for Ginger Rogers, who with her mother had a dairy on the Rogue River near Shady Cove. This was called "Ginger Rogers' Milk" and had a specially-designed glass milk bottle featuring her name. Their trademark, "Little Daisy, the cow," was out in the late 1950s, and their son, John W., had a daily column then in the *Medford Mail Tribune* entitled, "Moos and Musings," which featured the Little Daisy logo.

John W. was appointed in 1950 to fill a vacancy on the Medford City Council, and he served three terms on the council. Becoming mayor of Medford from 1956 to 1962, he was elected at age thirty-eight, becoming one of the city's youngest ever, and served three two-year terms. During his administration, Alba (Italy) became Medford's sister city.

Later, John W. sold its Pepsi Cola bottling and distributing business. In 1963, Arden Farms acquired the Snider Dairy & Produce Company's wholesale milk accounts and Cloverleaf Dairy took over its home deliveries. The building at 28 North Bartlett was demolished, and the land is now part of the parking structure across from Lithia Motors' headquarters. PepsiCo — the parent company of Pepsi, Frito-Lay, and Tropicana — now owns the bottling business, and operates this from the facilities at Airport Road and Avion Drive, across the street from Bicoastal Media.

When John W. died in 1994, area dairying had diminished — the family, however, was in other businesses and careers. His son, John Jr., owned his own Medford-based advertising company before working for years as District Director for Congressmen Bob Smith and later Greg Walden, then very active with the Holly Theatre renovation project. Doug Snider is a successful architect in Medford and has designed several local schools and hospital facilities. The tradition of family success was continued.

Sources: Scafani, *Southern Oregon Heritage,* 2003; *Medford Mail Tribune*: "Since You Asked," 1999.

The Grange Co-op

*D*URING THE DEPTHS OF THE GREAT DEPRESSION, ninety-nine farmers in the Valley invested $10 each in 1934 to form a cooperative. By joining together, they could pool their produce for better prices, secure a lower price for livestock feed, and purchase needed equipment and supplies at bulk prices. The cooperative has grown since into a multi-million dollar business with numerous services to meet this region's agricultural and individual needs.

Local farmers and ranchers can now obtain sacked or bulk feeds, certified organic and produced locally. The feeds are available for animals ranging from sheep, goats, cattle, and horses to rabbits, hogs, poultry, and llamas. When the bulk fertilizer plant was built next to the feed mill in the 1960s, the Grange Co-op provided farmers with both conventional and organic fertilizers—blended at the plant to requirements. Crop protection products such as herbicides, insecticides, and fungicides are available, plus renting different spreaders.

Rising 135 feet above Central Point, the Co-op's grain elevator is an imposing landmark. It is the tallest manmade structure in Southern Oregon; an area monument since its 1947 construction, a 1961 fire destroyed it. Rebuilt one year later at the same location and to nearly the same specifications, the structure is still the only major feed plant in Southern Oregon.

The facility holds thirty-five commodity bins that hold up to 2,000 tons of wheat, corn, barley, oats, soybean meal, and beet pulp. This flexibility allows the Grange to meet nearly all of a farmer's or rancher's livestock needs. Purchasing wheat, barley, or oat grains from regional farmers (the great bulk from the Mid-West), the shipments are unloaded from trucks and railcars that pull up to its Central Point facilities. A

A local landmark—the Grange Co-op grain elevator in Central Point. (SOHS 06889)

mechanical bucket system fills the bins, as elevator employees check the levels. The feed is then mixed and shipped.

While other agricultural cooperatives have had difficult times, this Co-op has done quite well despite the Valley's shift from strictly rural/agricultural to being more urbanized. Its success stems from a decision made in the mid-1960s to expand its retail offerings to target homeowners and weekend gardeners. The Co-op has grown over the years to eight retail stores in Ashland, Central Point, Coos Bay, Grants Pass, Klamath Falls (expanded), South Medford, White City, plus a "Pet Country" (in Medford).

The Co-op still runs its feed and fertilizer plants in Central Point with field-crop analysts serving customers from the coast to the Klamath Basin, and from Douglas County into Northern California. It still delivers bulk gas, diesel, and heating oil, as started by its founders. The retail sales at its outlets make the difference, however, with a wide array of products: from farm and ranch to lawn and garden; from pet food, supplies, clothing, and footwear to patio furniture, barbecue grills, specialty food, and more.

Co-op members for decades needed to be full- or part-time farmers or ranchers to receive its annual dividends of cash and equity credits based upon their purchases. This dividend-paying program was extended later to individuals who applied for this membership.

With 200-plus employees and total annual sales of over $50 million, it has greatly expanded from its earlier Depression beginnings — and is today yet another Southern Oregon success story.

Sources: Grange Co-op: "About Grange Co-op," at its website; Sarah Lemon, "The High Point," *Medford Mail Tribune*, April 17, 2011.

The History of
Harry and David (and Bear
Creek Corporation)

THE BEAR CREEK STORY DATES BACK TO WEALTHY Sam Rosenberg, who built the luxurious Seattle Hotel Sorrento in the early 1900s. Rosenberg then sold it in 1910 to buy the 240-acre Bear Creek Orchard in Jackson County with its Comice pear trees for $300,000—and incorporated the Bear Creek Company. First hybridized in France in the 1700s and renowned for their fine texture and flavor, the Comice flourished in this area with its rich soil and sunny climate that proved better suited than their French birthplace.

Educated at Cornell's School of Agriculture, sons Harry and David took over the operation following Sam's death in 1914. During the 1920s, they bought more orchards and successfully marketed their Comice pears as a luxury item; renaming the Royal Riviera pear as a brand name, these were sold in quantities overseas and throughout the country.

Living in tents in the orchards and driving carts pulled by mules, migrant workers harvested the fruit. Local women packed the wooden boxes with ice and the fruit, and the full boxes were shipped by rail to their destinations. With their business success, Harry and David continued to buy land and plant more pear trees. The depression of the 1930s, however, put a cruel dent in their operations, including their overseas exports.

In 1934, Harry traveled to New York City with fifteen boxes of pears. After one week, however, he hadn't sold one. He hired an advertising expert, G. Lynn Sumner, who handwrote fifteen letters from Harry and David Rosenberg on Waldorf-Astoria stationery (where he was staying) and sent each one—with a box of the pears—to a well-known executive,

Bear Creek Orchards packing plant and loading dock—after Jackson & Perkins acquisition. (SOHS 05602)

including Alfred Sloan, David Sarnoff, and Walter Chrysler. This first direct-mail effort brought in orders for nearly 500 boxes of pears.

Harry and David next created a four-page flyer that they mailed out. Selling 6,000 boxes of pears in 1934, their shipments reached 15,000 in 1935. One year later, David ran a full-page ad in Fortune magazine with the theme of making a "royal" delicacy available to the common man. Its headline was: "Imagine Harry and me advertising our pears in Fortune!"

Buying land from struggling orchard owners, Bear Creek Orchards expanded its acreage during the late 1930s. They then began selling year-round with the world's first "Fruit of the Month Club." They also changed their family name from Rosenberg to Holmes to end the anti-Semitic boycott of their products in Germany. Following 600 Camp

White soldiers during World War II who picked the pears, German POWs ironically did this for one year.

In 1949, the brothers built the present Art Moderne-style packing house complex straddling the Southern Pacific Railroad tracks, and Bear Creek's growth during the postwar years became significant. After David and Harry died (1950 and 1959, respectively) their sons — David Holmes Jr. and John Holmes (Harry's son) — took over running the family-owned business until 1976 when it became a public company.

The company then acquired in 1966 Jackson & Perkins Roses — a rose-growing and marketing operation dating back to the early 1900s — and moved its headquarters to Medford in consolidating the operations. The company shipped railroad cars of rose plants from Medford to all points. Jackson and Perkins's promotion of its new "Princess Diana" rose — after the princess's death in 1997 — was highly successful, and the business grew to dominate U.S. rose production with twenty-four million roses sold annually.

The Harry and David store, Medford.

The company expanded its offerings with products from fruit cakes and preserves to dried flowers, holly, and miniature Christmas trees in the Harry and David catalog. Over time, it purchased or started different operations from the direct marketing of orchids to jewelry, toys, fishing accessories, and even travel-trailers. With satellite facilities in California and Ohio, Harry & David had opened its first outlet store in Medford in 1991, featuring catalog items plus frozen foods, picnic, and kitchen accessories; it ran forty-seven retail stores nationwide after closing 60-plus during the Great Recession of 2008.

After the family sold the firm to RJR Nabisco in 1986, the business changed hands several times. From publicly traded conglomerates to foreign ownership, the take-over Wall Street firm, Wasserstein & Co., purchased the operations in 2004 from a Japanese company for $254 million. Unfortunately, Wasserstein had saddled the operations with a mountain of debt that coupled with declining margins, a bad economy, the Internet, and increased competition forced Bear Creek to file for bankruptcy in March 2011.

The company exited its "pre-arranged" Chapter 11 proceeding in 2012. Three years later, 1-800-Flowers.com bought the operations for $142 million and is presently running it. With more than 2,000 acres of orchards in this area (3,400 total in Oregon), Bear Creek Corporation is one of the largest non-federal and non-timber landowners. Pears are still its biggest seller and it is still one of the largest private-company employers in this region.

Sources: "Fundinguniverse.com—Bear Creek Corp. History"; LaLande, *Oregon Encyclopedia*: "Harry & David/Bear Creek Orchards"; Moore, *Oregon Business*, 2015.

The Neuman Hotel Group

DOUG NEUMAN WAS A SANTA BARBARA DEVELOPER until relocating to Ashland in the late 1980s with his wife, Becky. He specialized initially in building custom homes and subdivisions in Ashland, Talent, and Jacksonville. They came across an old resort lodge and cabins near Klamath Falls, the Lake of the Woods, which needed extensive renovation. "But it had great bones," as Doug said later. They restored the Lake of the Woods and eventually sold it. This brought the Neumans into the hospitality industry. (Doug manages the overall restoration; Becky does most of the interior design and furnishings.)

Their signature turnaround was the conversion of the historic Mark Antony Motor Hotel in downtown Ashland into the Ashland Springs Hotel. Buying it out of bankruptcy for $1.6 million, they spent two years and $10 million to restore it to its former grandeur. In addition to the Ashland Springs Hotel, the Neumans purchased Lithia Springs Resort (on Ashland's north side) and the former Windmill Inn in April 2013 (on Ashland's south side) — and the "Neuman Hotel Group" was born.

The Windmill Inn had been closed since 2007, except for a seventy-suite structure known as the "Village Suites at Ashland Hill," which was still in operation. Located close to I-5, this revitalization centered on the hotel's existing guest rooms (including the Village Suites) and renovating the complete facilities. Renamed the "Ashland Hills Hotel & Suites," the fourteen-acre property is three miles from downtown Ashland. With mountain views, a courtyard patio, an outdoor pool and jacuzzi, as well as two tennis courts and a restaurant (named the "Luna Café & Mercantile"), the 1970s retro-modern, design now has over 100 larger guest rooms and suites.

Ashland Springs Hotel.

In August 2013, a complicated deal involving MURA, the City of Medford, and DHD, LLC (set up by Sid and Mark DeBoer), centered on the old Red Lion Inn, immediately across Riverside Avenue from The Commons. DHD bought the 8-acre property for $2.8 million to sell the hotel back to Doug and Becky Neuman as its developers with another part to the City. The couple had already completed its major renovation of Lithia Springs Resort and the Windmill Inn. The Red Lion's 185 rooms decreased to 118 units, since the city needed to demolish numerous rooms to one side in constructing a public parking lot. Naming the hotel as "The Inn at the Commons," the Neumans also completely remodeled Red Lion's restaurant and named it, "Larks — Medford."

Not to be undone, the next acquisition was the Circle of Teran. In 2003, hand surgeon, Scott Young, and his wife, Robin James, built a mansion on a 1,100 acre Ashland property on Butler Creek Road that they named the "Circle of Teran." This 11,000-square-foot residence had eleven bedrooms, most with private baths and balconies; a commercial-grade kitchen; a great ten-sided, double-story room with inside balcony and giant stained-glass skylights; and a climate-controlled, glass-tropical conservatory where bananas, mangos and plumeria grow. Other features included ponds, a 5,000-square-foot barn with horse stables, a 200-foot-wide lavender maze (that takes thirty minutes to walk through), and windmill-and solar-generated power.

The Youngs had invested $8 million in their Circle of Teran Ranch, but newspaper accounts stated they were not disappointed when it sold for only $1.5 million—to Doug Neuman on July 1, 2014. While at the Medford airport, he had placed the winning bid over the phone and—to his surprise—won. Doug transferred the house to a group that created the Circle of Trust, a high-end drug and alcohol recovery center. The house was put on the market for $8.2 million, and it appears that the Neumans retained a sizeable amount of land.

Continuing on, the Neumans in April 2016 purchased the 3.1 acre Nunan estate (including its large 1892 Victorian home) on Oregon Street in Jacksonville. In addition to the Neumans, Mark and Sid DeBoer are partners in the endeavor (named the Nunan Historic, LLC). The entity purchased this from the owner for only $10 in cash, but also for "considerable non-cash value." The Neumans are adding suites that already included five bedrooms in the main house and three large rooms in another structure. A leased-out restaurant operation (named the "Onyx") now operates from what was once the Carriage House restaurant; patrons can sit at an onyx bar that wraps around the kitchen and watch the chefs at work.

The deals put together by Doug and Becky Neuman are breathtaking, and Southern Oregon is so much better off for their contributions—as we wait for the next ones.

Sources: Powers, "Neuman Hotel Group: How it all began…"; Cook, *Oregon Business*; Boom, *Medford Mail Tribune*, April 11, 2016; Darling, *Medford Mail Tribune*, April 13, 2016.

The Roots, Sabroso, and Tree Top

W HEN MYRON ROOT IN 1932 LOST HIS JOB during the Great Depression, the optimistic man started Myron Root and Company, a fruit packing and shipping business. The operation grew for twenty years, and when Myron retired in 1952, his sons, Don and Bob, took over. Eleven years later, a U.S. Department of Agriculture employee suggested they could make the "cull" fruit—or what was rejected before sending the rest—into a puree for different products. This was hardly done in this country, but was a common practice overseas.

Since the Root family didn't like throwing away 20% of their "cull" crop, they decided in 1963, along with partner Dunbar Carpenter, to start a new subsidiary, Sabroso Company (Sabroso is Spanish for "tasty"), which would market the puree made from the rejected fruit.

It wouldn't be until five years later, however, that Sabroso decided to market its puree as an ingredient for baby food; this endeavor over time became its largest market. With the growth of its purees and competition over the packing and shipping of fruit, the Roots decided to end the Myron Root and Company's operations and work on Sabroso's products.

Jim Root, grandson of Myron Root, was a college graduate with his BA from the School of Agriculture at Oregon State University and an MBA in International Business from the University of Oregon. With years of experience at Sabroso, he took over the operation's management in 1988 from several family members. Over time, he increased the number of fruits that the business processed, from four prime types (apples, apricots, peaches, and pears) to nineteen (including strawberries, mangos, guavas, and papayas).

Ten years later, the company used nearly twice as much fruit as the entire Rogue Valley grew and over five times what it had processed in 1988 (20,000 tons then). Sabroso in 1998 processed 110,000 tons of fruit (including Bear Creek's pears) from the West Coast, Mexico, and Canada, into its fruit puree and concentrates, ultimately sold to make baby foods, fruit snacks, and fruit juices.

The family-owned, Medford-centered business was so successful in marketing overseas that it already was the world leader in producing and selling concentrates, as well as receiving the State Exporter of the Year Award from Governor John Kitzhaber. It also began to expand its plant along Grape Street in Medford.

Owing to CEO Jim Root, Sabroso was a leading supporter of the arts. For example, the company started the campaign to redo the Craterian. It donated $275,000 over time that kept the fund drive alive. The business was so supportive, it was included in the 1999 national selection of the Best Companies Supporting the Arts (BCA 10), alongside large, recognized companies such as the Lincoln Financial Group, PNC Financial Services Group, and the Fort Worth Star-Telegram.

Sabroso by 2008 had grown substantially. With manufacturing facilities in Medford, Woodburn (Oregon), and Oxnard (California), it was also producing dried fruit flakes and fruit preparations for manufacturers and food service providers, including ingredients used in many items such as ice cream, yogurt, bakery goods, and drinks. Still the leader in making fruit purees, it was selling its products to twenty-six different countries.

These successes caught the attention of Tree Top, Inc., a grower-owned cooperative with 1,300 members in Washington, Oregon, and Idaho. With its Tree Top brand, the company was the largest supplier of dried apple products in the world, finding their way into the nation's top brands of cereals, breakfast pastries, cake mixes, and snacks. It manufactures, distributes, and markets juices and fruit-based products under its Tree Top brand name, as well as ingredients to the world's largest food companies and food service operators. With its four production plants in Washington and one in Rialto, California, the two firms were ideal for one another.

Tree Top offered to buy Sabroso and it accepted, closing the deal in November 2008 whereby Sabroso became a wholly-owned subsidiary. The amount paid was not disclosed, but it was reported as being "substantial." After staying on in an advisory capacity, Jim Root created his own consulting company, "Jim Root and Company." He also spends time in managing the Root family's "business portfolio" and continues with the family to support this community.

Sources: Davis, *Medford Mail Tribune,* May 9, 1999; Stiles, *Medford Mail Tribune,* January 19, 2000; Stiles, *Medford Mail Tribune*, October 27, 2008; "Jim Root and Company" at its website.

The Vintners and Their Wine

OREGON HAS CONSISTENTLY RANKED WITHIN the top four wine-producing states behind California, Washington, and New York, based on acres planted and number of vineyards (third on number of wineries; fifth on tons produced). Although Southern Oregon enjoys similar warmth within our state, it receives considerably less rainfall than the northern wine-growing regions (i.e., 40% less than the Willamette Valley). The diverse climates in our valleys, however, allow both cool- and warm-weather varietals to be grown.

The Federal Bureau of Alcohol, Tobacco and Firearms designates regions as American Viticultural Areas (AVA), which allows defined geographic areas to label their wines as produced from that region. As the southern-most of Oregon's eighteen approved AVAs, the Rogue Valley AVA (created in 1991) includes the Applegate Valley AVA (established in 2001) with four main growing areas: the Bear Creek Valley, Valley of the Rogue, Applegate Valley, and Illinois Valley.

This region has over 150 vineyards growing over 70 different varieties on roughly 3,500 acres and producing annually nearly 10,000 tons of grapes. The production is roughly 65-70% red varieties and 30-35% white. These three valleys differ in territory and climate; for example, Bear Creek Valley to the east (running parallel to the I-5 corridor) is warmer and dryer. Its climate is deemed similar to the warmer regions of France, Spain, Portugal, and Italy with varietals including cabernet sauvignon, merlot, chardonnay, pinot gris, sauvignon blanc, malbec, tempranillo, and syrah.

The Applegate Valley (south of Grants Pass) follows the Applegate River, but it is not as warm and dry as Bear Creek Valley: Its vineyards

In a Southern Oregon vineyard, 1907. (SOHS 12777)

are planted as at the Bear Creek Valley, but includes more Zinfandel and Pinot Noir. Being generally wetter and cooler than the others, the Illinois Valley (following its river) with its coastal mountains produces cooler climate varietals such as Pinot Noir, Gewürztraminer, Riesling, and Pinot Gris (along with Chardonnay and Pinot Blanc).

Arriving in the Rogue Valley in 1852, pioneer photographer Peter Britt planted the first vineyard two years later in the Rogue Valley with Mission grapes from California that he had purchased from an Italian peddler. Britt began experimenting with different grapes and fruit trees, ultimately bringing cuttings of over 200 different wine and table grapes. He developed a twenty-acre orchard and expansive grape vineyards on a ranch one mile outside Jacksonville.

Having named his business "Valley View Winery," he had experimented by the 1870s with his 200-plus varietals to determine grape-growing suitability. Conducted first in his basement, his winery is believed to be the first one established in Oregon. By the 1880s, Britt had planted numerous varieties, from cabernet sauvignon and zinfandel to riesling, sauvignon blanc, and merlot. More than a dozen grape growers were reported in 1890 in the Jacksonville area (including Ashland and Phoenix) with over 100 acres planted. Upon the death of Peter Britt in 1905, his winery ceased operating.

Pioneers in the different valleys planted a variety of grapes, but the advent of pears, apples, and peaches (and the early 1900's Orchard Boom) overshadowed all. Prohibition shut down most of the industry, but bootleggers continued producing. Although the 21st Amendment in 1933 ended national prohibition, the depression, World War II, and other industries such as timber and farming put a crimp on further development of vineyards and wineries.

The planting of vineyards finally started up in the 1970s as people looked at earning a living by selling the grapes to wineries outside the area. Valley View Winery (in the Applegate Valley) and Siskiyou Winery (the Illinois Valley) in 1978 became the first wineries to operate and sell wine again to the public. Wineries and vineyards began to sprout up throughout Southern Oregon during the following years.

The industry has experienced sustained growth from 1984 to 2015 (for comparison): The number of growers increased (20 to 235); number of wineries jumped (3 to 125); and planted acres increased from 310 to 6,000. As striking is that the tons of grapes produced increased from 530 to 18,100; the total crop value skyrocketed from $130,000 to $36 million.

Regardless of the valley or place, the interest in converting rural acreage or farmland into vineyards continues strongly. Very much like the Orchard Boom of the past, real estate agents look to sell undeveloped land to "gentleman farmers" and especially those from out of state, due to Oregon's state tax breaks and lower acreage cost. Vineyards and wineries now dot the region—a far cry from when Peter Britt created the first vineyards and winery well over 150 years ago.

Sources: Kingsnorth, *Jacksonville Review*, July 2014; Stiles, *Medford Mail Tribune*, August 20, 2015; *Wines Northwest*: "Rogue Valley and Applegate Valley"; email from Greg Jones, Ph.D., to author, August 19, 2016.

Tucker Sno-Cat

ONE OF THIRTEEN CHILDREN, EMMETT TUCKER was born in 1892 in a log cabin, and he grew up in a stone house built by his father in 1901 near the tiny town of Trail (above Shady Cove). Overlooking the Rogue River, the area is remote, scenic, and heavily snowbound during the winter. As he worked his way to school through deep snows, the young Emmitt was already thinking about how he could build something to transport people over the unpacked snow.

He began to work on different devices; and in the early twenties, Tucker had built several spiral-driven machines with skis on the front and sides. A motorcycle engine drove it, but he wasn't satisfied with the performance. His goal was to build a snow vehicle that could travel over deep, soft snow but with a minimum of expense and mechanical problems.

In 1938, he finally came up with the idea that would work. Revamping his approach, he centered on a machine that used pontoons with a revolving steel track and three skis, one in front and two for balance in the rear. It had taken him nearly twenty-five years of persistence and ingenuity. With this revolutionary design, Tucker built his prototype in his spare time from salvaged parts. Fiberglass later replaced the steel pontoons, plus a design change where wheels worked a rubber track forward.

While testing this in 1941 at Crater Lake, he met a stranger who managed a mine near Mt. Shasta. So impressed by the test model's performance, he bought it from Tucker right then. Moving in 1942 to Grass Valley, California, Emmett set up his first production line. Using a six-cylinder Chrysler industrial engine, Tucker sold seventy of these, primarily to the railroads. Three years later, he demonstrated his snow

Tucker Sno-Cat at Crater Lake, circa 1940s. (SOHS 12294)

vehicle over snow-packed trails and logging roads on a 600-mile, midwinter trek from Mt. Shasta to Mt. Hood. In 1951, Tucker invented the four-track design with an independent suspension system that didn't need the balancing skis. This allowed the machine to traverse rugged terrain.

In the historic first motorized crossing of the Antarctic, four Tucker Sno-Cats were used in the 2,100 mile trek over four months that concluded in March 1958. One of these is on display at its Medford headquarters.

In the 1990s, all-rubber tracks replaced the metal cleats, allowing the cats to cruise over environmentally sensitive areas; this allows all-season use from oil and gas exploration to avalanche control. Over time, Sno-

Cat models would employ a four- or six-cylinder diesel engine with standard automotive parts. The predominate use of a sharp orange color was due to Emmett's belief eight decades ago that this was the best color against white snow if someone became lost.

Carrying everyone from actors in far-away film locations (such as *The Shining*, *White Out*, and *National Treasure*) in ice-ridden spots, Emmett Tucker's dream became the world's oldest and most successful manufacturer of snow vehicles.

Sources: Ed Battistella, *Oregon Encyclopedia*: "Tucker Snow-Cat"; Stiles, *Medford Mail Tribune*, April 14, 2010; see generally "Tucker Sno-Cat" at its website.

William B. Smullin:
Communications Pioneer

W HEN HE WAS TWO-YEARS-OLD, WILLIAM SMULLIN'S family moved in 1909 from Pennsylvania to Hood River, Oregon. After graduating from Willamette University in Journalism in 1929, Smullin worked for a Coos Bay newspaper as its managing editor. He met Harold Hanseth, who owned a small radio station, KOOS. The two set up a new station in 1933 in Eureka, California — KIEM. Smullin had seen the viability of radio and its advantages.

One year later, Hanseth created a company, "Redwood Broadcasting Company," to own the radio stations; Bill Smullin (then the commercial manager) acquired a part interest. He purchased the remaining interest in 1938, becoming also KIEM's president. Prior to then, Bill envisioned a regional media presence, which he called the "Redwood Empire": KIEM was the southern "tip" and Grants Pass to be at the northern end. Gaining the interest of the *Grants Pass Daily Courier* publisher Amos Voorhies, the two worked together to bring KUIN in 1937 to the city. This station in the 1950s became known as KAGI, and Smullin donated this radio station later to Jefferson Public Radio.

Bill Smullin had a remarkable ability to convince others to partner with him on radio stations, and then over time with their success, either purchase the remaining interest or sell his. He looked to smaller, rural areas in a regional context. Along with the stations owned in Humboldt County and Southern Oregon, he branched out to start and/or own radio stations in other cities, such as Corvallis, Redmond, and San Jose.

This was just the start, as he realized television would be the next key media. On August 1, 1953, he launched KBES-TV (now KOBI-TV), as the first VHF television station in Oregon. Three years later, he put KOTI-TV (Channel 2) on the air in Klamath Falls. As these were television's first days, everything from commercials to programming were created on the spot. Automobile commercials were done first by taking Polaroid pictures of cars and putting them on a strip with a wooden track. With a camera fixed on the frame, an employee pulled the strip to show the different cars. They then drove them around the studio for the commercial shots.

Smullin figured out his programming and advertising by continually watching television sets at the studio, or in his living room. Not relying on today's rating services, he observed the reaction of his children, their friends, or others as they watched the two competing TV stations. He then made his decisions.

When CBS began televising Phil Silvers' "You'll Never Get Rich" show with the lead character of Sergeant Bilko, even Medford's City Council became involved. Its members and mayor were so interested in watching this show, they didn't want to attend any council meetings on Tuesday night. This is the reason why the council meets on Thursday evenings, as Tuesday's time then was "Bilko night."

With his operation of KOTI, he also became very interested in the future of cable television. As with radio and TV, he bought or started cable TV systems in Humboldt County (Eureka), Southern Oregon (Grants Pass, Medford, and Klamath Falls), Redding, and Roseburg. Needing a way to relay TV programming from distant cities such as San Francisco and Portland, he started Pacific Teletronics, which served as a microwave relay for these signals.

Over time, studio TV locations changed and transmissions became more complex. The name change to KOBI came when the station's transmitter site in 1968 was changed from Blackwell Hill between Gold Hill and Central Point. KOBI's signal doubled to 60,000 watts with greatly expanded coverage by moving to the much higher King Mountain that is near Wolf Creek.

Forced to choose between owning either his cable or broadcast businesses due to the U.S. government's anti-trust concerns, he sold off the cable systems in 1982. Two years later, he stepped down from the presidency of his company, California Oregon Broadcasting ("COB" that owned his broadcasting interests), in favor of his daughter, Patricia (Patsy) Smullin.

Bill Smullin received countless awards for his vision, drive, and abilities in bringing city-market media to our local, more rural areas. He was a board member of the National Association of Broadcasters and in 1990 received its Distinguished Service Award. He was a pioneer in broadcasting from radio and TV to cable and even public TV by working to create these in Eureka, Medford, and Redding. COB is the longest, continuously independent broadcast group in the West and one of the three oldest in the country.

Patsy Smullin continued on with these traditions. She has served as president of the Oregon Association of Broadcasters and also on the board of the National Association of Broadcasters. She also has been a trustee of Willamette University and a board member of the Southern Oregon University Foundation, the Oregon Children's Foundation Board, AAA of Oregon and Idaho, among others.

In 1990, Bill founded the nonprofit "Patricia D. & William B. Smullin Foundation," to serve the needs of Northern California and Southern Oregon. Since its inception, it has granted over $13 million dollars (through 2016) into this region by grants to higher education and for food, housing, and other health related necessities of the needy. Scholarship funds have been established at six educational institutions, including Humboldt State, Rogue Community College, and Southern Oregon University.

Bill Smullin died in 1995 at the age of eighty-eight; his contributions are everlasting and a tribute to his life.

Sources: Kramer, *Pioneer Mikes*, 2009; Kramer, *Western States Museum*: "History of Radio in Southern Oregon"; Stiles, *Medford Mail Tribune*, August 3, 2003; Darling, *Medford Mail Tribune*, April 24, 2016.

Blackstone Audio

*F*OUNDER CRAIG BLACK HAD EXTENSIVE business experience prior to starting up Blackstone Audio with his wife, Michelle, in 1987 in their Medford living room. Craig had been a retail store manager, supervisor, and in corporate development for Hickory Farms. He worked for the large conglomerate, Tenneco West, where he managed the House of Almonds—a mall-based specialty foods store—that grew within eight years from two anchor stores into more than 250 locations and $50 million in sales revenues. After earning an MBA from Pepperdine, he discovered his passion for audiobooks and launched the company.

Craig and Michelle first chose the name of "Classics on Tape," but later decided on "Blackstone" in honor of the British literary magazine (which also is a derivative of their name). When the decision was made on where to locate their production studios, they decided on Ashland with its Oregon Shakespeare Festival and acting pool for narrating their books on tape. The company started with three employees.

Navigating the firm's ups and downs along with the economy, the founders put at the forefront their love of books, audiobooks, and quality. The corporate culture formed accordingly. Its contracts with digital download companies brought audiobooks to libraries and direct to consumers, while selling its audiobooks and other recordings through its website, Amazon.com, iTunes, and other venues.

Keeping abreast of new technology developments ahead of others was another key factor in the company's growth: It was the first audio publisher to create the condensed MP3-CD format. The firm developed an app (named "Downpour") allowing readers to forward a digital book to their iPad, iPhone, or even car device, but even jump to a precise page on the book. The technology developed also included the ability to move back and forth between the ebook and audiobook, regardless of the type of device being used.

Blackstone Audio grew to near 200 employees with offices in California, Portland, New York and New England—with most employees in Ashland. Located on Mistletoe Road, its Ashland complex houses two buildings with over 40,000 square feet of office and warehouse space; the firm has five in-house, state-of-the-art recording studios located here alone. From partnerships with major book publishers to Disney, the company is also acquiring the exclusive audiobook rights to old classics, ranging from authors as Ayn Rand and Ian Fleming to George Orwell and William Shirer.

Blackstone has distributed over 11,000 audio book titles (being in the top three largest ones) and has branched into publishing print books. It has been awarded five Grammies and over fifty Audies (audiobook) awards. Further, in recognition of his standout career, AudioFile magazine lauded Craig as a "pioneer of the audio industry," and he was honored with the Audio Publishers Association Special Achievement Award in 2012.

In the three decades from working in a living room to their present Ashland headquarters and far-flung operations, the success story of Craig and Michelle Black stands out. And it has been an amazing journey that all of us can enjoy.

Sources: Mann, Danielle L. *Oregon Encyclopedia*: "Blackstone Audio, Inc."; Darling, *Ashland Daily Tidings*, February 15, 2016; Blackstone Audio at its website.

Fire Mountain Gems

$\mathcal{F}$IRE MOUNTAIN GEMS AND BEADS, INC. provides beading and jewelry making supplies to merchants, designers, and artists around the world. The company operates as a distributor and retailer of branded as well as their own products. Based in Grants Pass, Fire Mountain sells and distributes beads, jewelry supplies, stringing material, wire-wrapping wire, jewelry and gifts, and other items.

The company started as a hobby in 1973 in Stuart and Chris Freedman's garage in Southern California. The hobby was lapidary, or cutting faceted stones, which was perfect for an engineer with the angles, optics, and gemology, not to mention his love of turquoise. Soon they had to sell the finished stones to keep going, especially after having four people in the garage cutting full-time. They started off with small ads in trade magazines and flyers to sell the cut and uncut, rough germs.

The name came about when brainstorming possible company names with friends — and the topic of volcanic eruptions came up. Discussing the heat and pressure process through which all gemstones were formed during volcanic eruptions millenniums ago, Stuart wondered, "What might a Native American call one of those volcanoes?" He answered his own question, and "Fire Mountain" was born.

With a desire to share the knowledge of beading, this led to a full-time business in a Studio City rock and gem/silversmithing shop. Working together, Chris and Stuart soon knew how little information was available about beading. This ended up in publishing the "Beadmakers' Handbook," which also served as their catalog, and set the standard.

In 1986, after thirteen years of business in their North Hollywood location, they decided to relocate to rural Cave Junction, Oregon, and the "natural beauty of Southern Oregon." Realizing the area couldn't support their shop, they decided to start a mail-order jewelry-supply company. By 2000, Fire Mountain's business had outgrown their building space, and it moved forty miles to Grants Pass. Fire Mountain Gems and Beads had by then grown into a well-known direct marketing company.

Over time, the privately-held company has grown to employ "hundreds of employees" and operating from the huge building complex at 1 Fire Mountain Way, off NE E. Street and the Redwood Highway (Hwy. 199). Showing an ability to prosper on the Internet and mobile applications — as well as listening closely to customers — it is now the leading catalog and e-commerce direct marketing company in the jewelry supply industry. Importing jewelry-making supplies worldwide from countries such as Peru and Argentina to China and the Philippines, Fire Mountain has over 115,000 items on the web. And all starting from a hobby started inside a garage.

Sources: Fire Mountain, "The History," at its website; Craft Business, "Meet the Maker (the Freedmans)," at its website.

Dagoba Chocolate

*F*REDERICK SCHILLING WAS BORN IN 1971 in Minnesota, and his father had been an IBM corporate manager, but who retired later at age forty-nine to live life non-corporately. His son followed the example. Frederick left Ohio Wesleyan while on a lacrosse scholarship, intending to study religion and satisfy his spiritual needs. He attended a music festival in Telluride, Colorado, however, and then decided on a music life. Playing the guitar, he wrote songs and became the lead singer in a band. He moved to Boulder, where he could ski and live the life. To make ends meet, Schilling became a chef in a high-end restaurant and discovered the joys of using cocoa and the bean selection.

He learned that the early Mayans revered cacao as a drink of the gods, and that Aztecs used cacao beans for currency. In 2001, Shilling became intrigued by this and started making his own organic chocolate. The first ingredients included Chai tea spices, chilies, and dried rosehips.

After experimenting extensively in his home kitchen, Shilling quit to start up his own business. With his girlfriend, Tracey Holderman (whom he later married and divorced), Frederick traveled in 2001 to New York City to attend the Fancy Food Show and launch Dagoba, his organic-chocolate company. (The name is derived from the Sanskrit word for "temple".) Although Dagoba didn't have employees or orders, it did have a small industrial building lease, wrapped organic bar samples, and the financial backing of his family (an initial $20,000 investment).

Making cold calls to sell his chocolate, it took time to build the reputation. He hand-poured the chocolate into molds and wrapped the bars for the first two business years. An East Coast distributor later ordered 10,000 of the chocolate bars. Schilling poured each one (over

Entrance to the Ashland headquarters of world famous Dagoba Chocolate.

ten eighteen-hour days), and his mother, who lived in Minnesota, flew in to help with others.

In the summer of 2002, the company made its first million dollars in sales. As business grew, he decided to move the operations from Boulder to the Rogue Valley (after looking at other areas), due to the area's lower costs, less congestion, and close-by outdoors. From a 3,000 square-foot, Central Point space, they moved to Ashland in 2005 and nearly 40,000 square feet (on Benson Way). They added new machinery and employees; product lines expanded into cocoa powder, chocolate syrup, truffles, bars with different tastes and ingredients; and more.

The awards flowed in: "Best Chocolate," "CNN-Money," 2003; "Tops the List," *Money* magazine, 2004; "Best Dark Chocolate, Organic Style," *San Francisco Chronicle*, 2004; "Best Flavored Organic Chocolate," *Time* magazine, 2005. And so did the orders: In 2005 the company produced more than 700,000 pounds of chocolate. The marketing featured wrappers touting the percentage of pure cacao used and the region where the cacao beans were grown (primarily organic farms in the Caribbean and Latin America countries such as Peru, Ecuador, and Costa Rica). Encouraging farmers to grow organic crops, partnerships were created with cacao growers and their towns.

Hershey then paid $17 million for the business and kept it in Ashland. Bored afterwards, Shilling began moving into closely connected fields. He's a partner and co-CEO in a global organic coconut product firm, "Big Tree Farms," that sources its raw material from 14,000 small, Indonesian farmers, primarily on the islands of Bali, Java, and Sulawesi; it operates four factories with 400 employees. He had met Big Tree Farms co-founder Ben Ripple, who was working in Bali, and from selling bulk cocoa beans in the commodities market, he and Ripple moved into cold-processed, organic cacao powder and butter. Big Tree then expanded into organic coconut sugar and nectar as an alternative to cane sugar (although less expensive). It's now Indonesia's largest organic food company and the biggest producer and manufacturer of coconut sweeteners in the world.

Beginning in 2008, he became a partner in AMMA Chocolate, a Brazilian organic company with a factory in Salvador and headquarters in Sao Paulo. Frederick Shilling still has an Ashland home (although traveling extensively abroad) — not bad for an ex-songwriter, musician, and chef.

Sources: Buford, *The New Yorker* magazine, October 29, 2007; Squires, *Ashland Daily Tidings*, October 18, 2005; Stiles, *Medford Mail Tribune*, December 28, 2016.

PART IV

The Outdoors and Landmarks

Where Past Meets Present

The Siskiyou Summit
(and Pass)

*T*HE SISKIYOU PASS IS THE HIGHEST POINT at 4,491 feet that crosses the divide between the Rogue and Klamath Rivers, formed by the older Siskiyou Mountains to the west with the younger volcanic Cascade Range to the east. Now replaced by Interstate 5 (I-5) between Oregon and California, the Siskiyou Pass on Oregon Route 273 (also known as "Old Highway 99") is distinguished from the Siskiyou Summit that is 4,310 feet high on I-5; this height is set as the sign on I-5 reads: "Siskiyou Mountain Summit, Elevation, 4310 feet, the highest elevation on I-5."

The Summit and Pass is not only the highest of any I-5 pass, but it's the heaviest used and the most historically significant one in Oregon. The original pass is some five miles north of the California-Oregon state line and less than a half-mile west of present I-5. The treacherous pass and summit are called the Siskiyou Mountain and later the Siskiyou Mountains.

The first non-Native Americans to traverse the Siskiyou Pass are believed to be a group led by Peter Ogden, a Hudson Bay Company fur trader, with his trappers. After leaving Fort Vancouver, they traveled south along the far side of the Cascade Range and headed into Northern California for its rich beaver, otter, and other animal skins. They reached the Klamath Basin, but turned around in the winter to head north over the pass in early 1827 to the Rogue Valley.

Two years later, another Hudson Bay Company fur trader, A.R. McLeod, crossed the pass to the Mt. Shasta area, but was forced to retreat back during a bitterly-cold blizzard. Most historians believe that

The Siskiyou Summit today.

the name of Siskiyou was derived and given due to this steep, ill-fated journey in which horses perished. The Cree-Indian word of "Siskiyou" is the name for the type of bob-tailed horse that died on McLeod's unfortunate journey over the pass. Although their homeland was not here, the Cree were likely part of this expedition.

Others followed this original trail over the pass, as wagons and stagecoaches began to cross in spite of the difficult way. The discovery of gold in the Rogue and Shasta Valleys in the 1850s brought more people over this crossing. In the mid-1880s, Southern Pacific from the California side agreed with the reorganized Oregon & California Railroad to connect the two states over the Siskiyou Summit — and both started construction from their respective sides.

The completion of Tunnel No. 13 beneath the Siskiyou Pass in 1887 allowed Southern Pacific to connect California and Oregon by rail. On December 17, 1887, Charles Crocker, the Vice-President of Southern Pacific, drove in the golden spike in Ashland (the district center) that connected from north and south the track over the Siskiyou Mountains. The heavy snows and snowpack on the pass, however, during the winter completely stopped rail travel for months at a time. Even with track clearing procedures instituted later, weeks of delay continued until after the 1910s when powerful locomotives were used to push large snowplows and snowblowers.

Located a short distance east of the historic pass, the grades on both sides of the Siskiyou Summit are steep. The three young D'Autremont brothers saw this as the ideal place to pull off what's considered to be this country's last Old-West-style train robbery. On October 11, 1923, they jumped on it as the train was slowly ascending the steep grade north of Tunnel No. 13's entrance. Intent on robbing the mail car, the brothers dynamited it, killing the postal clerk inside, and then shot to death three railroad employee. They escaped without any loot. Later found, tried, and convicted of their crimes, the three brothers served long prison sentences before being paroled towards the end of their lives.

Southern Pacific Railroad in the 1920s completed its Natron cutoff over Willamette Pass. Traveling from Oregon's Eugene and Klamath Falls to Weed in California, this route took less time and was less expensive than the Siskiyou Pass. Trains consequently have rarely used the route over the Siskiyous since the early 2000s.

Automobiles and trucks competed with the railroad in transportation dating back to the 1920s. By 1923, Jackson County was the first county west of the Mississippi to have a continuous, paved route from border to border, and the two-lane Pacific Highway (Highway 99) was completely paved from the Columbia River to the California border. As with the railroad, the Siskiyou Summit's snowstorms were a constant barrier to winter travel by car—even now with the four-lane I-5. Even during the summer time, the steep, winding way could be difficult.

In the mid-1960s, Interstate 5 was completed and the older Highway 99 was deactivated over the pass. Despite this, winter can be still daunting—although not nearly as bad and measured by a short day or two—as the way over can be completely closed. When that happens, long lines of trucks snake on I-5's side for miles south of Ashland before the climb begins. Travelers head to a local motel for the night, and once reopened, chains are typically required.

From fur traders to wagon trains and stagecoaches, and then from railroad trains to cars, the Siskiyou Pass and Summit have experienced the transition as Southern Oregon and Northern California developed — but the winter ice and snows can still be a challenge.

Sources: LaLande, *Oregon Encyclopedia*: "Siskiyou Pass"; *Medford Mail Tribune*, April 22, 2007.

Mt. Ashland Ski Area

MT. ASHLAND IS ON THE SISKIYOU CREST — six miles west of Siskiyou Pass — at an elevation of 7,532 feet. Ashland Creek starts from there to flow north and with snowmelt provides the city's water supply, eventually cutting through Lithia Park. Over 250 inches of snow usually falls each season on the mountain, and the ski season is typically from early December to mid-April.

The Civilian Conservation Corps built a road in the mid-1930s from Ashland to the mountain, as well as a small ski slope along the road. Constructed 3,000 feet below the summit, this work included a gas-engine-powered rope tow and a "warming" hut. The mountain became a popular destination during the 1950s for local back-country ski enthusiasts.

But residents wanted more. By 1963, the Mount Ashland Corporation (MAC) had raised the needed $120,000 (more than half provided by Medford Chamber of Commerce President and businessman, Glenn Jackson) to clear trees, grade the terrain, build better access roads, and construct a T-bar lift, rope tow, and a four-story ski lodge. In 1970, however, three straight years of winter drought ruined snowfalls and ski runs. The MAC folded later. The Southern Oregon College Foundation took over management after Jackson County residents financed the purchase of the ski area.

A local businessman, Dick Hicks, brought it in 1977. Six years later, a resort and real estate developer — Harbor Properties of Seattle — purchased it. Although Harbor built two new lifts and installed night-skiing lights, it again fell on hard times. Needing more money for another project, Harbor put the ski area back on the market in 1991, saying that it would dismantle the chairlifts and move them to a Seattle ski slope, if a buyer wasn't found.

Northern California and Southern Oregon residents once more began raising money. From local Rotary Clubs and kids knocking on doors to the media donating free ad space, the citizens in 1992 raised $1.6 million dollars, which with a $500,000 grant of state lottery funds (the Oregon Economic Development Fund), amounted to $2.1 million. The City of Ashland received the donations, allowing these to be tax deductible. Since the Mt. Ashland Association (MAA) had not yet been formed, the City of Ashland was named on the U.S. Forest Service's (USFS) special use permit; a lease agreement between the City and MAA, as business operators, was later executed.

Realizing the limitations of Mt. Ashland's steep, short runs, the MAA in 1998 re-affirmed its plan for an expansion with two new chairlifts, two surface lifts, a four-acre tubing facility, three guest service buildings (a new lodge was included), 220 new parking spaces, plus more night lighting, utility lines, storm-water control, and watershed restoration projects. As this dated back to an initial 1991 USFS approved expansion plan, everything seemed well and good. Local conservationists objected, however, citing concerns about soil erosion in Ashland's municipal watershed, along with protecting old-growth forests and certain endangered wildlife species.

The USFS issued its first draft environmental impact report (EIR) in 2000 on the proposal. The EIR drew over 6,000 public comments, half of which supported MAA's plan and half being opposed. One year later, the USFS said it would prepare a new draft EIR to address problems claimed to be in the first study.

The final EIR was issued four years later, along with the USFS's approval of MAA's plans. Three environmental groups (the Sierra Club, Headwaters, and the Oregon Natural Resources Council) in 2005 sued the UFSF, arguing that the EIR was still deficient. The prime arguments were that the expansion would cut down seventy-two acres of trees (less than 1% of the 9,477 acre McDonald Peak area); erosion and watershed damage (in the ski-area); and endangerment to the Pacific Fisher (a weasel that eats porcupines), along with endangerment to species from the Northern Spotted Owl and Mountain Salamander to mountain lions, black bears, and the Arctic Blue Butterfly, to name a few.

When the U.S. District Court rejected these claims, the ski area began its plans to expand. The groups appealed to the 9th Circuit Court of Appeals, however, which in 2007 blocked the expansion until certain

The ski lift and lodge at Mt. Ashland. (Photo by Jordan Alec Boyd, Ashland Ski Area)

EIR corrections were made. At the same time, the City of Ashland got into the act, ending up in litigation with the MAA, in which a Jackson County Circuit Court judge later ruled that Ashland had unreasonably interfered with MAA's rights to operate — in fact, the city had "revoked" the association's authority to deal directly with the USFS on its expansion plans. The City of Ashland was directed to pay $400,000 in settlement costs and legal fees.

The USFS then prepared a supplemental EIR. In August 2012, the U.S. District Court held that it had corrected all of the EIR problems identified by the 9th Circuit. The opponents promptly announced they would appeal again to the 9th Circuit, along with "on-the-ground protests" if the expansion moved forward. It didn't.

Mother Nature then interceded. Poor snow conditions caused the area to close for the entire 2013-2014 season; a $750,000, low-interest, twenty-five year loan from the Small Business Administration was taken out to stay afloat. The next season was nearly as bad, and the ski lifts only operated for slightly over one month. Finally, the 2015-16 season had fine winter snows and the area operated well in the black and back into financial solvency; the next season's snowfall was also excellent.

Despite the expansion roadblocks, the park was able to increase parking, install solar panels, widen several ski runs, and maintain restoration sites to prevent erosion from affecting watershed streams. It announced in early 2017 that a $1.4 million fund drive was underway to renovate the 1964-built lodge, replace the roof, and repaint the exterior, among other modifications. This region can be justifiably proud of this well-run, maintained, and convenient ski area.

Sources: LaLande, *Oregon Encyclopedia*: "Mt. Ashland"; "Mt. Ashland Ski Area: A Historical Perspective," at its website; Fattig, *Medford Mail Tribune*, August 18, 2012; Ristow, *Medford Mail Tribune*, April 14, 2013; Boom, *Medford Mail Tribune*, April 20, 2016.

The Table Rocks

RISING 800 FEET ABOVE THE NORTH BANK of the Rogue River, the Upper and Lower Table Rocks overlook the Rogue Valley with exquisite views. The "upper" and "lower" refer to their positions relative to each other alongside the river; Lower Table Rock is located downstream, or lower on the river, from Upper Table Rock.

Approximately fifty to thirty-five million years ago, the Rogue River and other rivers deposited sandstone and other materials in the area of the Table Rocks. The formation of the Rogue Valley took place some ten to twenty million years ago with the uplifting of the nearby Klamath Mountains. A large volcano built almost entirely of fluid lava flows (called a "shield volcano") erupted seven million years ago, and a huge lava flow spread over the valley, from the Prospect area to Sams Valley.

This lava mass caused the landmass to rise to the height of the Table Rocks. Over the last seven million years, the ancient Rogue River meandered through the valley, eroding and carving away most of the lava rock. Over the countless millenniums, the Rogue washed away 90% of the lava-filled ground to the Pacific Ocean, leaving behind a few large rock masses and the two horseshoe-shaped buttes know as the Table Rocks. It is believed that the shape of these steppes was owing to the swift river curving around their now outlines.

The Table Rocks also have historical significance. The Native tribes and the U.S. Government negotiated a peace treaty in 1853 that brought about a temporary end to the continuing bloody conflict between the Indians and the white settlers and miners in the area. The peace treaty was entered into with the Shasta, Takelma, and Dakubetede Indians, collectively named the Rogue River Indians.

Lower Table Rock as seen from the south.

Its provisions established a temporary reservation on the north side of the Rogue River that included the two Table Rocks, Sams Valley, and the Sardine and Evans Creek watersheds. It also provided for goods and services for the Indians to farm and ranch, as well as the building of nearby Fort Lane to protect both sides from each other.

A small fort was quickly erected on a hill that overlooks what's now Gold Ray Road and that pointed towards the Table Rock Reservation. Enlisted men and officer barracks, a guardhouse, hospital, camp store, kitchens, and a blacksmith shop were contained within the walls.

In October 1855, a mob from Jacksonville, Oregon, killed twenty-eight Indians near the Table Rock Reservation. This also killed the peace and brought about the "Rogue River War, 1855-1856" between the Native groups and white settlers. The Takelma, however (and unlike other tribes on the reserve), stayed on the reservation and at peace; numbers sought refuge and protection at Fort Lane. When the conflict ended, they were moved in 1856 to a reservation west of Salem. By the end of the year, Fort Lane was abandoned with scant evidence now left as to its ever having existed.

During the decades following this and into the present, residents and tourists alike enjoy hiking the trails, picnicking, and seeing the marvelous sights. The Bureau of Land Management and Nature Conservancy of Oregon manage the Table Rocks, both with public-access trails. "Memorandums of Understanding" were signed in 2011 and 2012 with the Confederated Tribes of the Grand Ronde and the Cow Creek Band of Umpqua Tribe of Indians that are to "allow the coordination of resources to protect the Table Rocks" for the future.

Sources: BLM: "How Did the Table Rocks Form?"; LaLande, *Oregon Encyclopedia*: "The Council of Table Rock"; Miller, *Medford Mail Tribune*, March 28, 2010.

Mt. McLoughlin

*W*HEN DRIVING SOUTHWARD ON I-5 TOWARDS Medford, the near-perfect, mirror-image of Japan's Mt. Fuji appears. Although Mt. McLoughlin at 9,495 feet high is the tallest peak between Mt. Shasta and the South Sister (of the Three Sisters), its base size is dwarfed by the much taller Mt. Shasta (14,162 feet high with near thirty times more volume) and Crater Lake's Mt. Mazama (ten times) — but this one dominates the lower valley. From distant Medicine Lake in California, around Crater Lake's rim, or along I-5 between Yreka (California) and Medford, Mt. McLoughlin is easily recognized.

The symmetrical shape appears when viewed from the south or southeast. It becomes apparent that a large part of the mountain is missing when viewed from a different direction; for example, from the north along Crater Lake's rim or east from Klamath Lake. This was due to late Ice-Age glaciers that shaved away the mountain's northeast side, lowering the summit by 300 feet and gouging out a large bowl-like hollow.

The mountain is geologically young. Formed by a series of eruptions and cooled lava flow over long periods of time, geologists have determined that its steep-sided, lava cone is less than 700,000 years old. Indicating later eruptions, its western and southern flanks suggest that the bulk of its form is no older than 200,000 years, with much of this probably younger, perhaps as late as 20,000 to 30,000 years ago.

Leaving Fort Vancouver to trap beaver and otter for sale in England, Hudson Bay Company's Peter Skene Ogden traveled through Central Oregon to the Rogue River Valley. Ogden's journal has this notation for February 14, 1827: "I have named this river Sastise River. There is a mountain equal in height to Mount Hood or Vancouver; I have named

Majestic Mt. McLoughlin. (Photo by Richard Verstrate)

(it) Mt. Sastise. I have given these names from the tribes of the Indians."
Historians believe that he actually spotted the Rogue River with Mount
McLoughlin, and that this would have been the first recorded observation.

The name tributes John McLoughlin, one of the most influential figures
in the early 1800s in Pacific Northwest history. The Oregon legislature
renamed the peak from Mount Pitt to Mt. McLoughlin in 1905, and the
U.S. Board of Geographic Names in 1912 recognized that change.

McLoughlin was Canadian born and didn't become an American
citizen until he was sixty-seven years old. However, he had been a frontier
doctor, British fur trade officer, the founder of Fort Vancouver (1825) and
of Oregon City (1842). When he was the Chief Factor (Superintendent) of
the British Hudson Bay Company (HBC), based at Fort Vancouver on the
Columbia River, American pioneers arrived there without supplies. As
the last stop on the Oregon Trail for many, they asked McLoughlin to help

them survive their first winter in Oregon. He did — although this later cost him his job. Dr. John McLoughlin's key role in Oregon's early history prompted the state legislature in 1957 to name him the "Father of Oregon" on the 100th Anniversary of his death.

On July 1, 1927, a two-foot diameter pipeline began carrying water from Mt. McLoughlin by gravity flow to Medford (and eventually other cities in the Bear Creek Valley). Its snowmelt percolates through the porous, volcanic soils to emerge again at Big Butte Springs (a 2,700-foot elevation) near the town of Butte Falls and provides the area today with the great majority of our water needs.

The access to Mt. McLoughlin is considered "remarkably easy" via Oregon Highway 140 between Medford and Klamath Falls. Held in high esteem by residents, the thick conifer forests around its base and nearby mountains provide enjoyable hiking and fishing. After the snow has melted from the trail, hikers have a relative hard hike ahead, but the views are magnificent — and a continued tribute to this Southern Oregon landmark.

Sources: McLoughlin Memorial Association; LaLande, *Oregon Encyclopedia*: "Mt. McLoughlin."

Crater Lake

*T*HE FIRST NON-NATIVE AMERICAN TO VIEW Crater Lake is generally credited to John Wesley Hillman, a California prospector who was searching for the fabled "Lost Cabin Mine." As the story goes, Hillman rode his mule in June of 1853, to a rim, where if it hadn't stopped a few feet from the edge, he would have pitched over to his death. As his group marveled at the sight, a vote was taken on its name between "Mysterious Lake" and "Deep Blue Lake" with the latter chosen. The discovery was also referred to later as "Lake Mystery."

Created after a violent eruption of an ancient volcano, Crater Lake formed 7,700 years ago by an explosion calculated to be forty-two times as powerful as the 1980 Mount St. Helens eruption. The mountain then was 10,000 to 12,000 feet high and later named Mount Mazama. A basin or caldera formed when the volcano's top 5,000 feet collapsed from the ash and lava that exploded out. When the lava flows sealed its bottom, the subsequent rainfall and snowmelt over countless years filled this with 4.6 trillion gallons of water. The collapsed basin is roughly 3.7 by 5.5 miles, and the ash settled in a distinct layer over several thousand square miles.

The deepest lake in the U.S. was thus formed at 1,932 feet (sonar mapping in 2000 came up with an average depth of 1,943 feet) — and the seventh deepest in the world — that today is half-filled with water. A small volcanic island named Wizard Island is on the lake's west side. Surrounded by black, volcanic lava blocks, its cinder cone rises 760 feet above the lake with a small crater at its summit.

The lake's water is so clear that it holds a world-clarity record of 142 feet. The dramatic deep-blue color is due to its great depth, water clarity, and the way light interacts with water. Water molecules absorb the

Overlooking Crater Lake and Wizard Island, 1906. (SOHS 12782)

longer wavelengths of light better (reds, oranges, yellows, and greens). Shorter wavelengths (blues) are more easily scattered than soaked up. In the deep lake, some of the scattered blue light is redirected back to the surface to where the color is visible.

Peter Britt took the first surviving picture of Crater Lake in 1874; in 1902, President Roosevelt signed the law designating Crater Lake as the 6th National Park that now contains over 183,000 acres. The thirty-mile Rim Drive around Crater Lake is two-lanes with scenic overlooks. From mid-October until mid-June, the north entrance and Rim Drive are closed due to deep snow and ice buildups, although the lake rarely freezes over.

Although visitors can fish (non-native rainbow trout and kokanee salmon) and swim, the surface water is cold but "warms" up in the summer to 55° to 60° fahrenheit. The "yellow stuff" floating in the water then is simply pine pollen that later settles to the bottom.

More visitors from California than from Oregon have visited lately, and total visitations (including overseas visitors) number now over 700,000 people every year. This is one of the premier landmarks in Southern Oregon that people have marveled at since the first roads and treks led there.

Sources: U.S. National Park Service: "Crater Lake: Frequently Asked Questions"; Mark, *Oregon Encyclopedia*: "Crater Lake National Park"; Crater Lake Institute: "John Wesley Hillman."

The Oregon Caves

ELIJAH DAVIDSON DISCOVERED THE Oregon Caves in 1874 while hunting deep inside the Siskiyou Mountains. After shooting a deer, he followed his dog to a large hole in a mountain (now renamed Mount Elijah after him). With the sounds of fighting echoing from the inside, he waited until hearing his dog howl weirdly. Making his way carefully into the black darkness, Davidson lit match after match to find the silhouettes of caverns, stalactites (hanging down like icicles) and stalagmites (from below, sticking up).

Forced to leave when out of matches, his dog soon followed—but unhurt. With the sun setting, he decided to spend the night at his camp; before doing so, however, he set the deer by the cave entrance to entice the bear out. Returning the next morning, Davidson found a "monstrous" black bear lying by the carcass. Telling others about his discovery, labyrinth of caves, chambers, and connecting passageways, the news and location became fairly well known: Its remote location kept exploration for only the adventurous.

Experts determined that rainwater from the ancient forest above had dissolved the underlying marble to create one of the world's rare marble caves. In 1907, Joaquin Miller—the fabled "Poet of the Sierras"—visited the caves and was so impressed that he wrote an article about its unique beauty. Published by *Sunset Magazine* and entitled "The Marble Halls of Oregon," this publicity gave the caves nationwide exposure. As a result of the continued advocacy, President Taft designated the 480-acre Oregon Caves in 1909 as a national monument.

The completion of now Highway 46 in 1922 allowed the general public to visit the site. With this established, the U.S. Forest Service granted a concession to the Oregon Caves Company for accommodations and guide

Top: Oregon Caves King's Palace, circa 1923. (SOHS 11928)

Bottom: The Oregon Caves Chateau.

services that is still in effect. The access also brought about the formation of "Caves City," later incorporated as Cave Junction in 1948, at its junction with the Redwood Highway (Highway 199).

Grants Pass businessmen financed the lodging and staff to run the resort, while the Forest Service (later the National Park Service) provided oversight and infrastructure, including cave lighting, trails, and a water system. During this venture, the Grants Pass Cavemen formed with their exploits of "imprisoning" women in a rolling cage during parades, imitating U.S. Presidents, and cavemen "appearances" at different, official functions.

Located twenty miles east of Cave Junction on Highway 46, the rustic-style structures include a chalet (1923, rebuilt in 1942), seven cottages (1926), a dormitory for cave guides (1927 with additions in 1940 and 1972), along with the magnificent six-story Chateau (built in 1934) that spans a stream canyon with one running through its dining room. The chateau is not overly fancy with rustic rooms, but its bark siding and look is unique — as is the entire magnificent park that exists close to us.

Sources: U.S. National Park Service: "The Underworld of Oregon Caves: Human Story"; Mark: *Oregon Encyclopedia*: "Oregon Caves National Monument."

Mt. Shasta

*L*OCATED FORTY MILES SOUTH OF THE California border in Siskiyou County, Mt. Shasta is 14,162 feet high. The U.S. Forest Service manages this prominent landmark as part of the Shasta-Trinity National Forest, and it's the second highest of the fifteen major volcanoes in the Cascade Range. This major mountain range of western North America extends from southern British Columbia through Washington and Oregon to Northern California.

Mt. Shasta's volcano has erupted at least once every 800 years during the past 10,000 years, the last one in the 1780s. These eruptions have formed lava domes, lava flows down slopes, and massive mudflows extending over twenty-five miles into the valley. Geologists warn that future eruptions could wipe out the towns along Shasta's base, and several hot sulphur springs near the summit indicate that the mountain is still active. Such an eruption, however, is not now deemed to be very likely.

Led by Captain E. D. Pearce of Yreka, an eight-man party in 1854 made the first recorded, successful ascent of the summit. Rising nearly 7,000 feet above the timberline, the grassy tundra areas, large rocky fields, and glaciers prominently cover most of a treeless region on that route. Owing to being 10,000 feet above land, the mountain is famed for its prominent and widely-photographed lens-shaped clouds.

Although severe weather conditions can occur year-round, it is not a difficult mountain to climb. At least fifty people have died when climbing the slopes, however, owing to falling rocks, falling over the wrong side, or hypothermia. Some 5,000 people annually reach the summit.

Like so many awe-inspiring mountains, Mount Shasta is the focus of numerous legends, myths, and stories. Native American lore held that Shasta is inhabited by the spirit chief Skell, who descended from heaven

Mt. Shasta as seen from Shasta City, CA.

to the summit. Since then, various other faiths and spiritualists are attracted here—from Buddhists to New Age groups—and more than any other Cascade volcano.

Some believe that survivors of Lemuria, another lost continent that sank under the Pacific Ocean with Atlantis (owing to a thermonuclear war between them), live within the mountain in a city named Telos. An 1894 novel, *A Dweller on Two Planets* (written by Frederick Spencer Oliver), tells how Lemuria sank and its people came there. Oliver claimed that the tall Lemurians lived in an underground complex with multi-levels and tunnels, were seen walking on the surface in white robes, and were a super-human race that could change from the physical to spiritual state.

Arguing that aliens use the cloud camouflage to hide their spaceships, some consider it to be a UFO landing site, or have seen everything from

Lemurians to Yetis. New Agers view Mt. Shasta as an energy-power center. When a unique planet alignment occurred on August 16-17, 1987, Mt. Shasta was one of the few centers selected (along with the Egyptian pyramids, New Mexico's Chaco Canyon, Mt. Olympus, Machu Picchu, and Mt. Fuji, among others) as part of the first worldwide, synchronized meditation.

Believing Shasta to be one of the few, worldly acupuncture points for "cleansing energy," 1,000 people camped on its slopes and another 1,000 packed the area's hotels, all there for the long-awaited planetary purification—with annual anniversaries or celebrations held since then. This mountain certainly has something for everyone.

Sources: Climbing.About.Com: "Facts about Mount Shasta"; Weisman, *Los Angeles Times*, August 16, 1987.

PART V

Foundations and Non-Profits

Bill and Florence Schneider

$\mathcal{B}$ ILL AND FLORENCE SCHNEIDER MADE TWO MOVES in their married life that stood out to themselves. The first was their moving to Tucson, Arizona, in 1949 where they founded and successfully operated the Treehaven School for twenty-five years, which was a private boarding and day school conducted on a ranch. Florence became the first female president of the Arizona State Association of Independent Academic Schools. Bill Schneider invested wisely in Tucson real estate and both built up their assets.

The second was when they moved to the Rogue Valley in 1976, fully intending to enjoy their retirement lives. They did but in a way that greatly helped this community. With her background at Treehaven and education—a bachelor's degree at Brooklyn College (1934), master's at Columbia University (1935), and a doctorate at Bryn Mawr College (1939)—Florence Schneider taught as an adjunct professor at Southern Oregon State College (SOSC) in the Department of Sociology. (SOSC was renamed Southern Oregon University, or SOU, in 1997.) They taught English to non-native speakers. The Schneiders endowed the first academic chair at now SOU, the Florence Hemley Schneider Chair in Social Science.

They also decided that the college had a place for music and theatre, but there wasn't a perfect one for art. The Schneiders jumpstarted the fund-raising for the university's art museum in 1983 with a $50,000 endowment. The State Board of Higher Education later approved the naming of the museum for Samuel and May Schneider, Bill Schneider's parents. Three years later, the Schneider Art Museum opened its doors to the public. A grateful university in 1981 awarded SOU's Alumni Association's Outstanding Service Award, and in 1984 the first President's Medal for Outstanding Service to SOU.

The couple, however, didn't limit their efforts to art and education. They were major contributors to many charitable, cultural, educational, and religious organizations, including the Rogue Valley Symphony, Oregon Shakespeare Festival, Rogue Valley Opera, Temple Emek Shalom, Bryn Mawr College, and endowments to Providence and Rogue Regional Hospital, among others. In 1991, they donated a large parcel of land to the Ashland Community Hospital Foundation where the Mountain View Senior Living facility is now located.

They received the prestigious Governor's Arts Award in 1992, among numerous accolades from a grateful community, region, state leaders, and organizations. The couple with others supported the art museum in 1995 so that it could start a second construction of two new galleries with more staff office space; the new wings of the museum opened in early 1997.

Bill Schneider died in 1996 and his beloved wife, Florence, died three years later. Giving generously to so many causes—from large foundations to a single student that needed assistance for her last semester—the family today continues Bill and Florence Schneider's legacy. It's a legacy that stands the test of time.

Sources: *Medford Mail Tribune,* December 30, 1999; *New York Times,* December 31, 1999.

Dogs for the Deaf

R OY KABAT WORKED WITH EXOTIC AND DOMESTIC animals in Hollywood for the movies and television. He trained the animals, for example, in *Dr. Doolittle* and *Swiss Family Robinson,* Elsa the lioness in *Born Free,* and the cougar for the Mercury automobile commercials. He also produced syndicated children's TV shows as "Chucko the Clown" and "Circus." In 1971, Roy retired from the entertainment industry.

After moving to the Applegate Valley in Southern Oregon, the American Humane Association ("AHA") in Denver contacted him for his help. A Minnesota deaf woman had lost a dog that had trained itself to let her know what was happening around her. As she lost more hearing, the dog alerted her to more events. After her dog died, the woman realized how much she depended on the dog for help and needed someone to train a new one. The AHA wanted Roy's advice. After spending two weeks in Denver, Roy returned to Oregon and started "Dogs for the Deaf."

Beginning initially outside Jacksonville, Roy began training twenty or more dogs of all sizes and types at a time, most saved from nearby Humane Societies, saying, "They're the dogs that otherwise might be put to sleep." He trained "Hearing Dogs at Home" to alert an owner to important household sounds: buzzing fire and smoke alarms, ringing telephones, oven timers, alarm clocks, doorbell/door knocks, and name calls (sometimes even a baby's cry). Once placed with their deaf partner, the dogs learned to respond to other sounds—a microwave, tea kettle that boiled dry, or washer/dryer—and take their hearing-impaired owner to the problem. For a "Hearing Dog in Public," additional training was given for specific sounds such as a siren or honking horn, and to react so that the dog's deaf partner was aware of the danger.

Dogs for the Deaf trainer Jenny with certified hearing dog Enzo. (Photo courtesy Dogs for the Deaf)

Dogs in training initially are given food when they react properly to the noise of an alarm clock or telephone. But over the four to six months of training, they gradually are weaned from food to a kind word or pat on the head. By the 1980s, his nonprofit organization with the help of volunteers was delivering hearing dogs to deaf people throughout the United States. As the operation grew, Roy died in 1986 at age sixty-five, but his daughter, Robin Dickson, succeeded him as its CEO/President.

In 1989, the facilities moved to its current forty-acre site at the base of lower Table Rock on Wheeler Road in Central Point. Placing hundreds of dogs over time free of charge to the hearing-impaired, the investment in just one is approximately $25,000. This includes the dog's selection, initial veterinary care, training, placement, and follow up for the team's life. Dogs are also trained to watch out for autistic children, as well.

"Career Change Dogs" — happy and healthy but not suited as a program dog — are adopted out as regular pets to area homes. Our region can be justifiably proud of his and this nonprofit's accomplishments.

Sources: Dogs for the Deaf: "History"; *Los Angeles Times*, November 7, 1986; Pet Meds Blog, October 17, 2012.

Kids Unlimited
and Its Power

KIDS UNLIMITED BEGAN IN 1998 AS A grassroots movement from Tom Cole's recognition that kids from high-poverty elementary schools had little access to quality after-school programs. Cole's drive stemmed from meeting and working with disadvantaged youths while studying at Missouri State University, part of a community service requirement. He worked for the Boys & Girls Clubs in Missouri, and then moved to the Valley in 1995 to start the first such club in Jackson County. Cole began those operations in a Quonset hut.

He left two years later to start a program to prevent teen pregnancy, and this effort morphed into Kids Unlimited (for five to twenty year-olds). With $500, volunteers, and his commitment, seventeen first-graders enrolled in the first Kids Unlimited ("KU") program. Although all were from families where none had graduated from high school, the program participants did; in fact, fourteen went onto college and a few returned afterwards to become KU counselors. With an emphasis on areas in Medford and other places that are economically distressed, KU provides programs ranging from daily after-school and summer programs, teen leadership courses, college preparatory help, mentoring, and individual help. The curricula available ranges from the culinary arts and robotics to film and sports.

His VIBES program ("Vitality in Becoming Educated Socially") is now the largest after-school program in the Valley; opening its current facilities in a converted bowling alley in 2005, it provides tutoring at elementary and middle-school summer camps, as well as at five district schools. These programs are on every day, including weekends, and Kids Unlimited provides its services weekly to over 1,500 kids.

Kids Unlimited in Medford, OR.

When Tom started up KU, he also began a youth basketball program. The area basketball superstar and NBA starter, Kyle Singler, decided to help out; his Southern Oregon basketball open continues today. Cole added a girls' team in 2004 and worked with them. When South Medford had an opening three years later as the woman's basketball coach, he applied and won it. This was the first high-school coaching job that the then forty year-old ever had. The Panthers' team in the previous year didn't win one game and lost twenty-four. With his KU pipeline, he began developing this high school team.

His South Medford girl's team won eleven, twelve, eighteen and twenty-one games in the next four seasons. This culminated in Cole's team winning all of its thirty games in 2012, as well as winning the Class 6A state title at Portland's Rose Garden. No team from outside the Portland area had won the championship since South Eugene in 1999, and this was South Medford's first such title. The team also had the highest GPA of any girl's basketball team in Oregon; in 2013, they went back to the championship game—but lost this time. Since then, Cole's teams have continued their winning ways.

His KU players on these teams from disadvantaged families not only graduated from high school, but headed off to college with athletic scholarships or aid. Others went onto successful careers, even coming back to work with KU or being on its board. Tom was busily working also on a charter school named the Kids Unlimited Academy. In 2013, KU leased a facility on Riverside Avenue in Medford and began serving at-risk students in grades K-5 with more family involvement, longer school days, and a longer school year.

Growing to serving 300 students, it needed more classrooms to serve future 6th graders, and more space in future years for 7th and 8th graders. Its kitchen facilities needed more capacity. Raising over $2 million, KU purchased lots around its building in a blighted, gang-violent neighborhood to start its expansion program. After clearing the lots, construction began in 2017 on this $4.5 million project that includes a new, two-story, 30,000-square-foot, prefabricated addition (including ten more classrooms) behind the facility, as well as a commercial kitchen, second gym, commons area, and later soccer and track field. This work is substantially upgrading the once-dangerous neighborhood.

This is only the beginning as to what Tom Cole—its Executive Director and founder—with Kids Unlimited can do. Only a beginning.

Sources: "Kids Unlimited of Oregon" at its website; Ulmer, *Oregonian*, March 6, 2012; Thomas, *Medford Mail Tribune*, March 23, 2016.

The Carpenters and
Their Foundation

*T*HE ALLURE OF THE EARLY 1900's ORCHARD BOOM drew numbers of well-educated Easterners and Midwesterners to the Valley. Included in these newcomers were the Harvard-educated brothers, Leonard and Alfred Carpenter. After college, Leonard had been an electrical engineer and Alfred in the real estate and banking business. Although neither knew much about agriculture, the Carpenter brothers came here and planted a pear orchard in 1909 with a draft-horse team. The two men established their Veritas Orchard and took turns in managing the business.

Alfred decided to travel around the world in 1920, while Leonard with his wife of three years, Winifred, watched over the orchard. While on the cruise, Alfred met and fell in love with Helen Bundy, and they married in 1922 in Cairo. Helen's father, Harlow Bundy, and his brother had started a business in New York state three decades before that later owned the important patents for punch clocks. Named the Bundy Time Machine Company, the operation expanded, merged with others, and in 1924 with others formed International Business Machines (IBM). Helen and her two siblings would be the owners of very valuable stock.

Living for a few years in Pasadena, Alfred and Helen then returned to the Medford area in 1926. They bought land near Jacksonville on Old Stage Road, planted a small orchard, and built a "large and inviting" home that they named "Topsides." This became the center for their parties and social events, often for the benefit of nonprofits. Alfred managed their orchard and later became a board member of COPCO (which in 1960 became part of the mega-utility, Pacific Power) and the Medford Irrigation District.

During World War II, the Carpenters used their private funds to form the Jackson County Recreation Committee (JCRC), which provided entertainment and activities for the officers at nearby Camp White. Given these numbers, this was a large undertaking; first built and used by a telephone and telegraph company, the committee purchased the building for this use. (Alfred and Helen transferred the building's ownership in 1958 to the University Club.)

Although there was no further need to entertain the troops after the war, Alfred and Helen continued their charitable support: Scholarships were granted so that worthy students could attend college; and major donations were made to Medford's Community Hospital (now Asante Rogue Regional Medical Center), the Red Cross in Medford, and the Carpenter Center for the Visual Arts at Harvard University. Many of the individual or student contributions were made anonymously.

In 1958, the Carpenters reorganized the JCRC to become the Carpenter Foundation with a board of trustees; its aim was to "add opportunity, choice, inclusiveness, enrichment, and a climate for change for those living in the Rogue Valley." The Foundation's first grants included the Oregon Shakespeare Festival (OSF) and Rogue Valley Medical Center (RVMC, now Asante), and this support has continued over the years.

Alfred not only served on the RVMC board for nearly forty years, but he also served as its president for eleven years, and made a weekly visit to talk with the employees and physicians; he additionally served as the chairman of OSF's fund-raising committee. The funding assistance given to the Valley's arts and music is noteworthy. This support included substantial grants that supported major projects, including the development of the Angus Bowmer Theatre and Carpenter Hall at OSF, the Britt Music Festival, and others.

Helen Bundy Carpenter died in 1961, and Alfred later remarried Helene Salade Donker. Following into the foundation was Alfred's nephew, Dunbar Carpenter, whose father Dunbar (Alfred's older brother) had come to Medford during the Orchard Boom, but later returned to Boston. Dunbar was born in Medford in 1915, graduated also from Harvard, married, and during World War II flew the large Pan American Clippers for civilian contractors who were working with the military.

After World War II, Leonard and Winifred—then in their sixties— asked Dunbar and his wife, Jane, if they would be interested in taking over the orchard. They did and moved to Medford. When Alfred died in 1974, Dunbar (1915-2008) and Jane Carpenter (1915-2007) continued the foundation as a major charitable organization in this area. Jane was instrumental in starting a community action program that created Rogue Valley's first Head Start and Planned Parenthood programs. Their adult children, Emily Mostue and Karen Allan, took over managing the foundation.

The Carpenter Foundation since its inception has awarded $25 million in total grants, $3-plus million in college scholarships, and some 5,000 grants to Southern Oregon nonprofit organizations. It provides grants in the areas of human services, education, scholarships, the arts, and public interest. In an average year, it will make over 100 different grants, totaling as much as $750,000 in a given year.

Alfred and Helen Carpenter created a foundation that truly stands out. With their successors, its operation has brought about a very positive climate of change—for all of us living in this area.

Sources: See generally, "Carpenter Foundation," at its website; Kramer, *Oregon Encyclopedia*: "Carpenter Foundation"; Kramer (George), *Topsides*, 2004.

The Record
Powerball Win

*I*N OCTOBER 2005, BOB CHANEY WAS A seventy-two-year-old, retired security systems owner, and living with his wife, Francis, in Jacksonville. The Chaney's daughter, Carolyn, and their forty-eight-year-old son-in-law Steve West — a Medford landscaper — were living in a modest ranch house in Medford. As some noted, "They were very much your average folks." On October 19, 2005, Steve West and Bob Chaney bought a $40 lottery ticket that hit the largest single-ticket Powerball jackpot in history then of $340 million.

If they wanted, the $340 million could have been paid over thirty annual payments. They instead took a lump-sum cash award, which was $164.4 million. This amount was next allocated: Robert and Frances each received $34.1 million; Steve and Carolyn received $39.4 million each, all before state and federal tax withholdings. Other family members receiving amounts were Robert and Frances' son, Steven Chaney, $3.5 million; daughters Brenda Green, Robin Whitzel, and Sue Krammer, $3.5 million each; and Steve West's brother, Gary, $3.5 million. All prize amounts were before withholdings for state and federal taxes — and the total received by everyone after these taxes was $110 million.

In early 2006, Steve and Carolyn West moved four miles away to their new home. This was a much bigger place: It was located on six acres, the house totaled 6,400 square feet, and the grounds were complete with a hot tub, pool, and thirty-foot waterslide. When the astounded moving-van driver spotted the estate, he asked, "What did you do? Win the Lotto?" Carolyn West admitted, "Yes, we really did."

Their five-bedroom, five-bath expansive house cost "well over $2 million"; the expenses of an interior decorator and new, cherrywood furniture were extra, although they did keep their old house as a rental. Steve also built a 31' x 12' greenhouse for his orchids and tropical plants. Plus they bought a few new cars, such as a GMC Yukon for carpooling kids, along with a new champagne-colored convertible BMW 650i (for him) and silver BMW (hers).

With his some $20 million after taxes, Bob Chaney's first big purchase was a $50,000 canary yellow Hummer, which he always wanted and purchased days after receiving his winnings. Another large Chaney purchase was that of a French country-style house down the road from the Wests' new home. Steve and Carolyn took trips to Italy and Switzerland with their two daughters, while Bob and Frances headed away on vacations with their grown children.

Their joy was tempered by Bob Chaney's death on October 2nd, 2006, from a brain injury he had suffered after falling off a roof and hitting his head. He had lingering weakness after the fall, along with breaking his pelvis two years before, and then badly burning one of his feet. Other complications ensued and he died at age seventy-three, nearly one year after receiving the news of the grand win.

The families still seemed, however, to keep their centering. One year after receiving their money, Steve said that he still clipped coupons. He remembered back to the "embarrassing" bankruptcy he had to file in 1999 after losing his job at a lawn-care center. Liking her friends at work, Carolyn continued to work thirty hours a week as a bookkeeper, bringing home then "$500 to $600" every two weeks.

Although he hired a gardener to help mow his estate and gave his lawn-care business to his brother Gary, Steve worked with Gary to help with the fall plantings. The Wests noted that their friendships with others had basically stayed the same, although there were a few who didn't talk to them. Their newly-found wealth had changed how some of their friends saw them.

What stands out is that both families established substantial foundations that are within the top ten of Southern Oregon's largest, standing along with long-time ones such as the Carpenter and Smullin Foundations. Chaney's funding efforts included Missouri's Barry County, where they lived before moving to Jacksonville, and areas surrounding his hometown in Cabell County, West Virginia—along with Jackson and Josephine

Counties. The West Foundation contributes to numerous nonprofits also in Jackson and Josephine County. These foundations together have been donating some $700,000 annually.

The Chaney and West lottery win is still the largest Powerball jackpot in Oregon history. On May 19, 2013, the single winning ticket in Florida hit a Powerball lottery jackpot that was worth $590.5 million and is now the largest. The greatest jackpot so far in U.S. history is $656 million, split between winners in Maryland, Kansas, and Illinois, and won in the March 2012 Mega Millions lottery.

With the actual stories of how others squandered their winnings, what these Oregonians won and subsequently did with their winnings truly stands out. They remembered where they had been and wanted to improve the lives of others. They did — and certainly set a high bar.

Sources: Bane, *People*, March 26, 2007, Vol. 67, No. 12; See generally, "Robert & Francis Chaney Family Foundation," and "The West Family Foundation," at their websites; Sarah Lemon, "Giving Back," *Medford Mail Tribune*, May 31, 2007.

Wildlife Images

DAVID SIDDON GREW UP IN Los Angeles's San Fernando Valley in the 1940s when it was still rural country, and he was able to bicycle to near wilderness and see everything from condors and hawks to snakes and lizards. Siddon later pursued a career as a writer, photographer, and filmmaker that typically centered on his fascination with wildlife, as he traveled the world filming for TV productions that involved Disney or "Wild Kingdom."

Loving the outdoors, he and his wife left the Southern California "rat race" in the early 1970s when they heard about seventeen acres of wilderness property outside Grants Pass and near Merlin on the "Wild and Scenic" section of the Rogue River (on Lower River Road). They bought the land sight unseen and later acquired seven more acres. With this land, they could do more than raise baby owls in the laundry room or golden eagles in a backyard, as done before moving to the Rogue.

Obtaining the needed permits from the Oregon Department of Fish and Wildlife and U.S. Fish and Wildlife Service, there he could care for numbers of sick, injured, or orphaned wildlife. In no time, the public and law enforcement were bringing wounded animals to his place. Siddon found himself taking care of hundreds of animals each year and having to fund everything by himself.

With varying injuries, the wild animals treated included species from baby squirrels, raccoons, jack rabbits, bear cubs, and badgers to songbirds, hawks, bald eagles, herons, and owls. In addition to the yearly hundreds of baby animals brought in, the permanent "residents" augmented this when their injuries made them unable to be returned to the wild. In fact, two eagles — named Duchess and Phoenix — were there for over thirty years.

Wildlife Images cares annually for more than 2,000 injured or otherwise endangered animals.

With a flair for public speaking, Siddon appeared at places from TV shows to school assemblies throughout the Pacific Northwest in telling his story. To help with finances, many of the animals appeared in commercials and films, including the Buick automobile series with his red-tailed hawk named "Happy" who flew over the cars.

In 1981, J. David established it as a nonprofit facility with two important purposes: first, a place to provide critical care and rehabilitative services for injured wildlife; second, to provide education to the public. Wildlife Images accepts animals, birds, raptors (birds of prey), and even reptiles. Animals not accepted are opossums (a non-native species), coyotes (governed by livestock management regulations), and mountain lions (a risk to rehabilitate and release after developing human-comfort levels).

In 1996, J. David Siddon lost his battle with cancer. His son, Dave, left his job of twelve years in Portland at the Oregon Zoo to take over the management and ensure the continuation of these dreams. With a limited paid staff, its eighty dedicated volunteers and local vet-donated services, the facility cares annually for more than 2,000 animals.

Over a period of thirty years it released over 35,000 animals back to their natural habitat. Its release rate of intakes is near 50% each year — far above the national average of 33%.

Wildlife Images doesn't receive any local, state, or federal funding, but relies instead on individual donations of time, money, and services. It is a story that needed to be told.

Sources: Wildlife Images: "About Us" and "Message from Dave Siddon, Director" at its website.

Where Past Meets Present

PART VI

Medical and Other Facilities

Where Past Meets Present

Asante Rogue Regional
Medical Center

*F*ACED WITH A GROWING NEED FOR hospital facilities, the Medford community in the late 1950s raised $1.9 million in grants and donations to build a new hospital (a total cost of $2.8 million); on May 1, 1958, the Rogue Valley Memorial Hospital (RMVC) opened its doors with 80 beds and a 75,000 square-foot facility. Located "out in the boondocks" of East Medford on Barnett, the facilities were later renamed the Rogue Valley Medical Center. Government grants under the Hill-Burton Act (1946) supported the initial construction, as well as an East Wing in the 1960s that brought the total number of beds to 160. The same act allowed a new diagnostic/treatment center, child dental clinic, intensive care, coronary, and cancer care unit to be added during that decade.

Radiation and oncology facilities, linear accelerator, EMI or CAT scans, suture machines, cryo-surgery for early skin cancer detection, and laser treatments didn't exist then. Nurses performed anesthesia, and physician malpractice insurance was $250 a year (now, this can be $100,000 per year plus). Doctors took turns in the emergency room, and every physician was deemed able to care for whatever medical requirements came in.

Nobody received hip or knee replacements, and with no hurry to push patients in or out, short-stay units didn't exist. The cost of uninsured patients was spread among those who paid or carried insurance—and patients weren't turned away. Physicians didn't carry beepers, nor were unnecessary tests or practicing defensive medicine needed. A board of doctors examined claims, and the Rogue Valley Physicians Service, a doctor-owned insurance company, handled claim resolutions.

Top: Rogue Valley Memorial Hospital, 1962. (SOHS 16772)

Bottom: Asante Hospital today.

Competition between RVMC and Providence wasn't what it would become, and doctors served on the board of both hospitals. Nowadays, one hospital's physicians usually don't associate with those at the other. With the growth of patient-directed care, physicians over time lost authority from what they had then. With present managed-care requirements, critics argue that the present concept is: hospitals can make more money by doing less. With state and federal legal changes, hospitals must work so that patients don't return needing additional treatment for or arising from the same condition.

In the 1970s, services and facilities at RVMC were added for pediatrics, neonatal intensive care, mental health, cardiovascular, and open-heart surgery. In the 1980s, home health and hospice services were started. In the 1990s, a new addition on the north side was completed, a library constructed, and Three-Rivers Community Hospital in Grants Pass (then 125 licensed beds) was acquired.

By 1998, the Medford hospital had grown to some 500,000 square feet of facilities. In 2005, a major renovation and expansion was completed to bring a 210,000 square-foot, four-story parking garage with expanded emergency, surgical, and diagnostic centers. A 100,000 square-foot, six-story impatient bed tower was also built. And RVMC has over 375 licensed beds, nearly five times as much as in the beginning.

A board of directors of community members (local residents and physicians) governs its non-profit operations. In mid-2012, the board decided on the new name and logo of "Asante" — which means "To your health" in French. Community owned, the tax-exempt organization (with more departments not previously mentioned) covers the nine-county area of Southern Oregon and Northern California. Asante owns RVMC, the Three-Rivers center, Ashland Community Hospital (acquired in late 2012), Physician Partners, and additional healthcare partnerships throughout the region.

It continues to increase its medical presence with improvements. For example (among previous ones), as part of a $20 million medical equipment upgrade program in 2016, Asante purchased 416 new beds for all three of its hospitals in Southern Oregon; RVMC (257 beds), Ashland (32), and Three Rivers (127).

It is the largest private full-time employer at this time in both Jackson County and Southern Oregon — a far cry from its beginnings, but still very community and now regionally oriented.

Sources: See Asante website at http://www.asante.org/; Conrad, *Medford Mail Tribune*; Varble, *Medford Mail Tribune*, May 3, 1998; Mann, *Medford Mail Tribune*, April 15, 2016.

Providence Medford
Medical Center

$\mathcal{P}$ROVIDENCE MEDFORD MEDICAL CENTER (PMMC) is part of a large hospital network that includes hospitals in Hood River, Milwaukie, Newberg, Portland, Seaside, Willamette, and other Oregon localities. A young widow, Emilie Gamelin, was instrumental in 1843 in establishing a religious community of Catholic women in Montreal, Quebec. Soon called the Sisters of Providence (for their trust in divine providence), the nuns dedicated their lives to caring for the sick and oppressed, the elderly, and orphans. In 1856, they came to Vancouver in the Washington Territory; two years later, they had opened St. Joseph Hospital, the first hospital in the Pacific Northwest.

In Portland, the sisters opened the state's first permanent hospital—Providence St. Vincent—in 1875. Over time, their operations evolved into an extensive non-profit network of hospitals, health plans, physicians, clinics, and affiliated services throughout Oregon, as well as Alaska, Washington, Montana, and California. In Medford, PMMC today is a 168-bed acute and outpatient care facility, offering numerous services: From stroke care, rehabilitation, maternity, cancer, and home care to emergency, cardiac, spine health, and numerous other services.

During the early 1910s, trained (or untrained) nurses—supervised by some thirty doctors in "houses for the sick"—were the hospitals of the time. Medford's population then was 11,500 and with "fine wide street and concrete pavements." Wanting a modern medical operation, local physicians petitioned Portland's Archbishop and the Sisters of Charity of Providence to bring one here.

Some fifty years after establishing the Northwest's first hospitals and schools, three of the Providence Sisters arrived in Medford on May 26,

Sacred Heart Hospital, June 22, 1913 from the Sunday *Oregonian*.

1911 (during the Orchard Boom), and the first entry recorded in the "Chroniques de l'Hôpital du Sacré Coeur" — the original leather-bound, handwritten journals kept by the nuns in their native French for the first decade — was that day. They used a small, yellow house at South Central Avenue and 11th Street as their first hospital. Tending to fourteen patients the day after arriving, they set up a place to worship, noting that "the house is poor and very disorderly."

The nuns quickly instituted plans to construct a hospital on Nob Hill in Siskiyou Heights. Despite the doctors' chilly reception, residents agreed to raise money for the hospital. Seven months after arriving, the sisters with their patients moved on January 2nd, 1912, into the new red-bricked Sacred Heart Hospital (built for $150,000). Despite their modern facility and equipment, the Sisters were not "assured of any money for our daily bread," and listed gifts of winter hay that year for their two cows, along with peas, apples, eggs, tomatoes, and other produce from local supporters.

Providence Medford Medical Center today.

Sacred Heart at the end of its first year had served 350 meals to the poor. Providence today still designates one day per year when everyone can eat bread and soup in its cafeteria, regardless of the ability to pay. It accepts donations for St. Vincent de Paul Society's soup kitchen from those who so can afford. In its first fundraising event in 1913, Sacred Heart featured "fancy objects," such as "embroidery, laces, paintings, and a doll wearing a complete winter wardrobe." And its increased fundraising efforts continued to the present.

The Sisters helped hundreds of patients without charge over the first decade, gave free hospitalizations to many, and donated medicine to the needy. They visited the sick in their homes, as well as cared for the ill and needy in Sacred Heart Hospital. Growing over the decades, the hospital (with the shortened name of "Providence") moved in 1966 to its larger, current location on Crater Lake Avenue. Rogue Valley Memorial Hospital (now Rogue Valley Medical Center), however, made some inroads into the number of patients who came to Providence.

Over time, the Order sent its Medford hospital administrators until 1970, when Sister Carmelina stepped down and Jack Stormberg became Providence's first lay employee in that position. For over twenty years afterwards, however, Sister Carmelina folded sheets in the laundry room and made hospital rounds. The Sisters gradually reduced their hospital operations, as their numbers decreased. In 2010, the order relinquished governance of its five-state Providence Health & Services to a secular board of directors.

Providence provides in excess of $30 million in charity care each year for uninsured patients. In addition to locations in Central Point and Phoenix, as well as its own insurance plan coverage, this major area hospital continues to increase its presence. In 2015 (among previous moves), it purchased the Medford Medical Clinic (multi-specialty patient clinic); in 2016, it announced plans to build a 3-story, 64,000-square-foot medical office as a primary, specialty and urgent care center at the corner of Stewart Ave. and Highway 99. Construction of the state-of-the-art medical building began in early 2017.

Sources: Lemon, *Medford Mail Tribune*, May 22, 2011; Waymarking.com/Hospitals: "Providence Medford Medical Center"; Stiles, *Medford Mail Tribune*, March 8, 2016.

Rogue Valley Manor

*I*N THE EARLY 1950s, SENIOR FACILITIES DID NOT exist as they do now. When the Reverend Ross Knotts—then pastor of the Ashland Methodist Church—couldn't find an acceptable facility for his retired father, he decided that one should be built on Barneburg Hill in southeast Medford. An ecumenical group of Methodists, Episcopalians, and Presbyterians came together with him on this plan, and "The Manor" was incorporated in 1955. Different civic, professional, and other religious leaders joined together to push the concept into reality.

On November 4, 1961, the Rogue Valley Manor (RVM) held its opening ceremony, and the famed announcer, Paul Harvey, broadcasted his show from Medford's KMED that day about the new "Barneburg Hilton." Constructed on the highest hill in Medford, the city's tallest building at ten stories—turquoise-colored with a high center and two, twin ends—looks down over the Valley and was built by people of faith.

The Manor expanded afterwards to where it now includes three more multi-story buildings, apartments, private care suites, a healthcare center, nine-hole golf course, cottages, and other amenities. The retirement community covers many of the needs of the senior citizens who live there: independent living, assisted living, skilled nursing care, private care, and even memory care. Among different awards received, Hospitality Design and Lodging magazine in 1999 awarded to RVM its Gold Key Award for excellence in senior living design.

However, the story doesn't end here. To focus on reaching a broader community, the Manor's Board of Directors in the 1980s decided to form a completely new corporation to oversee this outreach effort. Incorporated in 1990, the new organization was named, "Pacific Retirement Services (PRS)" with RVM as a subsidiary. Today, PRS develops, operates, manages, and markets retirement communities throughout the U.S.

Rogue Valley Manor, circa 1960. (SOHS 16934)

It is the thirteenth largest nonprofit provider of senior living services and care in the nation, serving approximately 5,000 residents with 3,200 employees. The communities owned outright are: Capitol Lakes (Madison, Wisconsin), Cascade Manor (Eugene), Holladay Park Plaza (Portland), Mirabella (Portland), Mirabella (Seattle), Rogue Valley Manor, Trinity Terrace (Fort Worth, Texas), and the University Retirement Community (Davis, California); PRS manages retirement centers in Napa, San Mateo, Santa Rosa, and Saratoga, California, plus a fifth in Middleton, Wisconsin.

The Rogue Valley Manor today. (Photo by BG Photography, courtesy of Rogue Valley Manor)

In 2010, the Manor completed a $65 million construction project that included the Manor Terrace to the south (a four-story, 120,000-square-foot building). In 2013, differences arose between the RMV and its corporate parent, PRS, resulting in a settlement with an independent board of directors, a cap on PRS management fees for three years, and a credit back of certain monthly fees to the residents. In 2014, the initial-1961 building underwent an $8 million project to replace windows, change the building's color, and add new air conditioning and heating systems. These facilities stand out, as do the services to its residents.

Sources: Mann, *Medford Mail Tribune,* April 14, 2013; see "Rogue Valley Manor" at http://www.retirement.org/rvm/; see PRS at http://www.retirement.org/.

The Past and Present
of Mercy Flights

EORGE MILLIGAN IN THE 1940s WAS A Medford air traffic controller in the "old, civilian control tower." In 1949, a close friend of his with polio died during the long drive from the city to Portland for treatment. An ambulance was taking the young man to a saving, iron lung, but he died before getting there. Since polio vaccine wasn't developed until the mid-1950s, this was the only option for victims with a respiratory system paralyzed by the disease — and the closest one was in Portland.

George decided then to buy a surplus military plane and turn it into an air ambulance, the first such service in the country. With fundraising efforts by schoolchildren, the Boy Scouts, and other community members, Milligan raised enough money to purchase the first Mercy Flights airplane, a twin-engine Cessna known as the "Bamboo Bomber."

That same year, he created a membership program so that people not only could contribute to Mercy Flights, but also insure that they would be covered if they needed emergency air transportation. A friend, Earl Warren, was the first family subscriber at a membership fee of $2, and he also flew with George for a few years helping to transport people. When Earl Warren had a heart attack, he used his Mercy Flights membership, as well as after later incurring a severe head injury from a fall.

(Under its present annual membership program, Mercy Flights bills the insurance company for services provided and the payments are considered payment in full. If the member does not have insurance, the bill is reduced by 50%.)

Its operations grew each year to where more equipment, personnel, and support were needed to cover the numbers of patients requiring its help.

Mercy Flights' early planes. (SOHS 04737)

With a board of directors governing the non-profit operation, it does not depend on taxpayer funds but relies instead on its membership fees and billings. Unfortunately in 1985, however, Milligan and three others died, less than a mile from the Medford airport when their airplane lost power.

In 1992 - 1993, Mercy Flights purchased two area ambulance services to include ground services throughout Jackson County. By later agreements, it coordinates land ambulance services in Josephine and Douglas Counties with its air transportation. In 1995, it entered into a contract to provide emergency helicopter services to calls within a 150-mile radius of Medford.

Mercy Flights today employs 115 people, including 80 medically-trained staff and eight full-time pilots who fly two King Air C-90 airplanes. These powerful twin-engine turboprop airplanes are pressurized to 30,000 feet. Their coverage is of the Western U.S. within 1,000 air miles of Medford (excluding Colorado) and primarily used for transporting patients between medical facilities. It staffs its helicopter on a 24/7 day basis. The aircraft and helicopter have on board state-of-the-art, in-flight medical equipment and trained personnel, including a nurse and paramedic with physicians on contract; nineteen ambulances are now available for needed transportation throughout its regional coverage.

Mercy Flights today.

By ground ambulance, helicopter, and fixed-wing planes, Mercy Flights covers patients in Southern Oregon and Northern California. It responds to some 200 emergencies each year by helicopter, most of which are heart attacks, car crashes, and injuries related to hunting or outdoor sports. It is used mostly for critically ill and injured patients where time makes a difference. A helicopter can travel from Medford, for example, to a burn center in Portland in an hour and fifteen minutes, while ground ambulance takes at least six hours.

Mercy Flights has grown from its Spartan beginnings to being a leader in medical transportation. It has flown more than 15,000 patients throughout the Western United States, and its ground ambulance service currently serves annually more than 21,000 patients a year—and it's from this area.

Sources: Mercy Flights website; Asnicar, *Medford Mail Tribune*, April 24, 2016.

PART VII

Nature's Fury

The 1959 Ashland Wildfire

*T*HE DATE WAS AUGUST 8, 1959, WHEN, near the city of Ashland, two small fires jumped into a fiery maelstrom that burned out of control for miles and threatened the town's very existence. The conditions couldn't have been worse. The time was near one o'clock in the afternoon and there had been four days of triple-digit heat. The temperature on that very day was 105 degrees, and the winds then were 10 miles per hour.

Starting in the dry grass by Jackson Hot Springs — above the railroad tracks and near the intersection of Highway 99 with South Valley View Road — the winds and conditions quickly drove the fire through the Ashland Mine Road area towards Wrights Creek Canyon. Whipped by ever increasing winds, Ashland's largest fire ever eventually destroyed 3,800 acres in its five-mile march up Wrights Creek and the ridge above (on top of Strawberry Lane) to the western crest of the Ashland watershed above Lithia Park.

A suspicion was that two little kids had been playing with matches. An eyewitness account, however, maintained that a railroad train passing by Jackson Hot Springs had been the cause: Sparks from the track had ignited the tender-dry fields as it traveled by.

Once gaining momentum under the conditions, thousands of Medford and Ashland residents watched as "a dense multi-colored cloud of smoke covered the southern skies" with pillars of smoke "that thrust like an atomic cloud thousands of feet in the air" — according to a fifty-year anniversary issue of the *Ashland Daily Tidings*. Hundreds of firefighters and fourteen flights by borate-dropping airplanes weren't able to stop the conflagration. Lithia Park became a staging area for firefighter camps, toilets, water, and equipment for 300 men.

The 1959 Ashland wildfire. (Photo courtesy wildfiretoday.com)

Stunned people watched trees explode as the winds increased to thirty miles per hour that afternoon and by 6:00 p.m., the firestorm was out of control. At night, a production of Anthony and Cleopatra continued at the Oregon Shakespeare Theatre when the fire chief decided to keep traffic off the streets and at the theatre; the cast and audience alike watched the blaze and firefighting helicopters with a mixture of fear and awe. The question was whether the town would be destroyed — but no one would know until morning.

When their worse fears seemed to being realized, a sudden shift of wind came from the south around midnight. This stopped the fire's growth. On the second day, the temperatures dropped by ten degrees and the winds died down. Fire crews pumped 300,000 gallons of water from an abandoned mine and bulldozers came into action. The fire was finally brought under control late that next night.

The firestorm burned down sheds and barns but no homes. Today, this general area is populated with numerous people and homes — and a similar fire would wreak havoc.

Sources: John Darling, "The Fire of 1959," *Ashland Daily Tidings*, August 6, 2009.

The 1962 Columbus
Day Storm

*T*HE COLUMBUS DAY STORM THAT STRUCK the Pacific Northwest on October 12, 1962 with hurricane-force winds was the most powerful windstorm to hit the area in its recorded history. This "extra-tropical cyclone" killed forty-six people and caused $250 million in property damages alone (in 1962 dollars)—$200 million in Oregon—in a deadly swath from San Francisco Bay to Canada with gales gusting as high as 179 miles per hour. In today's dollars, it would be $5 billion in damages caused by the massive storm's destruction.

In a deadly, rare combination of conditions, it had started a week earlier as Typhoon Freda in the southwest Pacific tropics. When the warm, moist air met a cold air-stream from the Gulf of Alaska—along with cold air from the northerly latitudes—these conditions intensified and caused a storm of biblical proportions. More than fifteen billion board feet of timber overall was flattened—worth an estimated $750 million—from Northern California to Western Montana. That's enough wood to build 300,000 homes and three times greater than the number of trees knocked over in the 1980 Mount St. Helens eruption.

Surging northward only fifty miles off the Pacific Coast, the howling winds hit highs of 179 mph at Cape Blanco, 138 mph in Newport, 116 mph in Portland, 96 mph in Astoria, and 88 mph in Tacoma, as its force lessened. The Seattle Space Needle swayed, windows buckled, and a loudspeaker blared warnings of 80 mph winds. Airplanes were flipped over at Portland Airport and buildings lost all of their windows; bridges were crumpled, trees crushed cars, shattered glass severely injured those in its way, fishing boats capsized, and an escaped lioness even attacked a boy.

Over 100 million board feet of timber was flattened in the Rogue River National Forest. In Medford, the winds gusted to 58 mph, much higher

Damage from the Columbus Day Storm of 1962 in Newberg, Oregon. (Photo courtesy the National Weather Service)

in the mountains. Highways were plugged with fallen trees, some five feet in diameter with trees in the forests stacked twenty feet high. Families with small children huddled inside windowless homes and stared outside as huge trees snapped into the Rogue River. Like many across the state, people cooked in their fireplaces, since electricity was out throughout entire areas. All of the plate-glass windows inside one downtown Medford car dealership crashed to the floor after a customer opened the door, reducing the inside pressure.

Although removing felled trees, replacing glass, and repairing roofs and buildings took time, the memories of that "storm of storms" still remains. Weather experts believe that a storm of that magnitude happening today, moreover, would have a severer impact due to the larger population and greatly expanded infrastructure.

Sources: Fattig, *Medford Mail Tribune*, October 12, 2012; LaLande, *Oregon Encyclopedia*: "Columbus Day Storm (1962)."

The 1964 Christmas Flood

CUTTING THROUGH THE HOLIDAYS, A MAJOR FLOOD occurred in the Pacific Northwest and California between December 18, 1964, and January 7, 1965, named "The Christmas Flood of 1964." This 100-year flood was one of the worst in recorded history for Oregon and the worst on nearly every river in Northern California. The U.S. National Weather Service rated this flood as the fifth most destructive event in Oregon in the Twentieth Century. An extremely heavy snowpack accumulated in California, Oregon, and Washington that was followed by unseasonably warmer weather, heavy rain deluges, and huge snow melts that caused water to rush down and overwhelm river banks.

Many weather stations throughout the Pacific Northwest and this region measured the rainfall over the five days from December 19th to the 23rd as being the wettest ever recorded. When night arrived on Dec. 22nd 1964, the Rogue River raged over its banks. The monstrous waters destroyed nearly everything in its path, ripping houses apart, cutting away roads, slicing hillsides in half, and destroying small towns.

The Rogue River hit Shady Cove nearly the hardest. A portion of the bridge over the river washed away that night, as tons of heavy mill-logs and rooftops surged to race past and crush houses downstream. The town was totally dark as the power was already out, but anyone along the river could hear its tremendous roar.

The waters captured freezers, furniture, cars, and anything in its path, floatable or not. Normal placid streams became swollen. Bear Creek rushed into the Rogue, which surged over its banks to submerge much of downtown Medford. In Gold Hill, floodwaters were four-feet deep in the basement of a ranch house that was 600 feet from the river. The river crested at thirty-four feet — twelve feet above flood level — at the

Damage from the 1964 Christmas flood near Shady Cove in Southern Oregon.

City of Rogue River; it surged fifteen feet above flood stage in Grants Pass, swamping large areas of this city and heavily damaging homes, businesses, bridges, and even the sewage-treatment plant.

Afterwards, recovered possessions were useless, damaged beyond repair, or waterlogged. With the flood ripping through septic tanks, providing sanitation and potable water were priorities. Although no one died in this area, seventeen did throughout Oregon and the total damages were then in the hundreds of millions of dollars. Towns and residents banded together to help one another out; those on dry land took in friends, as the Salvation Army and other nonprofits opened their doors. Even without flood insurance, shops reopened and homes were rebuilt over time.

People do doubt that flood-control dams built after 1964, however, can restrain the next 100-year deluge, especially with the countless homes built later by riverbanks and those who are unaware of a severe flood's destructive powers.

Sources: Fattig, *Medford Mail Tribune*, December, 19, 2004; *Wikipedia*: "Christmas Flood of 1964."

The 1997 Ashland
New Year's Day Flood

JACKSON AND JOSEPHINE COUNTIES HAVE experienced eleven major floods over the last century, the landmark event occurring in 1964, which set most of the high-water records for the region. The area later experienced in late-December 1996 and New Year's Day of 1997 another destructive event, known as the "New Year's Day Flood." This impacted residents on both sides of the border in Oregon and California.

Similar to 1964, a warm rain followed weeks of heavy snowfall on the mountains, and the streams and rivers rose to 100-year flood levels, leading to flooding in both urban and rural areas. This caused multi-million dollars of damages to homes, businesses, and infrastructure in Southern Oregon alone (one estimate being as high as $50 million); more than 1,500 people were evacuated and over 1,000 properties damaged. In January 1997, President Clinton declared fourteen Oregon counties — including Jackson, Josephine, and Klamath counties — eligible for disaster assistance.

Over seventy landslides occurred throughout Jackson County, but Ashland was hardest hit when Ashland Creek surged down to cut the town in half. With turbulent, muddy, dangerous waters, the swollen creek pounded through Lithia Park. When logs, mud, and debris clogged the culverts under Winburn Way at the entrance to Lithia Park, the massive tsunami-like flood leaped over its banks to flood the park and downtown plaza.

Residents awoke on New Year's Day to discover that the currents had ripped through streets, caused massive infrastructure damage, and severed the main sewer and water lines with a twenty-foot waterfall that thundered down where an important street once was. The prime

Rushing waters inundate Ashland's main plaza during the 1997 flood, doing $4.5 million in damage to the city's infrastructure.

arteries of Main Street and Lithia Way through the town were impassable, and traffic needed to be detoured to I-5 and over out-of the-way back streets.

Depending on the area, running water and sewage service was cut for a week or more. Houses were flooded and people had to evacuate or scramble to higher floors. For days, residents put garbage cans out to collect rainwater, stood in line for drinking water from National Guard water trucks, and even pooled money to rent portable toilets for their neighborhoods. City residents couldn't drink city water for a week and others didn't have sewer service during most of January. Accounting for one-third of the county's losses, Ashland incurred $4.5 million in damages to its infrastructure, not to mention people's homes, cars, and businesses. Nobody thankfully was reported to be seriously injured.

Marty Bryant's "Caring Friends" supplied food, clothing, and furniture for 200 families whose homes had been flooded. As Ashland rebuilt, the city and residents turned Lithia Park back into the centerpiece that it is today. Learning the hard way about natural disaster preparedness, the town created a Community Emergency Response Team (CERT) program and has trained hundreds of volunteers in emergency preparedness. Despite this, the risk of these type of disasters is always present over time.

Sources: Plain, *Medford Mail Tribune,* January 1, 2007; Jackson County Emergency Management: "Floods" (at its website).

The 2002 Biscuit Fire

O N JULY 13, 2002, SOUTHWESTERN Oregon had endured nearly two months of drought and a searing heat wave was cooking the area. The forecasted weather was for a high of 105 degrees that day, and the Illinois Valley forests were dry as kindling. The conditions were a perfect storm for dry lightning strikes—so hot that the heat evaporates the rain before it reaches the ground—and which start one-third of all forest fires.

A series of electrical storms boiled over the mountains and just after 2:00 P.M. that afternoon, thunderbolts struck down onto the tinder-dry forests along the California-Oregon border. These bolts ignited five separate fires within twenty miles of one another inside Oregon's Siskiyou Mountains and the huge Kalmiopsis Wilderness. Without one drop of water cooling the land, 581 lighting strikes in total struck Jackson and Josephine Counties with twenty-three bolting down into the Siskiyou National Forest.

Despite immediate attempts to stop the first air-spotted fire, firefighting efforts failed and a second one—both on steep, rocky slopes—was spotted burning the next day. Observers then saw the additional smoldering fires. With most of the nation's fire-fighting manpower tied down elsewhere in the second worst fire season in fifty years (throughout eleven states), the small crews positioned there didn't have a chance to suppress the Kalmiopsis fires. In Oregon alone, a dozen major fires were already burning out of control inside 100,000 acres.

Dubbed the Biscuit Fire (after Oregon's Biscuit Creek, where the fires joined together), the fires burned into one another in days and a twenty-mile wall of flames sped through the wilderness of tall trees and thick brush. Only air-tankers could stop this, but the ten Oregon tankers were

Smoke from the Biscuit Fire billows above cars of local residents gathered for a meeting with fire officials. (Photo courtesy of wildlandfire.com)

already in use fighting fires in eastern and central Oregon. The small contingent of firefighters was forced to fall back, as the flames threatened the 17,000 residents in the Illinois Valley towns of Selma, Kerby, Cave Junction, and O'Brien.

With much of the fire inside remote wilderness (and skirting Highway 199), the Forest Service's efforts were intentionally limited to setting large backfires and building fire-breaks. With limited manpower and smoke filling the area, the Service decided to let the flames burn in different directions, but not into the Illinois Valley. On July 30th, however, one front blasted through 65,000 acres in twenty-four hours—an area equaling two-thirds the size of the city of Portland—racing five and one-half miles in only ninety minutes. At that rate, out-of-control fires would slam into Selma in less than an hour.

Easily seen from the I-5 corridor, mushroom clouds of thick, gray smoke reached as high as 30,000 feet into the sky. As the plumes topped, they then collapsed to spew embers and burning branches miles from the fire's edge. Along a twenty-mile stretch of Highway 199, the view to the west was an ominous string of plumes towering over the Valley. When 60 mph winds blasted flames 100 feet over the Illinois River, homes and lives there were directly threatened. Evacuation notices were issued for the entire Illinois Valley.

Worrying that these fires with the prevailing winds would burn to the Rogue River, the Forest Service brought in its best wilderness firefighters. As a steady stream of packed vans and campers headed away from the Illinois Valley, another convoy of bulldozers on huge flatbeds, fire engines (from three-dozen Oregon communities), and school buses filled with firefighting crews headed into the remote valley. Grants Pass motels offered discounts to residents fleeing the area, as smoke-filled air and cinders blanketed Southern Oregon for days on end.

By early August, equipment and over 7,000 people operated from three main fire camps near Cave Junction, Brookings, and Gold Beach; the efforts included firefighters from Mexico and technical personnel from Canada, Australia, and New Zealand. By August 10th, a combination of burnouts, bulldozed firelines, helicopter water-drops, firefighting "hotshots," and a near-miraculous wind shift formed a safety ring that saved the Illinois Valley.

Nearly two months after the lighting strikes, the fires—still burning out of control—were declared "contained." Even with this, the Biscuit Fire wasn't declared fully "controlled" until late November, and it burned until the winter rains came. On December 31st, the Forest Service finally declared it to be officially extinguished.

Although no lives were lost and structural damage minimal—limited to less than a dozen structures that were generally remote cabins—the burn area was 500,000 acres and Oregon's largest forest fire of record. Some forty percent of the 500,000 acres (200,000) within the fireline was reduced to charcoal and ash with twenty percent basically untouched.

A controversy developed over whether the fires could have been put out in the first days, especially as to whether California and Oregon fire supervisors had effectively communicated. A later GAO report stated that rapid responses were stretched thin by the outbreak of wildfires across the country and they had missed an early chance to put out the blaze, as regional "helitac" crews and smokejumpers were sent elsewhere. Leaving many forests choked with fuel, eighty years of suppressing wildland fires had compounded the problem. Despite learning that a wave of dry lightning strikes on a heated summer day can overwhelm small fire crews, it is possible that a fire of this magnitude could occur again.

In the years after the Biscuit Fire, despite the courts ruling for the Forest Service and that the salvage logging involved less than one percent of the fire-killed timber, protesters demonstrated against the efforts and blocked logging trucks. With U.S. Marshals and local police efforts, the logging proceeded as this became a battleground between the Bush administration and environmental groups over opening remote, road-less areas to salvage logging. At the end of 2006, helicopters removed the last of the salvage timber.

Sources: Savage, *RedOrbit*: "The Biscuit Fire"; LaLande, *Oregon Encyclopedia*: "Biscuit Fire of 2002."

Lost Creek Lake
(and Jess Dam)

B ILL JESS AND HIS BROTHER BEGAN CATTLE RANCHING in 1952 near Eagle Point by the Rogue River. A few months later, a flood swept away part of their ranch, although this one wasn't as bad as previous flooding. In 1955, the raging Rogue River again jumped its banks and caused $9 million in damages, including taking away more of Jess's land.

One month later, a group of fourteen people met in Grants Pass to push for dam flood-control, and they chose Bill Jess as their chairman. With support from others with this concern — including better water management — the "Rogue Basin Flood Control and Water Resources Association" formed in February 1956 and later that year became a nonprofit organization. Ben Day was a Valley rancher, attorney, and Oregon legislator (1949 to 1955, first in the House, then in the Senate); he joined and gave needed help to this movement.

Groups such as fishermen, guides, and tourist-based businesses, however, historically opposed dams and especially one on the Rogue River. With assurances that river flows and temperatures would be better controlled to help salmon runs and spawning, some of the opposition dropped. With the potential for more uncontrolled floods, momentum gained in convincing state and federal legislators.

Although Congress approved the dam in 1962, the funding wasn't appropriated until four years later, pushed by the disastrous 1964 flood, which was the Valley's worst ever in damages. With more funding delays and time required for surveying, permitting, and planning, the U.S. Army Corps of Engineers didn't start construction until 1972.

Located nine miles above Shady Cove and approximately half-way between Crater Lake National Park and Medford, construction was

Lost Creek Lake. This view is to the east from the dam; peaks in the Cascade Range are visible in the far distance.

completed in 1977. The dam — 345 feet high and 3,600 feet long — is earth and rock-fill construction with gated spillways on the south end; the outlets and powerhouse with two twenty-six-megawatt generators are located to the north.

The intake tower controls water releases through a unique technology that allows water temperature regulation by combining lake water from different depths in a mixing chamber before releasing it downstream. This cools the normally warm summer waters of the Rogue to improve conditions for the migrating salmon and steelhead. When part of the lake, the Rogue River still receives water from different streams, including lost Creek from one side and a second Lost Creek tributary from the other.

The Corps of Engineers at the same time built a fish hatchery, and the Oregon Department of Fish and Wildlife operates this facility. The Cole

M. Rivers Hatchery (named for a long-time Rogue River biologist) is one of the largest in Oregon and can annually produce 425,000 pounds of chinook and coho salmon, rainbow trout, and steelhead. The upstream barrier dam delivers the water that operates the hatchery, which is also open to the public and built to mitigate fish loss owing to the dam's presence.

The dammed Rogue River created a lake with 315,000 acre feet (674 square miles) that is ten miles long with a combined shore length of thirty miles. Its surface elevation is from 1,750 to 1,870 feet. Lost Creek Lake has over twenty developed parks that include campgrounds, picnic areas, trailheads, boat ramps, and fishing/shoreline access points. The Army Corps of Engineers maintains thirty miles of trails that surround the lake.

The river below the dam is popular with summer fishing, rafting, and tubing when the water is relatively warmer. Stewart State Park is along the southern shore, and the Oregon State Parks system operates this with over 200 campsites, a marina, store, café, and other amenities. Casey State Park is located on the Rogue River below the dam.

William Jess died in 1995 and one year later, Oregon Senator Mark Hatfield oversaw a bill that enabled Congress to rename Lost Creek Lake Dam as the "William L. Jess Dam and Intake Structure." With the removal of dams such as Gold Ray and Savage Rapids, the magnificent Rogue River now flows freely from The William L. Jess Dam at Lost Creek Lake for 157 miles to the Pacific Ocean.

Sources: Oregon Dept. of Fish and Wildlife: "Cole Rivers Hatchery"; Miller, *Medford Mail Tribune*, April 14, 2013.

PART VIII

Political and Community Leaders

Where Past Meets Present

Lincoln Savage of
Savage Creek

*J*AMES AND MARGARET ANNE SAVAGE CAME TO the Rogue Valley in 1853 after a six-month-long, arduous wagon-trail ride across the Midwest and West from Illinois. They took up a donation-land claim on what's now known as Savage Creek in Josephine County that empties into the south side of the Rogue River.

The small, unincorporated community of Savage Rapids—named after this pioneering family, including the rapids on the Rogue—is two miles to the west of the City of Rogue River on Highway 99 and eight miles east of downtown Grants Pass. The dam that was built much later and then demolished was also named after these pioneers.

Their sixth of thirteen children—Abraham Lincoln Savage—was born in 1864. Lincoln walked the three miles to school when growing up and had a strong interest in botany even then. He graduated from Grants Pass High School and later from the Southern Oregon State Normal School in Ashland. His three-year "Normal Course" degree was equivalent to today's bachelor of education, and Lincoln Savage had the highest grades and was the valedictorian of his twenty-three-student graduation class.

His passions being botany and education, Lincoln taught for thirteen years in the tiny towns of Butte Falls (Jackson County), Ruch (Applegate Valley), Wilderville (Applegate Valley), and Kerby (Illinois Valley), as well as being the high school principal at Ruch, Butte Falls, and Kerby. It is possible that these location changes were also due to his love of botany and the regional diversity. For sixteen years starting in 1900, Lincoln Savage was the Josephine County Superintendent of Schools.

Strongly believing in a standardized method of course and study, Josephine County became the first county in Oregon to create this system.

Marrying Ida Mary White in 1917, they had one son. Once elected as Josephine County's treasurer in 1924, however, his teaching career changed for one in government. Despite this, he continued with his love of botany, including field studies that dated back to his initial teaching responsibilities.

While principal of Kerby High School, he became friends with Albert Sweetser, a botanist at the University of Oregon Herbarium (a collection of preserved plant specimens). The two worked together, which later included Louis Henderson when Louis succeeded Sweetser at the University of Oregon; Henderson named a small plant in Savage's honor in 1931 for his work. With Lincoln's introduction of botany into his teaching curriculum, a number of his student's collections — along with more than 160 of his own (many from the 1920s and 1930s) — are in the Oregon State University Herbarium.

When Lincoln Savage died in 1950, he was considered to be one of Josephine County's most eminent residents. He had spent his entire life in Southern Oregon as a botanist, teacher, county school superintendent, and county treasurer. Eight years later, 540 of his plant specimens were donated to the University of Oregon's Natural History Museum.

This son of a pioneering family went onto being a pioneer in education and government. Lincoln Savage Middle School near Murphy and Lincoln Savage Reservoir are named in his honor, not to mention that the *Grants Pass Daily Courier* later heralded him as "Josephine County's Man of the Century." He certainly meets the criteria.

Sources: Lang, *Oregon Encyclopedia*: "Abraham Lincoln Savage (1864-1950)"; Blanchard, *Grants Pass Daily Courier*, September 11, 1995.

Glenn Jackson:
Mr. Oregon

G LENN L. JACKSON WAS BORN IN 1902 in Albany, Oregon; his father, W.L. Jackson, was the co-publisher of the *Albany Democrat Herald*, and his mother, Minnie, was a school teacher. Joining the California-Oregon Power Company (COPCO) as an appliance or "electricity salesman" in Medford — where he lived for nearly sixty years — Jackson became sales manager in 1921. Although he was expelled from high school, he graduated from Oregon State University in 1925 and earned increasing responsibility and assignments at COPCO.

World War II interrupted his career — like many others — but at its end, he had achieved the rank of colonel in the Army Air Corps, was awarded the Bronze Star and Legion of Merit, and had served in England, Italy, and France. Returning to Medford, he began working again for COPCO and continued for the rest of his corporate career.

Jackson also turned his attention to Jackson County. He led a group that acquired the interior of former Camp White and then worked to create the industrial center of White City. He not only helped to reinvigorate the Rogue Valley Country Club, he operated and owned it through his enterprise, Golf Holding Company. Jackson also was working on and developed a 12,000-acre cattle ranch on Highway 140 that he enjoyed for decades.

In 1949, he and his sister inherited the majority interest in the *Albany Democrat Herald* and later bought out the minority interest. Jackson built the business, the Democrat-Herald Publishing Co., to include the *Ashland Daily Tidings* and eight other newspapers. He delegated the day-to-day running to the managing editors, as he concentrated his priorities with COPCO and various civic activities.

Glenn Jackson.

Recognized then as a power broker, Jackson was a Republican, but he was non-partisan and supported the best person, regardless of party affiliation. He became an important out-of-the-public-eye supporter over time of different administrations.

Before he was on the Highway Commission, the proposed viaduct in Medford was debated at a public hearing in 1956. Businesses did not want the proposed I-5 to bypass them in favor of an alternate route along Hillcrest Road, believing that they would lose significant business if it didn't follow the downtown route of Bear Creek. The strongest opposition was largely from the orchardists, however, who didn't want the freeway going through their pear lands to the east and west of the downtown.

These interests made their case to Glenn Jackson and Earl Miller, Medford's Mayor, who agreed with their arguments. Although the central route brought important traffic closer, this would cut the town in half, had no place for on-ramps, and was expensive. Although the decision was controversial, the powers-to-be decided to put I-5 over Medford, and the I-5 Central Point to Barnett Road off-ramps opened in 1962.

In 1959, Governor Mark Hatfield appointed him to the Oregon State Transportation Commission, or Highway Commission, and three years later named him as the chairman of this important committee. Reappointed by later Governors Tom McCall and Robert Straub, his years of work in the highway-transportation area is where his greatest service was given for all Oregonians. He oversaw the planning and construction of 700 miles of highways and more than 800 bridges, including the Freemont, Astoria, and Marquam Bridges.

While doing this, Glenn Jackson first earned the title of "Mr. Medford," and then "Mr. Oregon." He maintained his priority of COPCO, however, not only heading it as its chief executive officer, but after it merged into Pacific Power & Light ("PP&L") in 1961, he later became PP&L's chairman. This entity became part of the giant utility, PacifiCorp, when it too was acquired.

When Governor Vic Atiyeh in 1979 appointed him as Chairman of the State Economic Commission, his twenty-year term on the Highway Commission (and its chairman for seventeen years) came to an end. He was still president of the Golf Holding Company, owners of the Rogue Valley Country Club, among other duties and responsibilities.

Glenn Jackson died a year later in 1980. He had started out selling electric appliances and had become one of the most influential people in Oregon's history. Aside from his tenure on the Highway Commission and COPCO/PP&L, he had been a director of the Rogue Valley Memorial Hospital, chairman of Executive Flight Services (the operator of Air Oregon, a commuter airline company), a trustee of Willamette University, and on the boards of U.S. National Bank, Fred Meyer, Standard Insurance, and the U.S. Chamber of Commerce.

He had been a five-term president of the Medford Chamber of Commerce. In 1963, he was the prime mover and jumpstarted the fundraising to improve the Mt. Ashland Ski Area by providing more than one-half of the required $120,000. The moneys were used to clear trees, grade terrain, build better access roads, and construct a T-bar lift, rope tow, and four-story ski lodge.

Capital Cities Communications in 1980 acquired his newspaper business. The members of the Rogue Valley County Club purchased these facilities from his heirs. The Glenn L. Jackson Memorial Bridge (or I-205 Bridge) across the Columbia River was named after him due to his transportation service for Oregon. Glenn Jackson was frequently called "the most powerful man in Oregon" — and he had spent his later adult life living up to this reputation.

Sources: Mahoney, *Oregon Encyclopedia*; *Medford Mail Tribune*, April 22, 2007; *Medford Mail Tribune*, April 22, 2007 (second article).

Robby Collins: Saving Jacksonville and the World

B ORN IN 1921 IN RIVERSIDE, CALIFORNIA, Robertson "Robby" Collins grew up in California and later graduated from Stanford University. After serving in the Army Air Corps in World War II, he moved to the Rogue Valley in 1948, where he was very successful in the lumber business. Moving to Jacksonville in 1962, he mounted a successful opposition in the 1960s to a proposed four-lane highway that would have connected Interstate 5 with the Applegate, destroyed or removed eleven historic homes and buildings, and cut Jacksonville in half.

Robby went onto bringing about the restoration of historic structures in Jacksonville and protecting them with historic preservation easements. This use creates the right of the designated organization to approve — or disapprove — any changes to the property and ensure that any proposal protects the structure's historic nature. In learning the ins-and-outs of restoring the town and its buildings, he became a heritage preservation specialist.

This culminated in a large swatch of Jacksonville in 1966 being designated a National Historic Landmark. The Landmark District is approximately 326 acres in size and includes 688 structures; this boundary is not the same as the city limits, nor is it the "historic core" area. More than 100 individual buildings also are specifically listed on the National Register of Historic Places.

Collins served on numerous boards, including the Southern Oregon Historical Society and the Historic Preservation League of Oregon, as well as being the past president of the Oregon Shakespeare Festival. No matter how busy he was as a businessman, however, he traveled all over

America and Alaska, sharing his experiences with other small towns that were struggling to save their heritage. He worked at local and state levels, eventually becoming a trustee and later vice-chairman of the National Trust for Historic Preservation.

He received the University of Oregon's Distinguished Service Award in 1980 for his role in Jacksonville's preservation; the governor three years later awarded him the Distinguished Preservationist Award. With his retirement coming, Collins began accepting overseas projects where he could use his Jacksonville and small-town experiences to assist third-world countries in their attempts to save their historic sites.

In 1984, he retired at age sixty-three from his lumber business and devoted full time to the international front. With these responsibilities, he later moved to Singapore for the rest of his life, from where he taught and consulted on historic preservation in countries ranging from Bangladesh, India, and Nepal to Thailand, Fiji, the Philippines, China, and other countries. Robby became the Chairman of the Cultural Tourism Committee of the International Council on Monuments and Sites ("ICOMOS"), an august group dedicated to these goals.

To share his expertise, Collins joined numerous travel-industry task forces (teams of hotel experts, bus, and airport operators) as the "heritage specialist" to help others assess and protect their heritage. He assisted the people in Macao (the land seaport accessed from Hong Kong) in developing a "heritage tourist package" that included their old Portuguese buildings and churches, not just the gambling casinos. In Cairns, Australia, he brought the residents to preserving an old railroad, coffee plantation, and vintage Queensland houses built by settlers a century before. Collins created plans to preserve sites such as Cambodia's famous Angkor Wat (an ancient Khmer temple complex in Cambodia.)

His commitment, energy, and enthusiasm for historical preservation around the world were legendary. Robby Collins died on May 23, 2003, in Singapore at age eighty-one from dengue fever.

Sources: Hoffman, *Christian Science Monitor*, July 22, 1988; *Medford Mail Tribune*: "Robertson E. Collins," May 28, 2003.

Ralph Wehinger:
A True Visionary

D R. RALPH WEHINGER WAS AN EAGLE POINT chiropractor who does not have a monument in his honor, a long-lasting business, or lived a long life. However, he was a true visionary and his passion for the outdoors and its wildlife is very evident today.

In the mid-1980s, Ralph was instrumental in the funding of the U.S. Fish and Wildlife Services (USFWS) Forensic Laboratory and its location in Ashland. Its Director, Ken Goddard, was working without a state-of-the-art facility and this need was striking. Wehinger was attending a USFWS forensic meeting in 1985 in Portland, when the agent explained that their efforts to stop falcon smugglers—a protected species—was enraging legitimate falconers, who had been wrongly accused of violating the Migratory Bird Act. The meeting's purpose was to tell the public not to take wild falcons from the wilderness without the required permits.

Wehinger questioned whether the agents had considered using DNA to see the difference. When the agent answered that the USFWS didn't have a forensic laboratory, Ralph got to work. Enlisting others, he lobbied Oregon Senators Mark Hatfield and Bob Packwood, who became involved in his efforts. Attended by the senators and other dignitaries, the Ashland dedication ceremony for the lab—the world's only dedicated wildlife forensic laboratory—took place in July 1989. Ralph received the credit also for bringing the lab to Ashland.

At the same time, he was working with Ron Lamb to create the Pacific Northwest Museum of Natural History in Ashland. With his success on the forensics lab—which would share a corner of the SOU property with the museum—Dr. Wehinger already had a track record with Washington, D.C. With federal Interior Department funds owing to Senator Mark Hatfield's efforts, private donations, and a state bond issue, the museum was constructed and opened in July 1994. Its exhibits, wildlife, and history were critically acclaimed; however, owing to not being able to meet the bonded debt, the museum closed in 1997. ScienceWorks now uses this facility for its museum, so all is not lost.

To make time for another endeavor, Ralph left the museum project in 1990: He also was working to obtain a Foreign Trade Zone designation for Medford Airport. This would allow for the international clearing of customs and duty-free manufacturing in Medford, plus the ability to clear wildlife directly to his proposed wildlife treatment center for injured birds and animals. He and Mike Burrill, Sr., set up a for-profit company, Ore-Cal Trade Co., of which Wehinger was the chief executive officer.

Due to these efforts, the airport in October 1994 became an international airport with a Foreign Trade Zone designation and creation of a U.S. Customs Service office. In March of the following year, the airport was renamed as the Rogue Valley International-Medford Airport due to this. One year later, the zone was activated at the airport. International shipments could be cleared there without needing to ship them through Portland or San Francisco. As an outgrowth of the Foreign Trade Zone designation, Dr. Wehinger in 1996 was named an honorary consul to Korea.

Ralph meanwhile was working on his dream of the International Wildlife Recovery Center. This center would be the only nonmobile facility of its kind in the western United States as a main responder for wildlife rescue in oil spills. Rather than dying at the spot, oily birds from any North American major spill could be flown to Medford. From there, they could be transported to his decontamination and rehabilitation center on Little Butte Creek, thirty miles east of Medford, in the remote wilderness behind his home—and nursed back there to health. The question was whether this could become a reality.

In September 2002, Dr. Wehinger announced the opening of the private, nonprofit center with receiving/inspection facilities at Medford's airport and the rehab center—with a heliport—on Little Butte Creek. A grant from the Department of Agriculture ($1.2 million) and other funding from the federal Oil Pollution Act of 1990 (passed due to the Exxon Valdez spill) brought about the $2 million development. His dream to save wildlife had been fulfilled.

One month later, the news came of Ralph's diagnosis of a brain tumor and his being in grave condition. Dr. Wehinger passed away on December 6, 2002, at age forty-eight. After his death, the Foreign Trade Zone and his International Wildlife Recovery Center became inactive. His chiropractic business was sold. The USFWS Forensic Center, however, and the former museum building (now home to ScienceWorks) continue on. Rogue Valley International-Medford Airport has its international designation.

Southern Oregon was so much the better for his vision — and so much was done in so little time.

Sources: U.S. Fish and Wildlife Service: *Our Lab's History*; Aleccia, *Medford Mail Tribune,* August 3, 1997; Denson, the *Oregonian*, June 7, 2009; Darling, *Medford Mail Tribune,* September 6, 2002.

PART IX

Rivers, Fishing, and Related Activities

The Rogue River

*T*HE MAGNIFICENT ROGUE RIVER HAS BEEN a source of drinking water, irrigating, fishing, boating, swimming, and many other activities dating from the first Native Americans to the present. Located in southwestern Oregon, the Rogue flows for 215 miles from Crater Lake to the Pacific Ocean. The snowmelt from Crater Lake is the initial source of its waters, percolating and flowing into Boundary Springs on the northern boundary. From there, these waters rush down into a stream that leads northerly from the park area.

Its name dates back to the early trappers. The first Europeans exploring the area were the French, who found their first experiences with the natives to be particularly troublesome. They called them "Les Coquins," or "the Rogues," and applied that name not only to the region, but also to the river which was such an important part of tribal life.

The Rogue River has three distinct regions: the Upper Rogue, Middle Rogue, and Lower Rogue. For forty miles, snowmelt and springs from the peaks of the Cascade Range—including Mt. Mazama of Crater Lake—feeds the river through the Upper Rogue from Boundary Springs to Prospect, as the main tourist route to and from the lake winds with it. The narrow, swift waterway cuts through thick forests of pine, oak, fur, and bank-lining alder, and it carved a steep canyon more then 200-feet deep at times for two miles, the Rogue River Gorge, which is a major tourist stop.

The middle stretch of the Rogue runs from Prospect to past Grants Pass, where it widens at times to more than 150 feet. The tributary flows through an ancient valley that was formed one-million years ago when Western Oregon slowly worked upwards to form the Pacific Coast

Rafters negotiate Mule Creek Canyon on the Rogue River. (Photo courtesy of Wikimedia/Northwest Rafting Co.)

Range. The Dakubetede, Takelma, Shasta, and Applegate tribes mingled throughout the area — collectively referred to as the Rogue River tribe — for countless centuries before the fur trappers, miners, and settlers came.

The gold discoveries in the 1850s triggered the influx that resulted in the towns of Shady Cove, Gold Hill, and Rogue River (in Jackson County), along with Grants Pass (in Josephine County) on the river. Its near prehistoric cutting resulted in the splendid Upper and Lower Table Rock formations that are easily seen from today's I-5.

Of the early river pioneers, Glen Wooldridge (1896-1986) stands out, as the monument in his honor at Riverside Park in Grants Pass attests:

Glen was a man without peer, who challenged and conquered the infamous Rogue River. Near this spot at an early age he forged a bond that forever linked him to this river. In 1915, he fulfilled a dream and became the first to maneuver a wooden drift boat from Grants Pass to the Pacific Ocean. In 1947, he made the first trip upstream using a twenty-two-horsepower outboard motor, fitted with a 'Jackass' lift he developed, on a 20 foot plank boat. Over the years a major industry, including excursion boating, river guiding, and driftboat fishing, evolved from Glenn's pioneering efforts on the Rogue River.

Owing to it being one of the initial eight rivers included in the Wild and Scenic Rivers Act of 1968, the Lower Rogue section starts seven miles west of Grants Pass and ends eleven miles east of Gold Beach. This protected area is eighty-four miles in length and is internationally known for its pristine whitewater rafting, camping, steelhead and salmon fishing, scenery, and wildlife. Tiny settlements — such as Galice, Agness, and other hamlets — dot this region.

With significant tributaries such as the South Fork Rogue River (meeting the river upstream of Lost Creek Lake), Elk Creek, Bear Creek, the Applegate River, and the Illinois River, the Rogue River in flood stage is destructive and dangerous. Notable ones include the floods of 1964 — rated by the U.S. National Weather Service as the fifth most destructive event in Oregon in the Twentieth Century — and 1861 (which crested higher at different towns than the 1964 disaster). Given these inflows, even the construction of the William Jess Dam (and Lost Creek Lake) in 1977 is not seen by the experts to be able to meaningfully stem such flooding in a 100-year flood.

The unsurpassed beauty and serenity of the Rogue has been a magnet for notable personalities. A few who became connected with the river are: Jack London, Clark Gable, Myrna Loy, Bing Crosby, William Faulkner, Ginger Rogers, John Wayne, the famed author Zane Gray, Kim Novak, Tyrone Power, Myrna Loy, Carole Lombard, Oregon Poet Laureate Ben Hur Lampman, and modern day personalities from Kirstie Alley to Johnny Depp.

Given the towns that cropped up on the Rogue River, there have been countless bridges built over time. In fact, the section of Gold Hill (and slightly north and south) has had more bridges than any Oregon town over time other than Portland. With the removal of the Gold Ray and Savage Rapids Dams, the Rogue River now flows freely from Lost Creek Lake and its William Jess Dam to the Pacific Ocean; and the variety of state, federal, and city parks that are on or around the river allow for its enjoyment.

Its Hellgate Canyon in the Lower Rogue has been the scene for various movies and commercials. Municipalities such as Grants Pass, Gold Hill, Medford (supplemental), and others rely on it for their city water supplies. Jet boats ply upstream from Gold Beach and downstream from Grants Pass with delighted passengers. The stunning and impressive Rogue River provides activities ranging from today's boat rides, whitewater rafting, salmon and steelhead fishing, picnicking, and fine dining to gold panning, swimming, town festivities, scenic driving, and a magnet for authors, painters, and poets—not to mention the rest of us.

Sources: *Wikipedia*: "Rogue River (Oregon)."

Glen Wooldridge: The Rogue's Premier Guide

BORN IN 1896 AT HIS GRANDFATHER'S PLACER MINE near Gold Hill along Foots Creek, Glen Wooldridge loved the Rogue River. He built a twenty-foot boat of cedar two-by-fours, and in 1915 decided to run it from Grants Pass to Gold Beach with a friend, Cal Allen. The nineteen-year-old commercial gillnetter became the first person to do this, disregarding that two men in separate tries had drowned one year earlier. Not knowing what was before him, it took five days to conquer the dangerous rapids and canyons in the 120-mile trip to the Pacific Ocean, as they sold caught salmon to a cannery.

He became the first professional guide on the Rogue River two years later, now measured in the hundreds, and popularized the river as a sport-fishing mecca. He also designed and built driftboats that were modified with a small stern transom and tilted upwards at the prow. Ginger Rogers, Clark Gable, Herbert Hoover, Zane Grey, and countless others selected him as their guide for their adventure fishing trips.

Wooldridge figured out how to make the wild Rogue passable at its most dangerous places: He dynamited them. He made Blossom Bar navigable this way, then a half-day portage. He maneuvered by a large rock, as his bowman dropped explosives in a gunnysack on the other side, and then rowed quickly away. He did this numerous times to make Blossom Bar as it is now, among changing many other rock barriers to navigating the river.

While he built up his Rogue Valley boat-building and guiding business, Glen was busy adventuring. He navigated Alaska's Yukon River to California's Klamath, including the dangerous Idaho and

Glen Wooldridge.

British Columbia rivers. In 1947 he made the first-ever trip up the Rogue River in a motorized boat from the ocean to Grants Pass. He had fitted a twenty-two-horsepower outboard motor with a developed "Jackass" lift to pull the motor up over obstacles on his twenty-foot plank boat. At age seventy-nine, he was the first to run the fearsome Hells Gate on British Columbia's Fraser River and guided fishermen on the Rogue River into his eighties.

Meanwhile, his boat building business expanded as he set the standards for the Rogue. Wooldridge Boats are no longer made from wood, however, since the material of choice is now all-welded aluminum with its strength and lightweight; the products now include several different deep-water prop and inboard jet boats. In 1970, his grandson moved the family's boat business from the Rogue Valley to Seattle.

He died in 1986 at age ninety and a Josephine County creek is named after him. His history and that of his outdoor businesses have been chronicled in different books, magazines, and films. A memorial was built in Grants Pass Riverside Park by the Rogue River to honor his exploits, concluding that "a major industry, including excursion boating, river guiding, and drift fishing, evolved from Glenn's pioneering efforts on the Rogue River."

Field and Stream writer Ted Trueblood wrote in the foreword to *Rogue: A River To Run*, which in 1982 Wooldridge wrote with Florence Arman: "This is the story of a unique man. One of the definitions of unique in my dictionary is 'being without a like or equal.' That fits Glen Wooldridge to a 'T'. He is a river man. There are none like him, and I contend he has no equal."

Sources: Mark Freeman, "River Man," *Medford Mail Tribune*, April 14, 2013.

The Mean, Stream Machine

*I*N THE LATE 1980S, THREE YOUNG RAFTING enthusiasts — Bill Bednar (Medford financial planner), Dorian Corliss (Grants Pass banker), and Michael Neyt (Medford banker) — were enjoying a raft trip in Northern California. On the trip they spotted a crude device looking like a "homemade syringe" that shot water for a distance and thought that using one would be fun. Corliss built a four-foot-long "tube within a tube" as an experiment. With a hole in the front and plug in the back, the two PVC telescoping tubes could produce a distant water stream.

On a later trip in 1990 down the Rogue, the group was camping across from Zane Gray's cabin at remote Winkle Bar in the lower Rogue River canyon. When another raft floated by, one of their group grabbed the soaker and shot water over the passing boaters. With everyone laughing, the threesome felt that they had a great idea. Neyt and Bednar built their own prototypes at home to compare with Corliss's one.

As they experimented, they found that a one-inch diameter pipe fit just right inside a larger one-and-a-half-inch one. A groove on the inside PVC, an O-ring around the groove to keep compression, holes, and a cap on both ends did the trick. Forming a partnership, they hand-built 300 of the devices that could shoot water up to seventy feet. Outside Grants Pass over one weekend, Neyt and Bednar sold all of their devices for $20 each. They knew they had a money winner.

Incorporating their venture as Water Sports, Inc., the three men invested $10,000 each and got to work. They built the squirt guns inside Bill Bednar's garage over weekends, and over the next year, sold some 5,000 of them, which they named "Dipstiks." As all had demanding jobs, they next contracted with a Grants Pass company, SPARC Enterprises, to manufacture their product.

The curent version of the original Stream Machine.

When Bednar wanted to step up marketing and sales, Dorian Corliss decided he would rather concentrate on his profession and later sold his interest to Bednar, who by his own admission was the "ultimate dreamer." Corliss sold his one-third interest in 1992 for $170,000, and Bednar obtained the money by a loan from a friend.

When the "Dipstick" name turned out to be trademarked by another, the company needed a different name. Portland's Terry Whitlock later ventured down and said that he had developed a streamer named "The Stream Machine." This soaker was built in bright colors with a pistol grip handle, whereas the Dipstick was constructed from white PVC pipe. Whitlock said the decision was theirs: They could either take him into the company or he would compete against them.

Naming Whitlock as president in charge of marketing and sales, he was offered a 25% interest. Not wanting to be a minority owner and concentrate on his job, Neyt sold his interest back for $50,000, plus a 5% royalty on each unit produced. Sales grew from $600,000 in fiscal 1992 to $1.5 million in the following year. The sales volume didn't match up, however, with the much larger inventories later built up, and the company ran into financial difficulties that included lawsuits and bankruptcy. At the same time, a patent was issued on their device.

When the financial problems and litigation were settled with Bill Bednar in control of the company, sales again took off with major customers such as Bi-Mart, Fred Meyer, and Costco. At its highpoint through its Medford facility, 160 people were employed that produced 1,000 Stream Machines every hour. When its sales volume increased to $3 million annually, Bednar sold the business for $2.4 million in 2000 to his Chicago-area, brothers-in-law. With the patent having expired later, different companies now produce and/or sell the soaker without restriction.

Dorian Corliss, Michael Neyt, and Bill Bednar brought about the universal squirting device seen on the Rogue — and rivers around the world — along with money in the bank. Not bad for three rafting friends who were just having fun all those years ago.

Sources: Macomber, *Medford Mail Tribune*, July 2, 1994; Silow, *Medford Mail Tribune*, April 14, 2010.

Willie Illingworth's Driftboats

WILLIE ILLINGWORTH WAS A FISHING GUIDE on the Rogue River and thought that an aluminum driftboat would certainly be easier to work with. Maneuvering a twenty-foot, heavy boat made of cedar or plywood was tortuous to row or handle in the rapids, not to mention the constant maintenance due to splintered wood, rot, and leaks. The design generally in use then was from the McKenzie River near Eugene with a pointed bow at both ends.

His design of a high flared bow, squat stern, and steep curves would work well in the Rogue's swift, shallow rapids—but welding aluminum together was at best a difficult task. Willie asked the acclaimed Glenn Wooldridge, then building his boats with wood, to make an aluminum one. Wooldridge said "no." Although he had no money, no welding experience, and only one hand (due to an accident as a child), Willie decided to do it himself.

He convinced Jim Parsons—an Ashland sawmill owner and fishing client—into loaning him $4,000 to build six driftboats. Illingworth then spent the first three months in 1971 in shearing out patterns and welding the first aluminum boat in his Medford shop. When the prototype proved to be a success in being lighter and easier to handle on the Rogue, Willie set up in White City his boat-building company, "Alumaweld," just as the name implies. He had figured out how to leave cedar planks behind and use welded aluminum.

He sold his interest six years later and in 1981 formed Willie Boats, which continues to the present. Illingworth was as much a maverick in person, as he was in coming up with the idea that he could build an aluminum boat with nothing in his favor. Bill Monroe—for the *Oregonian*—wrote that Willie was, "A loud, mischievous, party-hearty,

An example of a modern-day Willie Boat.

hard-drinking and often profane exterior (that) masked a private, generous, caring, and delightfully intelligent personality."

When Willie knew that he was dying from brain cancer, he held his own living wake in January 2007. Passing around a signup sheet for vials that would hold his ashes, he said then, "I don't want to miss my own party." More than sixty friends signed up. After he died two months later, his friends took the vials of his ashes when fishing on the Rogue, guiding clients, traveling outside Oregon, or even halibut fishing in Alaska.

Willie Illingworth is credited with being the first among the many aluminum boat manufacturers of the 1970s. His determination and design created a huge boat-building industry in the Pacific Northwest with Medford still being a center of the aluminum driftboat and powerboat industry. Willie Boats manufactures some 250 driftboats with 100 powerboats annually at its Central Point facility—and Willie would still be proud.

Sources: Freeman, *Medford Mail Tribune*, April 14, 2013; Monroe, the *Oregonian*, May 29, 2010.

The Rise and Fall
of Gold Ray Dam

*I*N 1900, DR. C.R. RAY VISITED SOUTHERN OREGON to inspect a gold mine
for his brother, Colonel Frank H. Ray. The two afterwards bought the
Braden Mine near Gold Hill and acquired with it the rights to a power site
to be built on the Rogue River for supplying the mine with important
electricity. An extremely wealthy New Yorker, Colonel Ray had no
problem raising the money to build the power station, as he was an
organizer and vice-president of the American Tobacco Company.
Additionally, securities were sold on the New York Stock Exchange.

Construction of the original Gold Ray Dam began in 1902 by first
building a cofferdam to divert the rushing river. Jamming large timbers
into the bedrock and backfilling with rocks, workers then constructed a
dam that was seventeen feet tall and 350 feet long. The impounded
waters were diverted through a powerhouse, whose unique rope-driven
turbines two years later created the first hydroelectric power in Southern
Oregon.

Seeing more potential in selling electricity than mining gold, the Ray's
Condor Water and Power Company furnished power throughout
Jackson and Josephine counties, from Grants Pass and Medford to
Jacksonville and Ashland. This vital electricity powered residences and
businesses, ranging from machine shops to saw and flour mills. This
allowed Southern Oregon to develop with the rest of the state.

These operations became part of the California-Oregon Power
Company in 1921, which later became Pacific Power (now PacifiCorp).
The utility replaced the timber dam with a concrete one in 1941 and
added a fish ladder with a fish-counting station. Power grids from

Operational dam and plant at Gold Ray Dam. (GHHS)

outside the area, however, with large land-generator stations minimized the need for this power, and the utility closed the facility in 1972 after nearly seventy years of use. The company deeded the dam, powerhouse, and twenty-seven acres to Jackson County.

Jackson County in late 2009 contracted for an environmental assessment on the demolition of the 105-year-old dam. The study recommended removing the dam for environmental reasons, including that an estimated 400,000 cubic yards of silt had built up behind it and potentially contained contaminants such as arsenic and mercury.

When "stimulus" funds (under the American Recovery and Reinvestment Act) of $5 million dollars from the National Oceanic and Atmospheric Administration were earmarked to remove the dam, its demise was certain. Jackson County had requested the funds to employ fifty-four people at different times throughout the eighteen-month period of study and its removal.

Demolition plans were prepared with a cost of $5.6 million for its demise. In August 2010, a temporary cofferdam to drain the sloughs didn't hold. The river pushed through the nearby spit's soft sand and poured out in a torrent of muddy water. A few construction workers and heavy equipment were stranded temporarily on the earthen cofferdam, as police were called in to warn downstream rafters and gold dredgers of the extraordinary surge that was more than twice the normal river flow at its peak.

Once removed, environmentalists predicted benefits: more salmon and steelhead swimming upriver to spawn; more gravel carried downriver to replenish the riverbed; and more rafters enjoying the scenery of private and public property along fifty-seven miles of newly opened water. In its place, gold-dredgers also showed up from California to Texas and Washington, eagerly sifting through the tons of gravel for the precious flakes of gold once hidden behind the dam.

Using suction dredges, these licensed prospectors annually cluster downriver from where the dam used to be. These modern prospectors must follow stringent state rules, however, aimed at keeping a distance between dredges, substantially reducing the size of their hoses, and only allowing work in a short summer period when little or no spawning is under way. It should only be a matter of time before these efforts are prohibited.

The Rogue River once again flows freely into the Pacific Ocean. Unfortunately, the extensive, environmentally-sensitive Tolo and Kelly Sloughs behind the dam were destroyed (although created by the impounded water), a habitat for bass eradicated, and huge swarms of mosquitoes bred that swarmed after residents and hikers alike. No matter how environmentally sensitive people are, a cost is always associated with this. However, the river is now free to run.

Sources: Powers, *Oregon Encyclopedia*: "Gold Ray Dam"; Fattig, *Medford Mail Tribune*, July 1, 2009.

PART X

Sports and Athletes

Andy Maurer: Football Star and Coach from a Tiny Town

A NDY MAURER WAS BORN IN SMALL SILVERTON, Oregon (in eastern Willamette Valley), in 1948, and lived in even smaller Prospect (450 people, now) where he attended high school. Maurer played football on an eight-man team, but still stood out from that small town, earning All-American status in football and basketball as a 6′4″, 220-pound athlete to go with his track and field marks.

He continued his athleticism on the collegiate level at the University of Oregon and started in the first football game ever played at Autzen Stadium in 1967. His abilities again stood out—as a fullback, tight end, and offensive lineman at Oregon from 1967-69—being selected by Atlanta during the third round of the 1970 NFL Draft.

As an NFL offensive lineman (right guard and left tackle), he played four years with the Falcons, had two stints with the Minnesota Vikings and one year apiece with the New Orleans Saints, San Francisco 49ers and Denver Broncos—for a total of eight seasons. He was a starting guard for Minnesota in Super Bowl IX (won by the Pittsburgh Steelers), and for Denver in Super Bowl XII (won by the Dallas Cowboys). Maurer appeared in 109 regular season pro-football games, starting eighty-four of them; he started in all seven playoff games he had. Individually, he displayed durability as he put together a four-season consecutive games played streak (1970 to 1973).

After retiring from football, he moved to Medford and was a successful businessman. Maurer may have had his greatest impact when he founded and coached the Cascade Christian High School football program in 1992 (which then didn't even have a playing field) and ultimately amassed a 100-78 record with the Challengers in the 1A to 3A

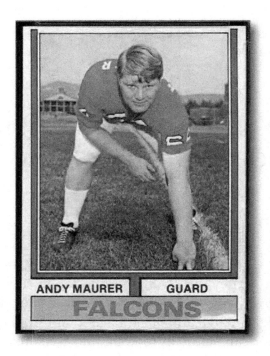

Andy Maurer trading card from his
days with the Atlanta Falcons, 1974.

class. The Challengers reached the state playoffs six times under him, winning the Class 2A crown in 2006 (returning to Autzen Stadium to lead Cascade Christian to its 27-18 win over Bonanza in the championship game). Cascade then moved up to the 3A level, and his teams reached the semifinal round in three of his final four seasons (retiring in 2010) while enjoying unbeaten regular seasons in 2005 and 2009.

His son, Marty, said, "He didn't just believe that he was training football players—he believed he was training husbands, fathers, future business owners and leaders, and he took that seriously as an important investment in the lives of the players he coached. Everyone has shared stories about how they've had their lives touched by my dad beyond football and it's pretty cool to hear that."

Andy Maurer died in early January 2016 at age sixty-seven after a prolonged battle with cancer.

Source: Henry, *Medford Mail Tribune*, January 5, 2016; Mims, The *Eugene Register Guard*, January 5, 2016.

Chandler Egan: Medford's Famous Golfer and Course Designer

ORN INTO A WEALTHY, CHICAGO FAMILY, twelve-year-old Chandler Egan began playing golf during a family vacation. Building a home-made course on the family's pasture land with friends, he honed his skills. Six years later in 1902, Chandler was at Harvard and captain of the golf team. He won individual honors as a sophomore that year, and the team won three straight national intercollegiate championships. In 1902, he also won the first of four Western Amateur titles, and captured two U.S. Amateur titles in 1904 and 1905 (placing second, four years later). His golf team in 1904 won Olympic gold, and he won a silver medal, the last time golf was held in these games.

Selling insurance and looking into other businesses after graduation, he and his newly-wed wife in 1910 took a train to Medford, Oregon; they were among the numerous Mid-Westerners seduced by the city's effective promotion to invest in the area's orchard industry. Strictly an amateur player and desiring to preserve this—like his later friend, Bobby Jones, who is considered the best amateur golfer of all times— Chandler wanted to start a successful business in an exciting new place, cash in on the "orchard boom," and provide for himself and his family.

He bought the 117-acre, apple and pear Bates Orchard in 1911 for $67,000 in East Medford in the oak-forested foothills and built a one-and-a-half story house for $2,600 on what is now Foothill Drive. He designed the arts and crafts-style house (with low-pitched, extended gabled roofs) to be both a residence and the offices for his Egan Orchard.

Photo of Chandler Egan, circa 1909.

The "raw" nine-hole course of the Medford Country Club — formed just two weeks before Egan first arrived — was "at the foot of his driveway."

Enjoying the orchard business, he headed back to playing amateur golf. In 1914 he was runner-up at the Pacific Northwest Amateur (PNWA), but won it the following year — and a total of four times over the next decade. After his first marriage failed, Chandler in 1916 remarried the former Alice Barrett of Chicago and they lived at the orchard house.

When the orchard business went bust, Chandler turned to golf-course designing, an endeavor bringing together both his design and golfing knowledge. He took on in 1917 his first paid job to design Portland's Eastmoreland Golf Course—and this led to others. In 1924, Egan's first nine-hole design for the Rogue Valley Country Club (RVCC) opened; he completed the second nine three years later. Together, this eighteen-hole course is still referred to as the "original course" at RVCC.

Over the twenty years of this work, Chandler Egan designed or redesigned over twenty courses in Washington, Oregon, and California. Ten are in Oregon: Coos Bay, Portland (Eastmoreland and Riverside), Eugene, Hood River, Lake Oswego, Klamath Falls, Seaside Golf Club, Medford, and Tualatin. He also designed courses from Atlanta to Spokane. His designed Indian Canyon in Spokane is a course regularly included among America's top-fifty municipal courses.

At the same time, he played amateur golf. Chandler won a fifth PNWA as well as the California Amateur Championship (1926), the first non-Californian to do so. He won two championship Walker Cups (1930, 1934); and he also played in U.S. Opens, Masters, and other tournaments. Egan partnered in 1929 with legendary golf architect, Alister MacKenzie, to renovate Pebble Beach for the upcoming U.S. Amateur, in which Chandler in his forties reached the semifinals.

Having finished designs in 1936 for the West Seattle Golf Course—and supervising construction of the Legion Memorial Golf Course in Everett, Washington—Egan came down with pneumonia. He died six days later at the age of fifty-one and his body was returned to Medford.

After his death, Alice became increasingly active locally. She was named the first lifetime member of the Oregon Shakespeare Festival in Ashland for her financial contributions, instrumental in the founding of the Medford Civic Theater, and provided the "seed" money to fund what became the Rogue Valley Arts Association. She lived at the house until her later years and died in 1964.

Chandler Egan was posthumously named to the Pacific Northwest Golf Association Hall of Fame and Oregon Sports Hall of Fame. His designed home on 2620 Foothill Drive (known as the "Egan Mansion") was placed in 1997 on the National Register of Historic Places.

Sources: Dear, "Favorite Designers: H. Chandler Egan"; *Wikipedia*: "Chandler Egan."

Danny Miles: Winning Coach in Basketball (and Life)

*B*ORN IN 1945 IN MEDFORD, Daniel "Danny" Miles went on to become one of the winningest coaches in the history of men's collegiate basketball, all at the Oregon Institute of Technology (OIT) in Klamath Falls. His father, Claude Miles, played semi-professional baseball in the early 1900s, and Miles Field in Medford was named after him owing to his successful career in Medford.

When Claude and his wife had three boys, he built a baseball field with a grass infield, backstop, and dugouts in the cow pasture behind the family home. Playing sports was their pastime. Danny was an outstanding athlete in three sports — baseball, basketball, and football — at Medford High School and was honored in 1963 as the school's outstanding athlete.

At the Southern Oregon College of Education (now Southern Oregon University, SOU), he earned All-American honors in football, was All-Conference in basketball, and named to the All-District baseball team. Danny was a four-year starter at quarterback for the Raiders, and set collegiate football's all-time record for all divisions by completing 77.9% of his passes in his sophomore year; his career percentage was an outstanding 66%. Miles led the nation in passing percentage in 1964 and 1965, and then in total offense in 1965.

After graduating from college, Miles coached the three sports at Mazama High School in Klamath Falls. After one year as the head baseball coach at Bend High School, Danny returned to Klamath Falls in 1970 at age twenty-four as an assistant coach in the three sports at OIT: that past year, their results were in basketball (1-21), football (0-9), and baseball (3-23). One year later, he became OIT's offensive coordinator for football and its head coach for basketball and baseball. He has never left the school, nearly a record in itself, which on his retirement in 2016 totaled forty-six coaching years.

Deciding to concentrate on basketball, Danny emphasized different aspects that most coaches didn't. Although he credits his assistant coaches and fans, most people center on his unique style of coaching. In evaluating players, for example, he created what he called the "Value Point System." Rather than focusing on someone's points-per-game and rebounding, his system computed the entire value of a player's contribution by including the missed shots, personal fouls, turnovers, recoveries, and assists, sizing up that person's team support. He freely substituted to give younger, developing players the chance to experience "game-on-the-line" times. He recruited from around the country, even the world.

Danny Miles emphasized sportsmanship and community service. He sponsored Special Olympic events where his team played basketball against the special team for over twenty years — and his players lost by one point every time. The field house reserved sections for those with special needs and the elderly; and he, his coaches, and players generated the money that allowed at least two African students to attend school. From working at an all-faith OIT chapel to reading at children's programs, his players put this philosophy into practice.

His approach resulted in achievements beyond comparison, and all at OIT with its low budgets, an enrollment of 4,000, in a city of 21,000, and in an economic region that has endured hard times. His "Hustlin' Owls" won three NAIA II national championships in 2004, 2008, and in 2012. This goes along with one national runner-up, a national third place, two elite eight's, fourteen district or conference titles, seven district runners-up, and being ranked in the NAIA's top-twenty on thirty occasions. They won a school record of sixty-five straight wins at home, the longest at the time in the country from November of 2009 to December 2011.

Miles led his basketball teams at OIT to an overall 1,040-437 (70.4% win record) with fourteen trips to the national NAIA II tournament. He was named the NAIA National Basketball Coach of the Year in 2004 and 2008, the overall National Coach of the Year in 2012, and ten times honored as the Cascade Collegiate Conference Coach of the Year. Miles led his Owl teams to numerous twenty-win seasons (thirty-two), twenty-five-win seasons (twenty-two), and ten, thirty-or-more-win seasons.

Danny Miles.

At the end of the 2015-2016 season, Danny Miles retired. He then had the third-most career wins of any collegiate coach—including more than notables such as Jim Boeheim (Syracuse), Bob Knight (Indiana and Texas Tech), and Dean Smith (North Carolina). On the all-time win list, he was only behind Harry Statham (Illinois' McKendree University) and Mike Krzyzewski (Duke). Several years ago, OIT had another round of athletic cuts, so even though Miles "retired," he stayed on as the basketball coach.

In 1966, he was inducted into the Oregon Sports Hall of Fame. Miles also is a member of SOU's and Medford's Halls of Fame. Southern Oregon University named him as its 2005 Distinguished Alumnus Award winner.

He coached at OIT for over four decades, working through the logging industry's collapse and decline of farming with the Klamath Basin water crisis. He turned down numerous coaching positions with much more money at bigger schools and in larger towns. Owing to tough financial times, OIT had to slash his budget so low that at times he almost quit; he had also been fired and rehired.

Danny Miles came a long way after taking over a basketball team that had only won one game before. After his retirement from OIT, Danny Miles joined Cascade Christian High School in Medford as an Assistant Athletic Director; in the summer of 2016, he was named its Athletic Director. He has been a most successful coach—in basketball and life.

Sources: Bishop, *New York Times*, February 22, 2012; Jones, "The Last Mile(s)," *Medford Mail Tribune*, February 6, 2016.

Dick Fosbury's
Ground-Breaking Flop

DICK FOSBURY GREW UP IN MEDFORD and when at Medford High School, he wanted to play different sports. By his own admission, he was a "fair" basketball player (but usually on the bench), a "terrible" hurdler, and tried football as a third-string end. He gave that up in his junior year, when his good-friend Bill "Earthquake" Enyart (who went onto playing in the NFL) blocked him so hard in one drill that Fosbury lost two front teeth.

He figured out that his "lankiness" shouldn't be as much a problem in the high jump. When using the standard "scissors" kick, he had cleared 5' 4" in junior high and had even won a meet or two. His varsity high-school coach, however, insisted on the Western Roll (kicking ones outer, rather than inner leg over the bar), but he just couldn't get it down.

In 1963, the sophomore was on the team bus for a Rotary meet at Grants Pass with twelve schools. He decided that he would do whatever it took for "one last jump." If he couldn't clear 5-foot, 4-inches, then he would always be a third-stringer. At the meet, he cleared that bar; on his next jump, he went two inches higher by arching slightly backwards. Driven by desperation, he added another two inches by reclining even more and heading more backward over the bar.

By now coaches and competitors alike were staring at his form. On his fourth attempt, he cleared another two inches for 5-feet, 10-inches and was completely on his back as he sailed over. To add six inches in height in high jumping—and in only two hours—was unheard of. The coaches began arguing: Was this move legal, allowable, safe, and what in the heck was it?

Dick Fosbury at a high school meet doing the "Fosbury Flop."
(SOHS 21133)

Fosbury had spontaneously created a style of his own, totally fracturing what had been taught or used before. It was on-site engineering, where he was driven—by any means possible—to get over a higher bar and beat his rivals. This was serendipity at its best. During the next full year of his upside-down technique, Fosbury began to lean with his shoulder about forty-five degrees to the bar, arch over on his back, and broke the school record of 6-feet, 3-inches.

The novelty continued. One newspaper headlined the image of one of his jumps: "The World's Laziest High Jumper." But it was the *Medford Mail Tribune* in 1964 that had the headline: "Fosbury Flops over the Bar." One reporter said that Fosbury looked like a fish flopping into a boat, and so the "Fosbury Flop" was born.

Fosbury placed second at the state championships in his senior year (1965), and then headed to Oregon State University. A contrarian at heart, Fosbury hardly practiced the Flop, saying that "there's no use wearing myself out." Promoters invited him to their events just due to the hype that followed.

Fosbury ultimately perfected his head-first leap by approaching the bar in a semicircle, pushing off his left foot, and landing full on his back. (The key was to land on ones shoulders, not the neck, and always on a foam pad.) The *Los Angeles Times* wrote that he "goes over the bar like a guy being pushed out of a thirty-story window." *Sports Illustrated* wrote, "He charges up from slightly to the left of centre with a gait that may call to mind a two-legged camel," and having flung himself over the bar back first, "he extends himself like a slightly apprehensive man lying back on a chaise longue that's too short for him."

He first cleared 7' 0" during the 1968 indoor season and won the NCAAs that year. He won the Gold Medal at the 1968 Mexico City Olympic Games by clearing 7 feet 4-1/4 inches, breaking the Olympic and American records. When he returned to Medford, a ticker-tape parade was held for him, but with no buildings on the route taller than two stories, the kids had to run along his car to shower him with confetti. He went on "The Tonight Show" and tried to teach Johnny Carson and fellow guest Bill Cosby how to do the Flop. He slipped, however, with his dress shoes on when he tried doing this. Other shows he appeared on included "The Dating Game."

He was top-ranked in the world following his 1968 victory, and Fosbury the next year won his second NCAA title before placing second in the National AAU meet, plus adding his third Pacific-8 championship. He graduated from OSU in 1969 and trained for the 1972 Olympics; but didn't make the team, having lost his competitive interest by his own admission. Turning professional in 1973, he joined the International Track Association for a few seasons and then retired.

Fosbury moved to Ketchum, Idaho, in 1976 and founded an engineering firm. He was elected to the U.S. Track & Field Hall of Fame in 1981 and the U.S. Olympic Hall of Fame in 1992. He was a past president and on the Executive Committee of the World Olympians Association, as well as vice president of the U.S. Olympians Association. He is retired now and living on a twenty-acre ranch south of Sun Valley, Idaho. Dick Fosbury is still remembered as one of the most influential athletes in the history of track and field, however, thanks to the Fosbury Flop that's now the standard for worldwide high-jumping.

Sources: Dick Fosbury's Official Website: "Dick's Bio"; Hoffer, *Sports Illustrated*, September 14, 2009.

Medford's Nike Connection:
Bill Bowerman

$\mathcal{F}$ ORMER MEDFORD HIGH FOOTBALL PLAYER and coach, Bill Bowerman, later went on to become a legend in coaching track—and a co-founder of Nike. He played for another stand-out, Prink Callison, whose Medford teams had a forty-four-game win streak at one time and won three state championships from 1926 to 1928. The 1928 Medford "Tigers" (as the team was called then)—one of the best teams ever in Southern Oregon—averaged thirty-six points a game, limited opponents to forty points for the entire season, and Bill Bowerman was their left end.

Born in 1911, Bowerman moved to Medford when he was ten years old. Raised by his mother and aunts (his father left the family when he was two), he was "a mean little kid," by his own admission. When he went out for football as a sophomore, Callison wouldn't put up with his antics and kicked him off the team to junior varsity. Bowerman credits both him and Superintendent Hedrick (for whom the middle school on East Jackson Street is named) as the disciplinarians who straightened him out. He also played basketball and edited the school newspaper.

After high school, he attended the University of Oregon (OU) and became a quarter-mile runner under the legendary Ducks' track coach, Colonel Bill Hayward; this coach became the mentor under whom Bowerman modeled himself and learned from the "concepts of greatness," as he reminisced. With his bachelor's degree in 1934, Bowerman decided to attend medical school, but he first had to earn the tuition.

Coaching for one year in Portland, he returned to Medford in 1935 to coach football and track. His "Tornado" football teams (newspaper

Two legends: University of Oregon track phenom Steve Prefontaine (*left*) and his coach, Bill Bowerman, deep in discussion.

sports editors coined the nickname) went 69-13-8 overall, while his 1935 and 1939 teams were 7-0-1 and 8-0-1. World War II intervened months before he was to start medical school and become a doctor. Having learned to ski in the Siskiyou Mountains, he headed to Colorado, trained for the 10th Mountain Division, and skied the Italian southerly Alps on patrol.

He returned to Medford after the war and coached for two more seasons, leaving in 1949 to coach track and freshman football at OU. For twenty-four years as the head track coach, he developed many of the world's best distance and middle-distance runners, among them being Steve Prefontaine and Alberto Salazar. His teams won four NCAA track and field championships, finished second twice, and coached forty-four all-Americans and nineteen Olympians. He is credited with turning the college town of Eugene, Oregon, into the running capital of the world.

With a commanding presence, Bowerman overlooked no detail, even hand-crafting his athletes' shoes. He created the first lightweight, outsole shoe from some latex, leather, glue, and his wife's waffle iron. In 1964, he joined with Phil Knight — a middle-distance runner who ran for him in the late 1950s — and each invested $500 into a company named Blue Ribbon Sports, selling initially 330 pairs of the shoes.

They sought to develop athletic shoes that were lighter and with more traction than the old, longstanding designs. More innovations came, including the wedged heel, the cushioned midsole, and lightweight nylon tops — not to mention developing rubberized asphalt runways. Propelled by the waffle-soled shoes, astute marketing, and the 1970's upsurge of interest in running and physical fitness, they built Nike, based in Beaverton, Oregon, into the world's largest athletic shoe and sports apparel maker. It became a multi-billion-dollar company and recognized around the world for its "swoosh" logo.

The Medford Linebackers club honored him in the early 1970s when they built Bowerman Field on what's now the North Medford campus. Giving back to the community, his foundation helped build or improve tracks at Medford's North and South High Schools, the Hedrick and McLoughlin middle schools, and St. Mary's. Receiving numerous honors during this time, he died at the age of eighty-eight in 1999.

Sources: The *New York Times*, December 27, 1999; Stiles, *Medford Mail Tribune*, December 17, 2010.

Rogue Valley Country Club

BY THE END OF THE NINETEENTH CENTURY, GOLF CLUBS in Oregon were to be found mainly in Portland and Eugene. These clubs were predominately used socially then and associated with the well-to-do. This association with the leisure class slowly eroded during the coming years when amateur stars such as Chandler Egan (see article in this book) brought interest to golf as a sport and not just for purely social reasons.

As Medford and Southern Oregon boomed in the early 1900s, a group of affluent businessmen from the Midwest and Eastern U.S. — who had flocked to the Rogue Valley during the orchard boom — decided to form a country club. In 1911, on property on Hillcrest Road east of Medford, the club opened with tennis courts, a skeet range, clubhouse, gardens, and nine holes of golf. Over the next ten years, the Medford Golf and Country club closed due to financial problems, re-opened at a smaller site, and closed its doors again due to its precarious financial situation. The failures were in no small part owing to the orchard bust.

In 1923, however, with the local economy improving, the group formed again and bought seventy acres of the original club property. It selected Chandler Egan, the former national amateur golf champion (twice) and a recognized course designer, to be its course architect. He had also won four Western Amateur titles, an Olympic silver medal, five Pacific Northwest championships (over time), and later two championship Walker Cups.

Egan thought that the land was ideal due to its "interesting terrain, attractive shade trees, and plenty of water nearby." He donated his services to the new club, as well as serving on the new club's board of directors. On May 3, 1924, the Rogue Valley Country Club (RVCC) opened on the original site with a nine-hole golf course and a limited

Legendary Rogue Valley Country Club golfer Eddie Simmons (who won six of the Southern Oregon Golf Tournament championships held there over the years) lines up for a putt in the 1954 tournament. (Credit: Rogue Valley Country Club)

100-person membership. Three years later, Chandler Egan designed the second nine holes to bring RVCC to an eighteen-hole course of play. After the second, nine-hole design, this play is referred to as the "original course."

The Rogue Valley Country Club in 1937 erected a drinking fountain as a memorial to its most famous member, Chandler Egan, who had died one year before. Bobby Jones, Egan's longtime friend and regarded as the best amateur golfer of all time, with Grantland Rice, the noted sportswriter, and others traveled to Medford to attend the ceremony. At Egan's memorial, Rice said Egan was "one of the finest gentlemen I have ever known." Over his twenty years of course design, Chandler Egan had designed or re-designed over twenty courses in Washington, Oregon, and California, including Pebble Beach.

Along the way, Glenn Jackson, or "Mr. Oregon," not only helped to reinvigorate the Rogue Valley Country Club after World War II, he operated and owned it through his enterprise, Golf Holding Company.

The country club's members purchased these facilities from his heirs in 1981 after his death.

Today, the RVCC has grown to its present complex with twenty-seven holes, 600 golf members, and 550 social members. Some of the amenities include: a driving range, three putting complexes, pro shop, tennis courts, a swimming pool, and a 38,000 square-foot Craftsman-style clubhouse with banquet facilities, offices, conference rooms, and lounges. The par-72 course is 6,666 yards long—proving that this club has come a long way since its original formation.

Sources: Rogue Valley County Club: "History"(at its website); see article on "Chandler Egan" in this book.

Southern Oregon's John Day:
Larger Than Life

O UR JOHN DAY IS NOT THE FRONTIERSMAN WHO WAS part of the 1811 Astor Expedition and died in 1820, with a river, dam, small town in eastern Oregon, and fossil bed named after him. Southern Oregon's one graduated from Medford High School, lived in Sams Valley, was larger than life, and passed away in 1986.

His father, Earl, had been a concert pianist, Oregon state senator, judge, and rancher. Born in 1910, John Stuart Day showed an early liking for exercise and taking risks. His father's motto was that if something was worth doing, it was worth doing well. This applied especially to father-son ax-throwing contests. While in his late teens and early twenties, John worked as a forest-fire fighter and ranger (at Crater Lake National Park), and also held the ax-throwing title at five Northwest national forests.

Educated at Oregon State, University of Oregon, and Harvard Business School (1937), Day returned to Medford and married Mary Parsons, the daughter of a well-connected Medford family. He was a rancher (the Blue Moon Ranch near Central Point), along with real estate development in East Medford and a large area off Highway 234 towards Sams Valley (Gold Ray Estates).

On top of a high hill overlooking the Rogue River (and then, Gold Ray Dam), Day built a spectacular home in 1956 that reflected his life. His ranch included 4,000 acres of land, five miles in one direction and one in the other. Deer multiplied there with herds of buffalo. He built a landing field on the neighboring Table Rocks to fly in his Hollywood friends. Liking to be different, he kept an African cheetah instead of a cat and drove a Volkswagen with a supercharged engine, instead of a Ferrari.

A ten-page, *House & Garden* feature story showed a long, winding road that led through his lands to his estate. A heated swimming pool, peacocks and wildlife, and a cheetah cage were outdoors; full-grown trees, a large waterfall, and a huge mounted Kodiak bear greeted visitors in the entryway. A spacious living room and 2,000 square-foot entertainment room followed. Bedrooms, laundry, and a small kitchen were located to the sides, with a mirrored gymnasium downstairs. A big-game hunter (with several listings in the Boone & Crockett Club record book), Day mounted different trophies—from goats and big-horn sheep to polar bears—throughout the house.

He played as hard as he worked, too. Often accompanied by his wife, Nan, and son, John P. (Jack), he traveled throughout Europe, South America, New Zealand, Canada, and the Arctic Circle. He hunted bear in Alaska, pursued jaguars near the Amazon headwaters, and was elected to membership in the Explorer Club, Adventurers Club, Boone and Crockett Club, and Polar Society. Photos of his were on the front covers of nine national magazines.

But it was his inordinate embracing of the outdoors that set him apart. Smoking four packs of cigarettes a day, the then forty-year-old man was diagnosed with arthritis and ulcers. He changed his lifestyle overnight, quit smoking "cold turkey," and began taking long walks. Soon his conditioning became extraordinary: Running four miles each morning, sprint-swimming in his pool, and doing sixty push-ups at a time were just a day's start.

When John and his wife were enjoying a 1956 Labor Day weekend at Lake of the Woods, he spotted Mt. McLoughlin one evening from a cabin. Day decided then that he was "going up that mountain before the next day dawned." By daybreak he was almost to the summit, "puffing and blowing." He tackled mountain climbing with the same drive and enthusiasm that he brought to his other ventures.

Deciding that U.S. mountains were too tame, John Day declared that they were open for foot racing and established a new sport. Accompanied by mountaineering friends (such as Jim and Lou Whittaker, nationally-recognized climbers) and his son, he tackled every mountain within reach. In seeing how many Oregon peaks he could speed-climb in one day, he made four. In the summer of 1958, Day climbed six Washington mountains in nine days; between July 4th and Labor Day, he scaled the West Coast's seventeen major peaks, from Mt. Baker to Mt. Whitney.

A pioneer endurance athlete, bicycle racing was next. Seeing how far he could cycle in twenty-four hours, Day started in Hood River and ended near Roseburg — and held several national age-group records. In 1960, he was severely injured from a fall on Mt. McKinley and had to be airlifted away with serious injuries, ranging from a broken arm to dislocated feet. After two months in hospitals, he knew that his mountain racing days were over. After seeing the 1960 winter Olympics, he decided to try cross-country skiing.

Strapping on a pair of skis for the first time at age fifty-two, he spent the next two winters working to make the U.S. Nordic ski team (with its average age of twenty-five). He spent a winter in Norway learning to race and covered thirty miles each day on skis. When the time came, however, he was selected to be an alternate, but couldn't race: He hadn't entered the qualifying races and was judged too old at age fifty-five.

Undaunted, he set up a Medford office to promote Nordic skiing throughout the U.S. and Oregon. Towing a snowmobile and setting tracks for people who wanted to ski cross-country, he drove throughout the state and raced. He and two friends co-founded the Oregon Nordic Club, an organization now with numerous chapters throughout Oregon. When John Day was seventy-four years old, he won a gold medal in international cross-country skiing.

Magazines such as *Sports Illustrated, Life, True, Argosy*, and the *Saturday Evening Post* wrote long articles about him. When he died in 1986, he was seventy-seven years old — and nothing seemed to be left to achieve. Beginning one year later, the Southern Oregon Nordic Club held its first John Day Memorial Cross Country Ski Race in his honor at Diamond Lake — and this continues to the present. If John Day were still alive, he would probably still be competing.

Sources: Horn, *Sports Illustrated*, February 3, 1964; Newberry, *Medford Mail Tribune*, February 22, 2013.

The "Greatest" Male
Southern Oregon Athletes

*T*HIS LISTING IS BASED ON ATHLETES WHO WENT onto the professional or world-class level in their sport. Folks will debate the "greatest" label — but that's the fun! With thanks to Tim Trower, Sports Editor of the *Medford Mail Tribune*, considerations can be: the impact on their sport (i.e., Dick Fosbury with the revolutionary "Fosbury Flop"); who competed at the highest level (i.e., Les Gutches, a world champion); or who was the best in high school (numerous).

Sonny Sixkiller: Lettering in football, basketball, and baseball at Ashland High School, Sixkiller was the starting quarterback in 1970 for the Washington Huskies as a sophomore. He led the NCAA in passing as UW posted a 6-4 record, a vast improvement over its 1-9 record in 1969. Although missing four games as a senior in 1972, he finished his college career with 385 completions for 5,496 yards and thirty-five touchdowns, and held fifteen school records. The Huskies posted consecutive 8-3 records in 1971 and 1972. Not selected in the NFL draft, Sixkiller had tryouts with different teams. Although he didn't play in the NFL, he did for two years in the World Football League before it folded.

Andy Mauer: Mauer played football for Prospect High on the Upper Rogue River, earning All-American honors in 1966, and then for the University of Oregon. He played eight seasons as an offensive lineman in the NFL for different teams, as well as playing in two Super Bowls. A coach for years with Cascade Christian High School in Medford, his football team won the Class 2-A State Championship in 2006. The complete story on Andy Mauer is in this section.

Chad Cota: Cota played football at Ashland High School and then the University of Oregon. A strong safety in the NFL, the Carolina Panthers drafted him in 1995; Cota played for the Carolina Panthers, New Orleans Saints, Indianapolis Colts, and the St. Louis Rams over eight seasons before retiring in 2003. Named to the Carolina Panthers, Ten-Year Anniversary Team as a safety, his interception in the end zone on the Steelers final possession preserved the victory to clinch the 1996 NFC West Division title. Living in Medford, Chad created a nonprofit foundation that raises moneys for nonprofits helping local kids, including an annual golf tournament. He also is part owner of Prime Time Ventures with its InfoStructure dba, an Internet/communications company with offices in Talent and Roseburg.

Jeremy Guthrie: Guthrie attended Ashland High School, where he excelled in basketball, football, and baseball, including the classroom where he was the class valedictorian. After high school, he attended BYU before transferring to Stanford, where he was a starting pitcher. Through the 2016 season — primarily with the Baltimore Orioles and Kansas City Royals — his record was 91-108 (wins-losses) in eleven full seasons with a 4.37 ERA (earned run average per nine innings) with over 1,000 strikeouts before being released. Jeremy led the fundraising for Ashland High's 2015 drive to convert its athletic field from grass to synthetic, including pledging $650,000 of the $1.2 million conversion price.

Kyle Singler: Singler attended South Medford High School and was a four-year letter winner in basketball, playing also football and baseball. In his last year, he was a first-team, Parade All-American and All-USA Today selection. Playing four years for Duke, his team won the national NCAA championship in 2010, and he is presently playing for the Oklahoma City Thunder. The complete story on Kyle Singler is in this section.

Les Gutches: Winning three state high school wrestling titles at South Medford High, Gutches at Oregon State won NCAA titles in 1995 and

1996. He received the Dan Hodge Trophy as the nation's 1996 top collegiate wrestler, was a three-time Academic-All American, and the 1997 world champion at 187 pounds. Gutches again medaled in 1999, when he won the bronze in the world championships. Other first finishes in international competitions were at the 1999 FILA Wrestling World Cup, the 1999 Pan American Games, and the 1998 Goodwill Games. An OSU MBA graduate, he is presently an executive with USA Wrestling.

Marshall Holman: Attending Medford High School, Marshall Holman's last PBA bowling title was in 1996 at the PBA Ebonite Classic, eight years after he had last won a title. The first bowler on the PBA to surpass $1.5 million in earnings, Holman won twenty-two titles (eleventh all-time), including two U.S. Opens and two Tournament of Champions titles. Holman was a large draw when bowling was very popular on television and the alleys.

He was the youngest-ever winner in the Tournament of Champions, topping the field in the 1976 event when he was 21 years old. He was a three-time winner of the George Young High Average award, and earned nearly $1.7 million on tour. Holman is ranked 9th on the PBA's 2008 list of "50 Greatest Players of the Last 50 Years." He resides in Medford and is a business owner.

Dick Fosbury: At a 1963 high-school track meet in Grants Pass, Fosbury (as a sophomore at Medford High) spontaneously created a high-jumping style of his own, totally fracturing what had been taught before. Leaning with his shoulder forty-five degrees to the bar, he arched over on his back, and later broke the school record. He perfected this approach and won the gold medal at the 1968 Mexico City Olympic Games. The complete story on Dick Fosbury is in this section.

Jonathan Stark: Stark grew up in Medford and attended South Medford High School. He played tennis for Stanford University, where he was a singles and doubles All-American in 1990 and 1991. He reached the NCAA doubles final in 1991. During his tennis career, he won two Grand Slam doubles titles (the 1994 French Open Men's Doubles and the 1995 Wimbledon Championships Mixed Doubles). Stark reached the World No. 1 doubles ranking in 1994. Over the course of his career, he won two top-level singles titles and nineteen tour doubles titles. His career prize-money winnings totaled over $3.2 million and he retired from the professional tour in 2001.

Jason Allred: Jason Allred graduated from Ashland High School, and was the 1996 Oregon High School golf champion, finishing second in 1995 and 1998. He worked as a whitewater raft guide after college (Pepperdine) and on his golf. His biggest thrills in golf included winning the 1997 U.S. Junior Championship and competing in the British Open and U.S. Open. Out of 152 golf tournaments, he has had ten, top-ten finishes and has made twenty-six, top-twenty-five cuts. The charities that he supports include Compassion International (third-world child sponsorship program), Young Life (Christian Youth Ministry), and College Golf Fellowship.

Sources: Using a search engine such as Google with the name and the sport.

Kyle Singler: One of the Valley's Best Athletes

ORN IN 1988, KYLE SINGLER ATTENDED South Medford High School and was a four-year letter winner in basketball. Playing also football and baseball, he made all-conference first-team as a tight end and defensive back in 2004, and was an all-state quarterback in 2005.

In basketball, he led the Panthers to a 110-10 record over four years, brought South Medford a 2007 state championship crown, and was named the 2007 Oregonian Class 6A Co-Player of the Year (sharing those honors with Lake Oswego's Kevin Love, now with the Cleveland Cavaliers). Singler averaged 29.3 points, 10.6 rebounds, 3.5 assists and 2.0 steals per game during his senior high-school season.

The 2007 state championship game against Lake Oswego, Oregon, featured Singler versus Love — one of the great match-ups in Oregon sports history, as Singler scored eighteen points in the 58-54 title-game win. South Medford finished the year ranked thirteenth in *USA Today's* "Super 25 national rankings," while Singler was a first-team, *Parade* All-America selection and first-team, All-*USA Today* selection. A year earlier, Love and Lake Oswego defeated Singler and South Medford for the state championship.

Kyle Singler comes from a family blessed with great sports talents. His father, Ed, played quarterback at Oregon State from 1978 to 1982, while his mother, Kris (formerly Kris Brosterhous), played basketball at OSU from 1973 to 1976. Five of Singler's uncles played on Division I football, baseball or basketball teams, including three who played for the University of Oregon.

Kyle Singler during his time with the Detroit Pistons.

His younger brother, E.J. Singler, played basketball for the University of Oregon, also after starring at South Medford. Another gifted athlete, E.J. was only the thirteenth player in school history to amass over 1,000 career points and 500 career rebounds. His career free-throw shooting percentage is the best in school history, and he was ranked second nationally in this in his junior year. E.J. was the 2009 Oregonian Class 6A Player of the Year. He currently is playing in the NBA Development League.

Kyle — a 6'8", 230 pound power forward — went onto playing four years with basketball powerhouse, Duke University. As a freshman, he finished the 2007–08 season with averages of 13.3 points per game and

5.9 rebounds per game, helping lead Duke to a 28–6 record. Singler was instrumental in Duke winning its fourth national NCAA championship in spring 2010; he was named the NCAA Final Four Most Outstanding Player in that tournament. He also was the 2010 Sporting News College Athlete of the Year, and Singler helped lead the Blue Devils to three consecutive thirty-win seasons, only the sixth time this had been done in NCAA Division I history. Teammate Jon Scheyer called him, "The toughest player I've ever played with."

Singler was the third pick in the second round (thirty-third overall) by the Detroit Pistons for the 2011 NBA Draft. In August 2011, he signed with the Spanish team, CB Lucentum Alicante until the end of the 2011 NBA lockout. After the end of the lockout, Singler exercised his option to leave the club and chose to join Real Madrid. Singler helped Real Madrid defeat FC Barcelona to win the 2012 Spanish King's Cup. Signing a multi-year contract in August 2012 with the Detroit Pistons, Singler was a starter on the team as a first-year player. He currently plays during the 2016–17 season as a reserve for the Oklahoma City Thunder.

He has hosted the Kyle Singler Southern Oregon Open in Medford in basketball during mid-May since 2007 with the proceeds benefitting Kids Unlimited. Now with his brother E.J., Kyle's open is the region's largest youth basketball tournament (grades five through high school) with teams representing Oregon, California, Nevada, and Washington. There is more to come — and he is only in his late twenties.

Sources: Kyle Singler at his website; GoDuke.com: "Kyle Singler"; *Wikipedia*: "Kyle Singler."

The Heyday of
Medford Football

PRINCE L. "PRINK" CALLISON WAS THE FIRST standout football coach for Medford High, and his teams manhandled nearly every opponent during a 47-game span from 1923 to 1928, winning state championships from 1926 to 1928. During those six seasons, Prink's teams won 45 games, lost none, and were tied in only two. A few of the victories were 102-0 (Roseburg, 1925), 94-0 (Roseburg, 1926), and 94-0 (Klamath Falls, 1927). After his successes at Medford, Callison in 1929 left to become an assistant football coach at the University of Oregon, later becoming its head coach.

Medford High School's football team nickname then was the "Tigers"—which makes sense given what they were doing to their opponents—although some newspaper stories referred to them as the "Pear Pickers" due to the Rogue Valley's chief crop. The sports editor for the *Oregonian*, L.H. Gregory, created the present nickname in the late 1920s when seeing another rout (probably when Medford beat Benson Tech 39-0 in the 1928 state championship game): "From out of the south, Medford swept over the field like a Black Tornado."

Bill Bowerman was the left end on Medford's 1928 team, earned a college degree at the University of Oregon, and returned to Medford in 1935 to coach football and track. Before he headed overseas due to World War II, his football teams won sixty-nine games, lost only thirteen, and his 1935 and 1939 teams were undefeated. Bowerman returned to Medford after the war and coached for two more seasons, leaving to coach track and freshman football at the University of Oregon, starting in 1949. From there, he became an outstanding track and field coach, not to mention founding Nike with Phil Knight—but that is another story.

Fred Spiegelberg followed Bowerman as Medford's football coach in 1948. He was born in 1919 near Omak, Washington, and attended

Washington State University (WSU), where he won the Pacific Coast Conference lightweight boxing titles as a junior and senior. He served in the Army during World War II, was wounded in France, but returned to WSU and graduated in 1948.

Once becoming Medford's football coach, Fred Spiegelberg turned Medford into a football dynasty. His teams had a 253-62-10 record in thirty-one years as its head coach. He guided the Black Tornado to three state championships, one co-championship, seventeen Southern Oregon Conference titles, and five conference co-titles. Medford reached the state final nine times beginning in 1956 with a title loss to Marshfield, and ending in 1980 with a title loss to Beaverton. Medford won state championship titles, however, in 1959, 1962, 1969, and 1977. He was named National Coach of the Year in 1971.

On Friday nights, Southern Oregon towns during this time jumped with excitement. The Medford-Grants Pass rivalry was so intense that they had to put in extra bleachers to handle 7,000 fans. Black Tornado season tickets were part of divorce settlements, and the fathers of gifted athletes were offered jobs to move to Medford. Residents fought hard to keep the one high school, and the intense rivalries affected business decisions for decades after big games. Given the population of Medford in the 1960s being around 25,000, a large percentage of the town showed up for these games, not to mention from the visiting team's area.

Fred Spiegelberg retired after the 1982 season. The former high school split into two schools in 1986 as North and South Medford High; North Medford continued with the Black Tornado mascot, while South Medford by student-body vote decided on the "Panthers." Grateful for his longtime impact, Medford named its football venue Spiegelberg Stadium in 1986 when South Medford High opened.

Today the stadium is the home to both South and North Medford High School football programs and can hold up to 9,250 fans. Spiegelberg was inducted into the WSU Athletic Hall of Fame (1983), the Oregon Sports Hall of Fame (1989), and the National Athletic Coaches Hall of Fame (1990).

Over the decades, Medford football has continued with success at both high schools — thanks in large part to great football coaches of the past, such as Callison, Bowerman, and Spiegelberg.

Sources: *Medford Mail Tribune*, April 22, 2007; see Bill Bowerman article in this book; *The Spokesman-Review*, March 24, 1996.

Chris Korbulic:
Paddling the Globe

SOUTHERN OREGON HAS ITS SHARE OF extreme sports enthusiasts from snowboarding and bungee jumping to extreme kayaking, such as Chris Korbulic. He has launched over the thundering, tallest waterfalls in Oregon and California to searching for the tallest falls ever survived, or most difficult whitewater in "expedition kayaking" throughout the world—and on film.

The 2004 Grants Pass High School graduate is a full-time extreme kayaker, earning a living from sponsors that include clothing giant Eddie Bauer, and from six years of appearing on Brazilian adventure television show "Kaiak." He and kayak partner Ben Stookesberry (Mt. Shasta, California) in 2015 were named two of the fifty most adventurous men by *Men's Journal* magazine.

Chris's parents, Mary and Paul Korbulic (then of Rogue River), are lifelong kayakers. Mary Korbulic paddled the remote Wild and Scenic section of the lower Rogue while pregnant with Chris. He started rafting from infancy, but didn't try hard-shells until taking a summer kayaking class. By the time he was at Grants Pass High, he was kayaking Class V rapids on the upper Rogue's North and Middle Forks. An interest in microbiology took him to Oregon State University, but his growing love of surviving massive waterfalls took over.

His fame grew with the size of waterfalls he ran, from a seventy-footer on Butte Creek outside Salem to an eighty-footer in the Salmon River Canyon. That talent earned him a sponsorship from Eddie Bauer to explore the world's most remote rivers. One of Korbulic's closest calls was in 2010 when he and two others were expedition kayaking the

Chris Korbulic: Brazilian reality TV star and one of the world's most accomplished expedition kayakers. (Photo courtesy eddiebauer.com)

Lukuga River in the remote Congo, to be the first to boat this wild, uncharted river fraught with danger from crocodiles and hippos.

Korbulic and Stookesberry watched in horror as a crocodile snatched their South African guide from his kayak. This was a part of an Eddie Bauer-sponsored expedition into the source of the White Nile led by guide Hendrik Coetzee. A fifteen-foot crocodile bypassed Korbulic underwater, launched into the surface, and snatched the third man from his hard-shell, all kayaking within mere feet of one another. Coetzee's body was not recovered.

His highest-ever waterfall jump was 120-foot Rainbow Falls on the Big Island of Hawaii in 2013. He later did a first descent on New Guinea, and helped guide an expedition at Murchison Falls on the Uganda Nile. In that year, he kayaked 400 miles north of Norway over glacial ice. Armed with only a WWII-era rifle, he and Stookesberry encountered polar bears and were "glacial kayaking": kayaking glacial waterfalls that thundered over the glaciers. A recent adventure included a quest to tame Iguazu Falls on the Brazilian-Argentine border, a Victoria Falls look-alike over 200 feet high. The authorities deemed this to be too risky. He'll get there.

Sources: Freeman, *Medford Mail Tribune,* August 7, 2009; Duewel, *Grants Pass Daily Courier*, May 3, 2015; Chris Korbulic's website.

PART XI

The Creative Scene

The Chautauqua in Ashland

EVANGELICAL CHRISTIAN ORGANIZATIONS HELD camp meetings and annual summer get-togethers during the nineteenth century in which the Chautauqua movement took hold. Methodist Minister John Heyl Vincent ran an 1874 summer camp at Lake Chautauqua in New York to train Sunday School teachers, where he held classes, lectures, and different recreational activities. This first Chautauqua and its idea spread throughout rural America, as communities competed for the opportunity to hold the ten to twelve days of lectures, activities, and music.

In Oregon, the first Chautauqua was held in Canby in 1885, but it only lasted for that one year. Other towns in this state then conducted them: Oregon City, Gearhart, Dallas, Ashland, Lebanon, Silverton, Monmouth, La Grande, and Albany. Oregon City and Ashland started theirs in 1893 and enjoyed the longest runs. Each of these two towns had a strong supporter who tirelessly supported the movement: Oregon City's author and suffragist Eva Emery Dye worked continuously for the Gladstone Chautauqua, held a few miles north of where the Clackamas and Willamette rivers joined; G.F. Billings did the same in Ashland and served as the Southern Oregon Chautauqua Association's President for most of its existence.

As with many of the Chautauquas, Gladstone and Ashland had large, beehive-looking, domed buildings constructed as the centerpiece for their activities with many of the same nationally-recognized speakers. Ashland was then the most populated town in Southern Oregon. Located on the hillside above the Plaza where Lithia Park begins, the first domed structure was constructed in one and one-half weeks and finished one day before its grand opening in July 1893. Those attending

Ashland Chautauqua Auditorium. (SOHS 02216)

could rent tents in Chautauqua Park, stay at hotels, live with friends, or be lucky enough to enjoy a horse-and-buggy ride back to home.

Classes were held in the morning on nearly every subject ranging from geology to physical fitness, and entertainment was provided at night, given that television, the Internet, and X-boxes didn't exist then. The summer affairs featured theatre, concerts, sports (particularly baseball), classes, theater, and important people of the times—for example, John Philip Sousa with his band, educator Booker T. Washington, evangelist Billy Sunday, politician William Howard Taft (the 27th President of the United States, 1909–1913), orator William Jennings Bryan, and "The Poet of the West," Joaquin Miller.

The first dome structure held 1,000 people, and it was rebuilt twice to increase the seating capacity during its thirty-one-year run, including in 1905 when the structure was enlarged to hold 1,500. The building was torn down in 1917 and completely replaced by another round, dome-covered structure. Even so, people were turned away from the most popular speakers. When the "silver-tongued" William Jennings Bryan arrived in 1897 (he ran for U.S. President three times but lost), so many attendees came that he had to give his lecture outside the dome. Theodore Roosevelt called the movement "the most American thing in America"; by 1924 an estimated thirty million people annually were attending the more than 10,000 Chautauqua summer assemblies being held across the country.

With competition from movie houses, radio, and travel by car, the Chautauqua movement throughout the country began to lose attendance and incur financial deficits. Ashland was no different. When the Chautauquas died out in the early 1920s, its structure fell into disuse and in 1933 the dome was torn down. Two years later, however, the Oregon Shakespeare Festival conducted its first production, "Twelfth Night," in a stage built within those very cement walls.

In any event, the Ashland Chautauqua reflected the times and was a grand movement in the town's and region's history.

Sources: Peterson, *Oregon Encyclopedia*: "Chautauqua in Oregon"; Oregon History Project: "Ashland Chautauqua, 1895."

Ben Hur Lampman:
A Man for the Ages

*F*OLLOWING HIS BROTHER, REX, TO GOLD HILL in 1912, Ben Hur Lampman became over time a nationally acclaimed poet, writer, and author. Following his father's passion for owning and managing newspapers from Wisconsin to North Dakota, the self-educated Lampman also pursed this profession.

His wife—a young high-school teacher by the name of Lena Sheldon—lost a child in infancy and had health problems. As his father and brother then were living in the Rogue Valley owing to a better climate, it was natural for the family to relocate here. Although his parents had switched from newspaper publishing to try their hand at farming, brother Rex was also the editor of the *Gold Hill News*.

Ben Hur sold his North Dakota newspaper and headed to the Rogue Valley, discovering that the climate was indeed better. When his brother sold the *Gold Hill News* to him and moved to Portland, Ben Hur became the newspaper's new owner and editor. He loved the town, its famed fishing, and the people he came to know.

Four years later, he moved north to join the Portland *Oregonian's* staff. Over time he became a renowned editor, essayist, short-story writer, novelist, and poet. Ben Hur won the prestigious O. Henry award for the best short fiction, authored six books, had a movie made about his life, was published in national publications (from the *New York Times* to the *Atlantic Monthly* and *Saturday Evening Post*), and was honored in being selected as Oregon's Poet Laureate for which he served three years.

Year after year, he returned to Gold Hill to continue his passion for fishing on the Rogue and keeping up with old friends. In recognition of

Ben Hur Lampman (*left*) sporting his "jaunty cap." (GHHS)

its "native son" who returned so often, Gold Hill held Ben Hur Lampman Day in his honor on June 21, 1947. Governors, ex-governors, and even Clark Gable, Tyrone Power, and David Niven—who had been fishing on the Rogue—joined an estimated 2,500 people who attended.

A long parade (with fire engines, trucks, bands, marchers, and floats), baseball game, horseback stunts, horse race, and a barbecued salmon feast were part of the festivities. A tract of land three-quarters of a mile long and opposite Gold Hill was dedicated as Ben Hur Lampman Park: It's still in use and alongside the road named for him.

Ben Hur Lampman died on January 24, 1954, and was buried in Portland. But his works live on. One of his best-known articles was a reader's inquiry on where was the best place to bury a dog. He wrote a long article which ended:

....There is one best place to bury a dog.
If you bury him in this spot, he will
come to you when you call – come to you
over the grim, dim frontier of death,
and down the well-remembered path,
and to your side again.

And though you call a dozen living
dogs to heel, they shall not growl at
him, nor resent his coming.

People may scoff at you, who see
no lightest blade of grass bent by his
footfall, who hear no whimper, people
who may never really have had a dog.
Smile at them, for you shall know
something that is hidden from them,
and which is well worth the knowing.

The one best place to bury a good
dog is in the heart of his master.

Sources: Colburn, *Oregon Encyclopedia*: "Ben Hur Lampman (1886-1954)"; Gold Hill Historical Society, *Nuggets of News*, September 1992, pp. 1-5.

Dorland Robinson:
The Talented, Young Artist

BORN IN 1891 IN JACKSONVILLE, OREGON, Regina Dorland Robinson was the daughter of a physician and drugstore owner, Dr. James Robinson, and Sarah "Tillie" Robinson. The family was well-off, her father was an amateur painter himself, and her parents became dedicated to her artistic growth. Having lost their first two children to diphtheria the year before her birth, Dorland's parents focused their attention on her and her talents.

Exhibiting a very early talent for drawing and painting, she started on her artistic path at age five, more than likely encouraged by her parents. Over time, Robinson learned various applications in the use of watercolors, charcoal, pastels, gouache (opaque watercolor painting with the pigment suspended in water), and oils — all in a variety of images.

When fifteen and sixteen, she had formal training in both California and Portland; while at the Oregon School of Art, her striking work in charcoal was considered to be some of her best work. In 1907, the *Oregon Sunday Journal* newspaper stated that the sixteen-year-old was a "prodigy", and her first exhibition was held that September in Grants Pass. When she was twenty years old, she studied at the Pennsylvania Academy of Fine Arts for seven months, after which she produced extraordinary, delicate floral watercolors.

She and her mother moved in 1911 to Oakland, California, where she became part of the Bay Area art community. Joining the prestigious Sketch Club in San Francisco, she met influential, "avant-garde" artists such as Anne Bremer, Arthur and Lucia Mathews, and Xavier Martinez.

Dorland Robinson, self portrait. (SOHS 489)

Dorland showed more of her art at the San Francisco Art Association in 1912 and 1913; by then, she was a practicing and showing artist. Returning to Jacksonville in early 1916, she exhibited thirty-five of her works in Medford; she also showed that year at the Portland Art Museum.

The French school of impressionism significantly influenced her artistry. This 1800s art movement emphasized short brush strokes, an emphasis on the interface of light, and the use of vibrant colors. Robinson painted and sketched Southern Oregon landscapes, portraits, self-portraits, and numerous still lifes (inanimate objects, such as flowers or fruit), receiving numerous praise for her works.

Her career was on the brink of escalating into prominence, when her life dissolved in 1916-1917. Earlier in 1916, she had met a traveling salesman living in San Francisco by the name of Charles H. Pearson, who was twelve years older. They married in October in Portland, traveled within the country, but then filed for divorce less than two months later. She had a nervous breakdown in December, never fully recovered, and committed suicide in a boarding house in San Mateo, California, on April 7, 1917.

Her mother discovered her body, a gunshot wound to her head with a revolver near her body that she would have dropped. A coroner's jury decided she had shot herself "by her own hand while temporarily deranged, suicidal." An obituary stated that her unhappy domestic experience contributed to the self-destruction, stating that: "Miss Robinson was of an unusually sensitive and intense disposition and could not throw off disappointments as readily as a less temperamental person."

Her paintings were then being shown in Burlingame on the San Francisco Peninsula; another exhibition of her paintings had been planned in Medford. In the ten short years before her death at age twenty-five, Dorland Robinson had created an impressive body of work in charcoal, oils, pastels, and watercolors; at least one hundred and fifty pieces are known to exist in private collections or at the Southern Oregon Historical Society which owns some two-thirds.

Buried in Jacksonville Cemetery with her two older siblings, Dorland Robinson was talented enough to have become a nationally recognized artist, had she lived long enough. Instead, she is known as a prodigy who accomplished so much in a very short life.

Sources: Curler, *Oregon Encyclopedia*: "Robinson, Regina Dorland (1891-1917)"; Fattig, *Medford Mail Tribune*, November 29, 2007; see also Dawna Curler, *A Lasting Impression: The Art and Life of Regina Dorland Robinson*, Medford, Oregon: Southern Oregon Historical Society, 2007, that includes images of her works.

Edison Marshall

E DISON T. MARSHALL'S FATHER WAS A newspaper publisher in Rensselaer, Indiana, where Edison was born in 1894. When he was thirteen, his father learned about the Rogue Valley orchard boom and moved the family there. Unfortunately, the venture in fruit growing was a failure to where Edison promised that whatever he did, he would make a "bountiful living." He was quoted later in *Grit* magazine, "I went after two big prizes, fame and fortune, and I got them both."

Marshall grew up in southwest Medford and graduated in 1913 from Medford Senior High School. Edison then attended the University of Oregon from 1913 to 1915 where he majored in journalism. His love of literature came from reading his father's library of classics while he was growing up. In his freshman year at college, he sold his first story to *Argosy*, which gave him the confidence that he could make a living at writing.

Edison joined the U.S. Army in 1918, served as a public-relations officer, and was stationed at Camp Hancock, Georgia. There he met his future wife, Agnes Sharp Flyth. He said later that his work in public relations and as a reporter for one summer were the only salaried jobs he ever had. In 1919, he wrote a short story entitled, "The Elephant Remembers," which was widely read and reproduced in a number of school textbooks.

After marrying Agnes, the two moved to Medford after World War I and lived a few blocks from the Marshall family home where he had grown up. The two-story, 1910 Craftsman-style home was on South Oakdale in the now South Oakdale Historic District (registered in the National Register of Historic Places). The two-level house contained some 3,000 square-feet of living space with four bedrooms on the upper

Edison Marshall with his books. (SOHS 10507)

level. In Medford, their two children — Edison Jr. and Nancy Silence — were born.

Edison Marshall was awarded the prestigious O. Henry Award for the best short-story fiction in 1921 for his work, "The Heart of Little Shikara." His adventure book, *The Strength of the Pines*, was also written in 1921 in an Oregon setting. Little, Brown, and Company was a widely respected New York City publishing house and published different works of his while living in Medford. These were: *The Voice of the Pack* (1920), *The Snowshoe Trail* (1921), *The Skyline of Spruce* (1922), and the *Land of Forgotten Men* (1923), in addition to *The Strength of the Pines*.

His first writing screen credit was for *Snowshoe Trail* in 1922, and with his previously published books and articles, Edison's career was well underway. Agnes grew homesick for Georgia, however, and the family moved to Augusta, her hometown. Despite this, Edison frequently returned to Medford to visit his family and friends. The *Medford Mail Tribune* featured these visits by the famed author in its social section and columns.

For twenty years, Edison wrote short stories and serials for magazines—including for *American, Good Housekeeping, Harper's Bazaar, Cosmopolitan*, and *Reader's Digest*—for which he was widely read. Marshall was a frequent contributor throughout the 1930s of serial novels to *Good Housekeeping* magazine and his name was featured on the cover.

Edison Marshall's genre was a storyteller of adventure. He traveled throughout the world and earned a reputation as a big-game hunter and adventurer in search of story material. Over time, many of his works were set where he visited (as when living in Oregon): Alaska, Africa, India, and China. Like Hemingway, the trophies of his big-game hunts lined the walls of his home. His short stories and articles had titles such as "Black Snake," "The Cave of a Million Buddhas," "The Fox of Zanziba," "My Lord the Elephant," and "A Strange Sea Story."

Edison Marshall returned to writing novels in 1941 with the publication of his first historical novel, *Benjamin Blake*, which was a Literary Guild selection and huge commercial success. It was a best seller in the United States, Sweden, Norway, Finland, and Denmark; the novel was made into a movie, *Son of Fury*, starring Tyrone Power.

Marshall then wrote a novel each year, totaling forty-nine such works. His popular fictional narratives over the next twenty years were typically based on historical figures, including *The Upstart, Yankee Pasha, Infinite Woman, and Castle in the Swamp*. Having lived for years in Edison Marshall's home on South Oakdale, Vicki Bryden wrote the cited article below and concluded: "Readers who know local history and names can catch references to his Oregon roots in his writing."

In 1941, the University of Oregon awarded him an honorary M.A. degree. Marshall had five silent movie screen credits and five "talkies" based upon his books. The notable movies were *Son of Fury, Yankee Pasha* (1954, staring Jeff Chandler), and *The Vikings* (1958, starring Kirk Douglas).

To the critics of his writing, his answer was that most of his books were on the best-seller list; they had been translated into nine foreign languages and made into ten films. When Edison Marshall died in 1967, his obituary in the *New York Times* concluded that he was the foremost author in the field of historical novels during the 1940s and 1950s.

Edison Marshall summarized his life as "Fifty years of making a good living from my pen alone with no other gainful occupation." And what a life it was.

Sources: Bryden, *Oregon Encyclopedia*; Augusta State University: Edison Marshall; Twitchell, *Medford Mail Tribune*, December 13, 1997.

Pinto Colvig:
Bozo the Clown (and More)

VANCE "PINTO" COLVIG WAS ONE OF seven children and born in Jacksonville in 1892; his parents were Addie and William—and his dad practiced law. William Colvig was in demand as a speaker and widely known as Judge Colvig, although he never had been one. "The only judge I've ever been," he loved to tell others, "was a judge of fine whiskey."

Vance received the nickname of "Pinto" due to his face being full of freckles when young. Descended from Rogue Valley pioneers on both his mother's and father's side, he grew up in Jacksonville and Medford, attending school and playing clarinet in the town bands. An extrovert like his dad, Pinto would try to get a part whenever vaudeville came to town. He enjoyed getting attention and worked at this, such as when he rode a calf through the town's main street. Pinto always "wanted to be somebody."

Studying art at Oregon Agricultural College (now Oregon State University), he played in the cadet band and drew cartoon illustrations for the college yearbook. Pinto would ditch his classes every spring, however, to travel throughout the country as a circus clown or play on the vaudeville circuit.

After graduating, he worked the vaudeville circuit and in 1914 became a staff writer and cartoonist in Reno, then later in Carson City, Nevada. Pinto Colvig was definitely the entertainer, as he then joined a circus. He married Margaret Slaven in 1916 and moved with her to San Francisco where four of their five sons were born.

In San Francisco, Pinto was a writer and cartoonist for the *San Francisco Bulletin*, drew "Life on the Radio Wave" (a United Features

Pinto Colvig with Capitol Record cover. (SOHS 20920)

Syndicate cartoon series) for the *San Francisco Chronicle*, and worked in the beginning days of film animation. In 1919, for example, he created "Pinto's Prizma Comedy Revue," which was an animated cartoon.

The Colvig family moved in the early 1920s to Hollywood, where during the silent movie era, Pinto wrote titles, gags, and scenarios for numerous films. While at the Keystone Film Company, he combined animation with live action by hand-drawing cartoons over film frames of live actors.

In 1930, Pinto's career took off with his signing of a contract with Walt Disney as sound pictures began. Although best known as the original voice of Disney's Goofy (and later Bozo the Clown), he did the voices for many characters including Oswald the Lucky Rabbit, Grumpy and Sleepy in "Snow White and the Seven Dwarfs," the Practical Pig in "The Three Little Pigs," and even the barks for Pluto the dog. Colvig worked not only for Disney, but also for Max Fleischer Studios, where he voiced Bluto in the Popeye cartoons and Gabby in "Gulliver's Travels." He did Munchkin voices in MGM's *The Wizard of Oz*, and also wrote the lyrics for "Who's Afraid of the Big Bad Wolf."

In 1946, he developed the Bozo the Clown character for a read-along children's record series that Capital Records produced. He made the first voice recordings, wrote some of the first songs, and made the first live appearances as Bozo. He played the grinning, red-haired clown from then into the early 1950s, and Colvig starred in "Bozo's Circus," a 1949 TV series broadcasted in the Los Angeles area, all while making appearances at children's hospitals and orphanages.

Notwithstanding his residing in Hollywood, Pinto kept up his local connections by returning to see friends and even serving on different occasions as the Grand Marshal of Jacksonville's Gold Rush Jubilee Parade. He kept up with his childhood friends, including one to whom he wrote letters "adorned with cartoons" to her for years. Pinto commented later that he "put all the hicks in the world into (the voice of) Goofy and all the mean, old codgers of Jacksonville into Grumpy."

A lifelong smoker, he died of lung cancer in 1967 at age seventy-five. Before his death, however, he worked with Oregon Senator Maurine Neuberger to promote her bill that required warning labels on cigarette packaging as to the risks of cancer.

Disney Studios posthumously honored Pinto Colvig in 1993 with its Disney Legend Award. In 2004, the International Clown Hall of Fame in Milwaukee, Wisconsin, inducted him. At that time, the organization named him as the original Bozo the Clown—instead of Larry Harmon, who had purchased the identity from Columbia Records in the mid-1950s and then played the character on network TV.

Pinto Colvig was able to live the life that he wanted—and, in turn, enriched many.

Sources: Curler, *Oregon Encyclopedia*: "Vance DeBar (Pinto) Colvig (1892-1967)."

Eugene Bennett: Noted Southern Oregon Artist

*B*ORN IN 1921 IN CENTRAL POINT, Eugene ("Gene") Bennett showed an early interest in the visual arts, along with different artistic talents. He credited his art teacher when at Medford's Washington Elementary School as being his first art mentor. He was a multi-gifted artist, being also an accomplished musician and studying piano at an early age.

He composed music, including one piece that was played in an Oregon Shakespeare Festival production in 1940; and even acted in a Shakespearean play that same year. World War II interrupted his music studies at the University of Oregon, and Bennett in 1943 joined the U.S. Navy. Discharged three years later, he decided to center on art rather than music, telling a friend that it was easier to carry an art palette around than a grand piano.

He attended the Art Institute of Chicago and used his G.I. Bill to pay for the tuition. While still a student at the Art Institute, he had a solo show at the Portland Art Museum. After his studies, Bennett taught art at a suburban-Chicago-area high school, painted and developed his artistic talents, along with traveling extensively to France and Italy. His love for Southern Oregon brought him back; in 1958, he returned to the Valley to live first in West Medford.

Gene became a founding member in 1960 of the Rogue Gallery & Art Center, and his achievements during the 1960s were as breath-taking as the awards that he received later in his life. Becoming known for his landscapes with their light and color, he also created art including sculptural poles that adorned the Oregon Pavilion's entrance at the 1962

Eugene Bennett. (SOHS 21165)

Seattle World's Fair; these combined ordinary objects such as colored foil, chicken wire, tacks, and roofing nails.

That same year, Bennett purchased the historic, 1850's Eagle Brewery and Saloon close to Britt Hill in Jacksonville for his home and studio— and began its remodeling. John Trudeau was arduously working at the time to bring about the Britt Festival, and soon Gene discovered that he had "an orchestra in his backyard." His lifelong friendship with the Britt had begun.

An easy walk to the Britt, his friendships with fellow musicians, and the setting, inspired him to paint there many times over the years, including the Festival's first summer concert season in 1963. A favorite place for painting or sketching was while sitting on the grassy Britt hillside, while he watched and heard the musicians practicing. His 1980 painting "Evening at Britt," became the first poster he created for the festival (used in 1984); his 1963 Britt Festival painting became the second poster (1992), and a 1991-sepia-toned one named "The Rehearsal" was the third (1996). His will provided a bequest that funded the Britt in purchasing the 1963 painting.

The 1960s were also when he met Robby Collins, who was leading the movement to save Jacksonville's downtown, and which culminated in a large swatch of Jacksonville in 1966 being designated a National Historic Landmark. He joined forces with his friend and helped to develop the Historic Preservation standards for Jacksonville, of which he became the first chairman of the Jacksonville Preservation Commission (among other committees). When Robby Collins was later restoring the U.S. Bank building, Bennett painted a scene on the safe at Robby's request.

He was the first recipient of the Arts Council of Southern Oregon's Lifetime Achievement Award, featured on the "Oregon Art Beat" television show (2001), and received the Governor's Arts Award for having "significantly contributed to the growth and development of Oregon's cultural life" (2002). A feature-length independent film, *Eugene Bennett: Portrait of an Artist*, premiered that same year at the Craterian Theater. In 2004, he and others founded the Eugene Bennett art scholarship for Jackson County youths as a permanent endowment through the Oregon Community Foundation; numerous local students have received tuition awards to attend different colleges throughout the country.

The colorful collections that represent six decades of work covered the walls inside his home studio. Posters for the Britt Festival and Taste of Ashland hung next to his many oils, collages, drawings, photographs, sculpture, and assemblages. Bennett's work had also been shown at the Brooklyn Museum, Museum of Modern Art in New York City, San Francisco Museum of Art, and in Alba, Italy.

In November 2010, Eugene Bennett passed away at age eighty-six. Long regarded as the foremost artist in Southern Oregon, he was a renaissance man. His visual arts talents were seen from the variety of these works to his watercolors and oil paintings. He also worked hard for the betterment of his community.

Sources: Byden, *Oregon Encyclopedia*: "Edison Marshall"; Specht, *Medford Mail Tribune*, Sept. 23, 2010; Specht, *Medford Mail Tribune*, Nov. 5, 2010.

The Holly Theatre

*M*OVIE THEATRES IN THE EARLY 1900s were more like palaces with a grandeur not seen today. For Southern Oregon, residents in 1930 had their first opportunity to experience a movie palace created solely for sound motion pictures. Workers began to construct the foundation in late 1929 at the corner of Sixth and Holly Street, one of Medford's prime thoroughfares.

John Niedermeyer owned the lot and was building the structure with Earl Fehl as the superintendent of construction. Later, the public was informed that a four-story brick theatre was being built at a cost of $100,000. Frank Clark, the pre-eminent Valley architect — and the most influential then — designed the theatre exterior and lobbies. The theatre opened on August 29, 1930, with the Great Depression underway.

A thirty-three-foot tower-like "Holly" theatre neon sign hung prominently outside, reportedly the largest outside of Portland. Inside, brilliantly-colored carpets spread out with two stairways from the inner foyer that led to an upper lounge. This large room extended the building's full width and gave entry to a magnificent 1,200-seat auditorium. The woodwork to the pillars and beams were decoratively finished in soft walnut, with the moldings striped in gold and reds. The entire interior was hand-painted with an exquisite scroll pattern to create a "venetian" scene.

The most advanced sound systems and motion-picture projection equipment were installed; and its sound system could broadcast live performances over the radio. Offices were located on the second and third floors, and an optometrist, chiropractor, and dentist (on the third floor) were among the first tenants. The projection room was fireproof and supported by concrete and steel columns. Well-appointed dressing

A crowd in line for a showing of *Puttin' On the Ritz* at Medford's Holly Theater, circa 1930. (SOHS 18357)

rooms were built to allow live performances, including to accommodate the theatrical and operatic troupes stopping in Medford on their way to and from San Francisco, Portland, and Seattle.

The Holly operated successfully, but the depression caused attendance at theatres across the United States to suffer—not to mention being a large theatre in small town with various others. In 1934, the Holly Theatre shut down for eight years. With the U.S.'s entry into World War II, however, and the thousands of soldiers at Camp White wanting entertainment, the theatre reopened. Admission in 1942 was thirty cents for a matinee, forty cents for the evening, and soldiers paid a quarter.

The theatre was an important part of these people's lives: growing up, first dates, first kisses, birthday celebrations, and even anniversaries.

Owing to multi-plex theatres and large chains, operations at the Holly shut down in 1986 due to low attendance, as did many downtown, single-screen movie houses over the years. Its doors were closed for years, until Art and Lea Alfinito ten years later bought it with their dream to restore and preserve the building's unique architecture and history.

In late 2002, the City of Medford Building Department ordered the building closed and its paying tenants leave, as one of the main roof trusses had cracked. The Holly's theatre, again, became soundless and vacant.

Nearly ten years later in April 2011, the JPR Foundation—a non-profit organization that raised money to support Jefferson Public Radio— bought the building to restore and return live stage performances. Jefferson Live! (which also operates the Cascade Theatre in Redding) is managing the Holly for the Foundation.

The thirty-three-foot neon blade sign and marquee were replicated based on the original design, and in a 2012 ceremony, the Holly was lit for the first time since the 1970s. The JPR Foundation is raising the money, securing grants, and engaging the city's support to bring the structure back to its 1930 appearance with total costs presently estimated at near $4.5 million.

With significant contributions by philanthropist Jim Collier, the Medford Urban Renewal Agency, the State of Oregon, and many others (including Jim Belushi, Robert and Suzi Givens, and Asante), the expectation is to start the major restoration in mid-2017, with completion expected in the following year. The foyer has been restored with additional interior work to start, and the theatre will comfortably seat 1,003 patrons, making it the largest indoor venue in Southern Oregon.

The exquisite architectural and historical value of this theatre is seen in its placement on the National Register of Historic Places—and the efforts of the community to restore it to its former grandeur. Before we know it, the Holly will once again be hosting performances.

Sources: See generally, "The Holly Theatre" at its website; Truwe, *Southern Oregon History, Revised.*

The Craterian

ESIGNED BY THE PRE-EMINENT ARCHITECT, Frank C. Clark, the Craterian was built in 1924 as a theatre with retail space, typical for the times; when opened, it had tenants such as law offices and shops. George A. Hunt leased the built theatre and ran a contest to select the best name with the winner receiving a $25 prize. From the 1500 entries received, he chose "Craterian" as it was derived from the region's Crater Lake, but it also was an adaptation of the time's favorite movie-house name, the "Criterion."

On October 20, 1924, a sell-out audience of 1,200 people attended the grand opening to watch a play, *The Havoc*, and listen to music played on the "grand" Wurlitzer organ. Movie projectors were installed later for silent films, and as typical of this era, theatre and vaudeville acts were booked. Eighteen months after its opening, fifteen-year-old Ginger Rogers appeared on the Craterian's stage and captivated the audience. The *Medford Mail Tribune* wrote: "Miss Rogers is a winsome little miss with captivating mannerisms and a pair of feet that make the most intricate dances seem easy."

When talking pictures were brought out, the theatre quickly exhibited them, such as Al Jolson in the 1928 film, *The Jazz Singer*. When the Great Depression overcame the state and country (and multiplicity of theatres), Hunt had to sell his lease to the chain of Fox theatres, but after their bankruptcy, he bought the lease back in 1933. The theatre operator remodeled the Craterian, reduced matinee prices to fifteen cents, and showed "first-run" films such as the *Thin Man* series starring William Powell and Myrna Loy. Despite these changes, revenues were hard to come by, and it took World War II with its nearby Camp White and thousands of soldiers wanting entertainment to make the times easier.

The 96th Infantry Band performing in front of the Craterian theatre for the "4th War Loan" rally, February 1944. A film featuring actor Victor Mature film was playing at the time and Mature appeared "in person" for the affair. (Photo courtesy George Kramer, Ashland, OR)

After the war, several operator and owner changes occurred with more building alterations, including the sale of the Wurlitzer organ as it was no longer needed. With the increase of home TVs and multi-plex theatres, audiences decreased and took its toll on these theatres. In late 1985, the Craterian was placed on the National Register of Historic Places as Medford's first "Movie Palace," but by then it was closed down. The old building was donated to the nearby Rogue Valley Art Association, the intent being to "foster community theatre activities."

Former Medford Mayor Lindsay Berryman (2000-2004) and other community leaders agreed that the Craterian needed to be completely refurbished, not only for its historical presence, but also to revitalize part of Medford's downtown and support the arts. Over several years, a total of $5.2 million was raised to completely renovate the building, including major structural changes. More than 600 individuals, foundations, the Medford Urban Renewal Agency, different state agencies, and businesses contributed. As one standout example, Sabroso (the Medford-centered, fruit puree and concentrates supplier) through its CEO Jim Root donated $275,000 over time — and the Roots individually also made substantial contributions.

The newly-revitalized Craterian opened in March 1997. The new auditorium was designed to be more comfortable with a seating capacity of 732, but the new stage easily handled large concert and theatre productions. The theatre was initially named for Ginger Rogers, the long-time Southern Oregonian who appeared when young and then much later to support the theatre.

In August 2012, the theatre was renamed the "Craterian Theater at The Collier Center for the Performing Arts," in honor of local philanthropist, James Morrison Collier, who was a long-time Craterian supporter and had donated a substantial, but undisclosed, sum of money. The stage at the Collier Center is named the Ginger Rogers Stage; the James and Valerie Root Auditorium, who were also long-time supporters, retained its name. The Collier Center also has named rooms and lobbies honoring other supporting individuals.

The Craterian shows numerous different events, from local productions such as the Rogue Opera and Youth Symphony to art shows, national productions, and exhibits. It is another historical place that is from the past, but with a strong presence now.

Sources: Craterian Theatre: "History" at its website; Varble, *Medford Mail Tribune*, August 31, 2012.

Camelot Theatre

C AMELOT THEATRE IS THE PRIME LANDMARK IN Talent, Oregon, a small city with less than 7,000 residents. Seldom does one find a theatre with its capabilities in such a little town. Named the Actors Theatre when founded in 1982, the theatre began productions eight years later in a building that once was a feed store. It had been built in the early 1950s and converted into a 104-seat theatre.

Although serving the theatre's needs, the control booth was miniscule, the low-ceiling stage crimped productions, and a beaten trailer outside served as the dressing room, costume shop, and office. If an actor needed to enter at the theatre's front, he first walked outside, whether it was raining or snowing. The audience could hear the flushing of the backstage bathrooms and the theatre didn't even have a curtain.

It struggled throughout the years, but its transformation didn't begin until 2002 when Livia Genise became the new Artistic Director. At the time, the board wanted to change from the serious dramas — although "good work" — that the then director was producing. Livia Genise also had significant experience in acting, directing, and running a theater conservatory program.

Starting her forty-year stage career at the St. Louis Municipal Opera, Livia had performed from Broadway (Rizzo in *Grease*) to Hollywood, guest starring on everything from "Three's Company" to "Hill St. Blues," including four-months on "Days of our Lives." She founded the Willows Theatre Conservatory for the Performing Arts and served as its director for four years. Before taking on the Camelot (and its new name), Ms. Genise had been the Education Director at the Marin Theatre Company.

The Camelot Theatre, downtown Talent, Oregon.

Livia changed the programming to a mixture of musicals, comedies, and dramas, in that order of preference. Revues were produced that paid tribute to famous singers such as Linda Ronstadt, Nat "King" Cole, and Rosemary Clooney. With the credit as the founder of the Camelot, she also acted and directed in its productions; her directing credits ranged from *Meet Me in St. Louis* and *The Crucible* to *An Evening of Cole Porter* and *Gigi*.

In 2007, however, the Talent Urban Renewal Agency (TURA) created a downtown redevelopment plan that included significant widening and realigning changes to Main Street. The Camelot's plays and musicals were housed in the old building at Main Street and Talent Avenue, right in its path. A retained consultant conducted a study that concluded it wasn't feasible to raise funds to construct a new theatre—and the economy worsened from there.

Not deterred, the theater's board started raising money. With significant help from Valley performing-arts-benefactor James Collier ($300,000 to start the campaign, plus more later), the Meyer Memorial Trust ($150,000), and many others, the group raised $1.9 million between January 2010 and April 2012. With the collaboration of South Valley Bank and Oregon Financing, the rest was secured by a $500,000, 20-year mortgage at 5% interest. Over 500 individuals, businesses, foundation grants and loans were given to raise the needed amount.

With the successful raising of the total $2.4 million (debt and equity) to purchase the land and construct a new theatre, the building project was competed ahead of schedule in May 2011. The new theatre has an Art Deco facade and is three prefabricated steel-sided buildings that are linked together. This design was to give the theatre an "old building refurbished" look to complement the surrounding area. It has a spacious lobby, has 164 seats, and is 60% larger than the old one; the stage has acoustic panels, baffling, and a heating/air-conditioning system for minimal noise. The new theatre provides the offices, dressing rooms, and rehearsal space that was lacking in the old one.

Camelot's brand-new home opened with the production of *Sweeney Todd* in the James Morrison Collier Theatre in June 2011. It joined then with other Valley theatrical organizations, from the Oregon Shakespeare Festival to the Craterian, in providing top-quality productions—but in the tiny town of Talent. Although Livia Genise left the theatre in early 2016 and an Interim Artistic Director was named, she was a prime mover for this entity with the Camelot making few changes in its then ongoing production schedule.

Sources: Camelot Theatre Company website; Hughley, *Oregonian*, July 23, 2011.

James Collier: The Patron
of the Performing Arts

*B*ORN IN 1938, JAMES (JIM) MORRISON COLLIER grew up in Des Moines, Iowa; he earned a B.A. degree in English from the University of Iowa and an M.A. in English Education from Drake University (1970). Jim taught English in Wisconsin and California during his thirty-five-year career, including twenty years at alternative high schools for troubled youths. Considered a kind and gentle man, he took on the role of a philanthropist after inheriting what was called a "significant" amount of money from his mother and stepfather, Mary and Raymond Baker.

Raymond Baker met Pioneer Hi-Bred founder Henry Wallace in 1926. Fascinated by Wallace's work with corn hybrids, Baker two years later became Hi-Bred's second employee. As Pioneer Hi-Bred's lead plant-breeder for forty-three years, Raymond Baker developed many of the company's hybrid seed corns and helped bring it to becoming the world's largest seed-corn company. He retired in 1971 as a vice president and died in 1999 at age ninety-two. DuPont bought for cash and stock the remaining 80% of Pioneer Hi-Bred in 1999 that it didn't already own.

In the early 2000s, Jim Collier made "generous" gifts to the Des Moines Opera, Drake University, Des Moines Symphony, and Roosevelt High School (his high school). He donated Steinway pianos, funded scholarships, endowed care for the elderly, and funded an Apprentice Artist program with the Des Moines Opera. For his donations to Drake, he was nominated in 2006 as the Outstanding Philanthropist of Central Iowa.

As his Master's thesis was written on Shakespeare's Julius Caesar—and with his deep interest in classical music and the performing arts—it was natural for him to be drawn to the Oregon Shakespeare Festival (OSF) and this area. After his retirement from teaching, Collier in April 2003 moved to the Rogue Valley Manor in Medford; once settling here, he became a major benefactor of the arts.

Jim Collier was the driving financial force with the building of the new Camelot Theatre with a "substantial but undisclosed" series of gifts; in appreciation, the Camelot's new 164-seat facility was named the James Morrison Collier Theatre. On opening night in June 2011, he dressed as a king and made an entrance to say, "Long live Camelot!" to the audience.

The Craterian was next. In August 2012, the long-time Craterian Theater supporter gave it a "very substantial," but also undisclosed amount of money. In appreciation, the board renamed it as the "Craterian Theater at The Collier Center for the Performing Arts." A few years later, the Holly Theatre restoration project released the news in 2016 that he had made a "substantial gift in the six figures" to pay for an elevator at the historic Holly Theatre.

Jim Collier frequently underwrites programs at the Rogue Valley Symphony, Oregon Shakespeare Festival, Youth Symphony of Southern Oregon, Britt Festivals, Rogue Valley Chorale, Siskiyou Violins, Southern Oregon Repertory Singers, and numerous others; these supported groups play throughout the region, including at the Collier Center, SOU's Music Recital Hall, the OSF, and the Collier Theatre (Camelot). Affectionately known as "the Piano Man," he has also donated eighteen grand and upright pianos (at this time) to organizations here and in Iowa. The Executive Director of the Craterian at its re-naming was quoted: "I'm not sure who he isn't supporting." And Southern Oregon is so much the better for this.

Sources: Drake University, May 31, 2006; Iowa State University: "Raymond F. Baker Center for Plant Breeding"; Varble, *Medford Mail Tribune,* June 26, 2011; Varble, *Medford Mail Tribune,* August 31, 2012; *Medford Mail Tribune,* February 24, 2016.

The Britt Festival

*T*AKE THE DREAM OF AN INDIVIDUAL, ADD an historic gold-mining town, and a nearly perfect summer climate, and you have the recipe for an outdoor summer music festival," wrote John Trudeau, the founder of the Britt Music Festival. In 1961, he and his friend, Sam McKinney, visited Southern Oregon as they searched for a site to produce a summer festival. Both worked then at Portland State College (now a University), and Trudeau would be there for thirty-two years, becoming a full professor, appointed department chairman, and ultimately selected to be the Dean of the School of Fine and Performing Arts.

Once in Jacksonville, McKinney and Trudeau heard that the 1850s-homesteaded estate of photographer Peter Britt was available. Taking thousands of photographs, Britt had chronicled fifty years of life and growth in Southern Oregon, from miners and ranchers to orchards and mountains. Peter Britt was also a premier horticulturist, who planted the first fruit trees in the region and opened Oregon's first winery.

The two men saw that Britt's hillside not only had a beautiful view, but excellent natural acoustics for outdoor presentations. They convinced Jacksonville's mayor and city council that their dream was doable. They recruited the first orchestra for its August 11, 1963 debut and two-week classical season; it was the only outdoor summer music festival then in the Pacific Northwest. Workmen constructed the temporary stage with plywood and canvas; the lighting came from forty-five, 75-watt bulbs hung inside #10 tin cans that were strung from above.

One year later, 100 valley residents formed the Britt Festival Society in a meeting at the Jacksonville Museum. Jackson County in 1971

Attendees enjoying one of the Britt Festival's outdoor concerts in 2014.

purchased the eleven-acre Britt property for $40,000 and agreed to a long-term lease with the Britt Festival Association. Fourteen years after the opening concert, a new pavilion with a saw-tooth ceiling and hinged glazed-panels replaced the temporary stage — and this allowed the Britt to offer more than its exclusive classical music. Bench seats were added later with handicapped access and restrooms.

Steve Sachs and David Zaslow in 1979 produced the first jazz concert at the Britt, and the festival has had performers over the years such as Mel Torme, Billy Idol, the Neville Brothers, Count Basie, Jean-Pierre Rampal, Christopher Parkening, Pinchas Zukerman, Diane Schuur, Dave Brubeck, Garrison Keillor, and so many more.

During the twenty-fifth silver anniversary in 1987, John Trudeau retired as its director and conductor; the conductor of the Oregon Symphony, James DePreist, replaced him. By the time of Trudeau's death in 2008, the festival had grown to a four-month-long performing arts event from June into September, featuring top names in classical, dance, pop, rock, and musical theater. Its present classical orchestra is twice the size of the first chamber orchestra.

With a maximum capacity of 2,200, the Jackson County Parks Department maintains the facilities while the Association operates them under the county's lease. As thousands enjoy the wonderful performances under the stars, many of Peter Britt's original trees are still producing fruit. The Sequoia sapling that Britt planted in 1862 (on the day his first child was born) stands more than 200 feet tall, down a path fifty yards from the marked home site. The setting is perfect.

Sources: Mason, *Oregon Encyclopedia*: "Britt Music Festival"; Britt Festival at its website.

Films Made in
Southern Oregon

S OUTHERN OREGON HAS HAD ITS SHARE OF feature films, independents ("indies"), and made-for-TV filmed here. In the 1975 film, *Rooster Cogburn*, John Wayne played the one-eyed, alcoholic, out-of-shape federal marshal who met and was won over by Katharine Hepburn's tough, New England schoolteacher character. The river float scenes were filmed on the Rogue, and dating back to this film, John Wayne made Deer Creek Ranch, located one mile west of Selma, his private hideaway.

In 1960, the television show "Route 66" aired two episodes set in Grants Pass, Merlin, and Wolf Creek. As Marshal Matt Dillon in "Gunsmoke," James Arness dove into the cold Rogue River waters while escaping outlaws; this series was the country's longest-running, prime-time, live-action drama that ran for over twenty seasons. The 1994 film, *The River Wild*, was filmed on the Rogue and with film stars Kevin Bacon and Meryl Streep.

Despite the rumors, it turns out that the famous cliff-diving scene in the 1969 film, *Butch Cassidy and the Sundance Kid*, did not happen at Hellgate Canyon. The Rocky Mountains provided the cliff and river scene with the precipice duplicated on a Hollywood soundstage. The filming of two stuntmen jumping from a crane into a water tank was combined with a painting of the river and bluffs on glass.

Jacksonville with its turn-of-the-century buildings has been another favorite. For example, *The Great Northfield Minnesota Raid*, was filmed there in 1970 and released two years later. Universal Pictures had the town appear like the 1870s where Jesse James and his gang had tough problems robbing a bank, including when an outlaw was locked inside the vault.

A scene from the movie *Wild*, starring Reese Witherspoon, filmed along the Pacific Crest Trail just above Ashland. (Photo courtesy of Fox Searchlight)

Planks were laid over concrete sidewalks, telephone poles removed, and streets covered with dirt. When the producers asked for extras, needing only 200, thousands of area residents showed up with many in Western garb. In addition, a prior remake of *Last of the Wild Horses* (1948) and a made-for-TV rendition of *Inherit the Wind* (1987) were also filmed in that town.

Owing to a favorable movie-making climate, more Indies are being filmed in this area now and with well-known actors and actresses. The great majority of the near–forty productions filmed in part or their entirety in Southern Oregon within the last ten years are Indies. Two recently made were *Redwood Highway* and *Night Moves*.

In late 2012, crew members working on *Night Moves* came to eat at Porters restaurant in the historic Medford downtown railroad depot. Liking the setting, one of the members approached a co-owner and asked if they could shoot a scene there. Porters agreed and later could add a film credit to its list of TV commercials. The movie is about three eco-terrorists who conspire to blow up a dam, and the production was filmed in Roseburg, the Applegate Valley, Medford, and Ashland. *Night Moves* features Jesse Eisenberg, who had the starring role as Facebook founder, Mark Zuckerberg, in the box-office hit, *The Social Network*, as well as Dakota Fanning, who has appeared in dozens of movies including *War of the Worlds*.

Redwood Highway tells the story about a woman (Marie) who was living in a retirement community in Southern Oregon, but embarked on an eighty-mile journey on foot along the Redwood Highway to the Pacific Ocean. Premiered in 2013, Marie is played by Shirley Knight—a Tony, Emmy, and Golden Globe winner—who was twice nominated for an Academy Award. Tom Skerritt, who acted in *Alien*, *Top Gun*, and *A River Runs Through It*, is featured in a supporting role. The locations ranged from Cave Junction and downtown Grants Pass to the Applegate River Lodge, Talent, and Ashland.

In 2014, the hit movie *Wild*, starring Reese Witherspoon, was filmed along portions of the Pacific Crest Trail in the mountains above Ashland. In addition, a lengthy scene involving Reese's character, Cheryl Strayed, was filmed on the Plaza in downtown Ashland. Again, locals were hired as extras to populate the Plaza. Witherspoon received an Academy Award nomination for her performance.

With the outdoors and amenities of this area, the snap of a clapboard with the shout for "Action!" is being heard more often than ever before—with new productions currently in progress.

Sources: Miller, *Medford Mail Tribune*, June 21, 2009; Pfeil, *Medford Mail Tribune*, October 23, 2012; Morgan, *Medford Mail Tribune*, May 23, 2014; on various names, an Internet search also brings citations.

Hollywood Lives
in Southern Oregon

*P*AST CELEBRITIES WHO HAVE LIVED OR BEEN IDENTIFIED with our region include Ginger Rogers, Clark Gable, John Wayne, Zane Grey, Rose Maddox, and Kim Novak, to name a few. Jim Belushi built an expansive house on the thirteen-acre former Elks picnic grounds near Eagle Point with 1,800 feet of river frontage, along with his commitment to helping the Holly Theatre finalize its renovation funding needs. It's even been rumored that Johnny Depp lives (or lived) in Kirstie Alley's former home that she owned in the Applegate.

It's easy to see why Hollywood's celebrities would choose to live here — with our rural setting, ease of movement, lack of congestion, and freedom from autograph seekers. They usually choose the anonymity; for example, Jim Belushi had owned his Rogue River land for two years before the story broke that his construction of his retreat complex was also the subject of a reality TV show named "Building Belushi."

The Rogue River, of course, is a favorite area. Kim Novak, who's probably best known for her role in *Vertigo*, lives on a ranch with her veterinarian husband along the river where the couple raise llamas and horses. Ginger Rodgers bought a 1,000-acre ranch near Shady Cove in 1940 before moving to Medford in the early 1990s.

Patrick Duffy lives along the Rogue River near Eagle Point and is routinely spotted around this area. Duffy was working as a house painter when he landed the role of Mark Harris in the TV series "Man from Atlantis" (1977). Two years later, he won the role of Bobby Ewing on "Dallas" (1978), which he starred in from 1978-1985/1986-1991 and has appeared in numerous TV shows and movies since then.

Director/producer Howard Koch (*The Odd Couple*; *Plaza Suite*; *Airplane!*; *Maverick*; "Hawaiian Eye"; and more) had a place on the river near Duffy's.

Jack Elam was nearly a fixture at Omar's Restaurant in Ashland. His genre was generally playing the "bad guy" in 1950's Westerns. Among his performances were co-starring with James Garner in the western comedies *Support Your Local Sheriff* (1969) and *Support Your Local Gunfighter* (1971). In an interview, he guessed that at least 300 of his movies and TV appearances had been Westerns. In 1997, he was inducted into the National Cowboy Hall of Fame after moving to Ashland from Santa Barbara.

Bruce Campbell was known for his role as Ash Williams in Sam Raimi's hit *Evil Dead* film series in the 1980s, and is probably best known for his role as Sam Axe, the former Navy SEAL and covert agent, on the TV series "Burn Notice." Campbell lives in Jacksonville and is also frequently seen around town and in Ashland.

Annette O'Toole has worked consistently in TV and film for more than thirty years. Among her credits are *48 Hours* with Nick Nolte and Eddie Murphy, *Superman III* (as Clark Kent's boyhood girlfriend), *It* (the Steven King novel made into film), and the TV series "Superman" for six years (as Superman's mother). She has been married to Michael McKean (*This Is Spinal Tap*) since 1999 and both were nominated for an Academy Award for Best Song in the film *A Mighty Wind* (2003). McKean has appeared in some 100 movies and television shows, including as Lenny on "Laverne and Shirley." They live part of the time in Ashland.

And there are more: In 1992, Kevin Hagan moved to Grants Pass and continued his acting career until his death in 2005; he was best known for his role as the kind Doc Baker on Michael Landon's "Little House on the Prairie" (1974-1983), along with roles on "Gunsmoke," "Bonanza," "Lost in Space," and others. Steve Reeves — the bodybuilder who won the titles of "Mr. America," "Mr. World," and "Mr. Universe" by age twenty-five — also starred in eighteen films (e.g., *Hercules*) and lived in the Applegate area.

Nationally recognized country singer, Rose Maddox, lived on a ranch near Ashland; her brother, Don Maddox, and surviving member of the Maddox Brothers & Rose team, owns and still works the ranch. In the 2000's, he was "rediscovered" as an artist.

Emmy-nominated writer, Sam Egan, lives in Ashland. He is probably best known for his five seasons of work on Showtime/MGM's "The Outer Limits," as the executive producer of the series. which ran on Showtime and the Sci Fi Channel. Before his five seasons on "The Outer Limits," Egan produced and wrote CBS's "Northern Exposure." Included in Egan's many writing and producing awards are nominations for an Emmy and four Gemini's (Canada's TV awards).

Rocker Steve Miller owned a house, recording studio, and huge barn (to house his tour bus) in the Williams area for ten years (1976-1986). He was there when he released his mega 1970's hits such as "Fly Like an Eagle."

Robert Clouse was a hard-working director who was probably best known for his two most successful films: *Enter the Dragon* (1973) and *Game of Death* (1978). He worked in cinema due to the fact he was completely deaf. Clouse used assistant directors who verified that actors had delivered their lines correctly; he died in Ashland in 1997.

There are and will be more added to this list — as time goes on!

Sources: Conrad, "Role Call," *Medford Mail Tribune*, April 17, 2011; *Medford Mail Tribune*, October 17, 2010; as well, a variety of articles on celebrities mentioned above.

The Ashland Independent
Film Festival

S TARTING IN OCTOBER 2001 AT Ashland's Varsity Theatre, the Ashland Independent Film Festival (AIFF) has steadily grown to become one of the standout independent, non-studio film exhibits of the 1,500 that take place throughout the country. A small cadre of locals during the late 1990s believed that an independent film festival in the small town would complement Southern Oregon's established cultural and artistic endeavors. With strong support from volunteers and others, the husband and wife team of Steven and D.W. Wood led the way to the non-profit AIFF's start.

The enterprise needed the strong support of John Schweiger, the owner of the Varsity Theatre and founder/owner of Coming Attractions, Inc., that owns and operates numerous theatres on the West Coast, including the Varsity Theatre and Ashland Street Cinema. Credited as the AIFF's Founding Advisor and Benefactor, Schweiger from the very start made the Varsity Theatre and office space available for the festival. The historic theatre with its Art Deco façade and lobby was perfectly suited for this.

The first AIFF sold 3,000 tickets and over four days showed seventy-three films with twenty-two world premiers, chosen from 157 entries. Despite the critical acclaim, however, the festival did not take place the following year, showing the need for more financial support. The AIFF returned in March 2003, adding advance ticket sales (3,500 tickets sold) with a five-day period; sixty-seven films were presented, forty-three being first-time theatrical showings, or world premieres. Quality films were shown and two selections of the 2005 AIFF made the final list to qualify for the Best Documentary Feature at the Academy Awards.

The Varsity Theatre in downtown Ashland, home to the
Ashland Independent Film Festival.

The festival presents short films and features in numerous ways,
including drama, comedy, documentary, and animation. Although
drawing throughout the U.S. and overseas, the AIFF is a prime place for
Oregonians to present their films from and about this state. The
audiences are predominately from a fifty-mile radius of Ashland, but it
also has drawn well known film personalities, such as Bruce Campbell,
Les Blank, Ed Hardy, Helen Hunt, Albert Maysles, Elvis Mitchell, and

Will Vinton, among others. The filmmakers interact with the audience at the AIFF's opening night party, after each screening, and at the awards.

Nine juried and audience awards are presented with film clips of the top five in each category, including Best Feature. Judges review entries in categories of narrative, documentary, experimental, animation, and student-produced films. Among the audience voted awards is the Gerald Hirschfeld A.S.C. Award for Cinematography that honors the Ashland resident whose films included *Fail-Safe* and *Young Frankenstein*.

The annual event now includes showings at the Ashland Armory, and ticket sales have reached 16,000. Grants from the Academy of Motion Picture Arts and Sciences, National Endowment for the Arts, Carpenter Foundation, Collins Foundation, Oregon Cultural Trust, and Oregon Arts Commission, individual contributions, and memberships have stabilized its finances.

Each year nearly 18,000 tickets are distributed with 7,000–8,000 attendees and some ninety documentaries, features, and short films being exhibited. More than half of the some 150 screenings are shown to capacity audiences and 80 percent of the seats are typically filled at the five-day, April event.

From volunteers in 2001, the AIFF now has an Executive Director, staff of four, and 300-plus volunteers. Coming Attraction Theatres and the Film Festival also produce annually the "Varsity World Film Week" in early October that showcases ten to twelve foreign films from countries ranging from Brazil, Norway, and India to France, Mexico, and Indonesia.

MovieMaker magazine has several times named the Ashland Independent Film Festival as one of the "Top 25 Coolest Festivals in the World." It is a showcase for this area, and before was just a dream by a few.

Sources: Ashland Independent Film Festival at its website; Battistella, *Oregon Encyclopedia*: "Ashland Independent Film Festival."

Bert Webber:
The Consummate
Researcher and Publisher

*B*ORN IN 1921 IN MARYLAND, Ebbert True "Bert" Webber was the first born; his father was in the military and his mother died when he was only six. He joined the Army Signal Corps in 1940 after his high school graduation. Stationed in Kodiak, Alaska, Bert developed a life-long passion for photography, which later brought him to the New York Eastman School of Photography. He was in Europe during World War II as an official Signal Corps photographer.

He and his wife, Margie, had first met in San Francisco as teenagers. Corresponding during World War II, they married in 1944; Bert headed overseas to Europe, while Margie completed her training as a nurse. After the war, the two resided in Washington, where Bert earned his living in different ways: running his own retail store as a commercial photographer and photo-finisher for ten years, a "stringer" for the *Seattle Post-Intelligencer*, and selling typewriters for Remington Rand.

He earned a bachelor's degree in 1965 at Whitworth College in Spokane, Washington, with a double major in Journalism and Secondary Education, and then moved to Lake Oswego as the high school's librarian and social studies teacher. While there, he obtained in 1968 a master's degree in library science from the University of Portland, while also publishing a bibliography on "The Pacific Northwest in Books" — and discovering his true calling.

Bert and Margie moved to the Rogue Valley in 1968 where he worked as a librarian at Medford High School. At this time, his fascination with Northwest history and love for research photojournalism drove him to publishing his own regional history books. Combining historical research, journalism, and librarian skills, from 1967 to 2003, Bert Webber authored eighty-six non-fiction books, the majority involving Oregon history. Many were collaborations with Margie and published through their Central Point business, the Webb Research Group and Pacific Northwest Books.

The books covered a remarkable diversity of subjects. From *Indians along the Oregon Trail* and *Battleship Oregon: Bulldog of the Navy* to *Flood: Ashland Devastated New Year's Day, 1997* and *Railroading in Southern Oregon and the Founding of Medford*. He tackled dredging for gold, logging and sawmilling, and beachcombing to railroads, the city of Jacksonville, and lighthouses.

Describing the overland passage was a favorite with several books being transcriptions of pioneer diaries, annotations, and maps. Bert and Margie wrote books on the Oregon Caves, the Southern Oregon Symphonic Band (in which he played the baritone horn), the Rajneeshpuram postal service, the lost Oregon coastal towns of Lakeport and Bayocean, covered bridges, and the DeAutremont train robbery of 1923.

Webber died in 2006 and his papers are in the Hoover Institution Archives at Stanford University. His family continues to manage Pacific Northwest Books and the numerous publications that he created.

Sources: Battistella, *Oregon Encyclopedia*: "Ebbert T. (Bert) Webber (1921-2006)"; "Obituary: Ebbert True (Bert) Webber," *Medford Mail Tribune*, April 23, 2006; see also, Pacific Northwest Books at its website.

Lisa Rinna: The Medford Actress Who Made It

$\mathcal{B}$ORN ON JULY 11, 1963, IN NEWPORT BEACH, California, Lisa Rinna grew up in Medford, after her family moved there. Her father, Frank Rinna, had graduated summa cum laude from the California College of Arts and Crafts; after working for the *San Francisco Chronicle* in the early1950s as a staff artist, he freelanced on different accounts that included Harry & David. While working on this, Harry & David offered him in 1970 the job of Executive Art Director, which involved moving to Medford. Frank retired from there in 1988 with his famed watercolors featured at the Britt and in different private collections.

A cheerleader from junior high through high school, Lisa attended Medford elementary school, junior high school and graduated in 1981 from Medford Senior High school. While in high school, she acted in musicals such as *Fiddler on the Roof* and *Hair*. While there, she dreamed of "a more fabulous life." She studied drama at the University of Oregon after high school, but dropped out after her first term when she was denied entry into the advanced acting program.

She moved to San Francisco where she pursued a modeling career. In 1986, she had her lips injected with silicone on a whim for that "pillowy" look, along with a "real big 'boob' job," as she said. She switched gears one year later and moved to Los Angeles to become an actress, landing early roles on TV commercials, guest appearances on "Baywatch," and appearing in low-budget movies. Rinna appeared in 1989 on her first TV show, "The Hogan Family."

Her career took off in 1992 when she took on the role of Billie Reed on the daytime soap opera "Days of Our Lives." This role earned her

Lisa Rinna modeling at The Heart Truth's
Fashion Show in 2008.

back-to-back *Soap Opera Digest* awards in 1994 and 1995, including
"Outstanding Female Newcomer." Lisa moved in 1996 to Fox's prime-
time soap "Melrose Place," where she played the scheming Taylor
McBride; this character was also an instant hit, and she soon met her
future husband, actor Harry Hamlin.

Hamlin had graduated from Yale University in 1974 with a BA in
Drama and Psychology. He then attended the American Conservatory
Theatre's Advanced Actor Training Program and earned a Master of
Fine Arts degree in acting. Hamlin appeared in the 1976 television
production of "Taming of the Shrew" and also had the title role in the
1979 television miniseries "Studs Lonigan" — but his big-screen break
was the starring role in the 1981 Greek mythology fantasy epic of *Clash
of the Titans.*

His career faltered, but after two miniseries, Hamlin's popularity skyrocketed when he starred from 1986 to 1991 on the popular NBC legal-drama series "L.A. Law," as the principled attorney Michael Kuzak. (In 1987, he was voted as *People* magazine's "Sexiest Man Alive.") After leaving the series, he acted in more movies and direct-to-video features. Lisa and Harry married in 1997.

Rinna created a stir in 1998 when she posed nude while six-months pregnant (with daughter Delilah Belle) on the cover of the September issue of *Playboy* magazine; she gave birth to the couple's second daughter, Amelia Gray, in 2001. Lisa was again the cover model in May 2009 — this time in a skimpy leotard, suit jacket, lacy peek-a-boo bra, and fishnets.

After "Melrose Place," she hosted or co-hosted several TV shows, including "Soap Talk," for which she earned four Emmy nominations in the "Outstanding Talk Show Host" category. Rinna joined the cast of the second season (2006) of "Dancing with the Stars" as one of the celebrity competitors. The appearance helped her (and Hamlin who was on this show during season three) land the lead role in Broadway's *Chicago* in 2007 — the same year she began being the red-carpet commentator for TV Guide Network at such events as the Emmy Awards.

Lisa Rinna has written three books, released a series of exercise DVDs, launched a fashion collection (Belle Gray) on TV's QVC, had a reality show with her husband ("Harry Loves Lisa"), served as Anderson Cooper's co-host on his daytime talk show — and in 2014 became a lead player in the reality series, "The Real Housewives of Beverly Hills," that continues at the time of this book's publication.

Lisa used her exotic looks, infectious energy, and savvy business acumen to become one of the very recognizable faces in Hollywood — and still visits Medford. It will be interesting to see how she continues with her career and life.

Sources: Wikipedia: "Harry Hamlin"; Varble, *Medford Mail Tribune,* November 28, 2014; Biography: "Lisa Rinna"; Morgan, *Medford Mail Tribune*, January 22, 2016.

P.K. Hallinan

P.K. HALLINAN WAS BORN IN LOS ANGELES in 1944 and spent his youth in Bethesda, Maryland, and the San Fernando Valley. By his early twenties (1967), he was a toy department manager for a major retailer (Sear and Roebuck) with two young sons. And bored to death: "I needed to make a change," he wrote much later in his book, *A Life That Matters.* He was earning a living but then paying it all out for bills. He thought that night about how to make something of his life: He decided to be a "famous novelist" and write the "Great American Novel."

"Well, it also helps if you know how to write, but that didn't stop me. I plowed ahead and churned out two really terrible manuscripts that are now in a landfill in Kearny Mesa, California, where they belong." And to do this, he left his retail job for another that gave him better working hours.

Christmas was drawing near and his wife asked him to write a "little children's book" for their kids as a Christmas present. Over the next two weeks, he scribbled out a story and drew some pen-and-ink cartoons of his kids. Much to his surprise, his kids, family, and friends liked it and said he should write more children's books. He did.

While he worked on his books, P.K. also worked as a project scheduler for Lockheed (1970-1973); in 1972, a publisher wrote that it wanted to publish one of his children's books. They hired an illustrator, however, paid him more than P.K., and the author was aghast at the illustrations. He decided to never let anyone else do his drawings on his books — which meant, he had to learn how to draw.

He started on his next book, and a publisher accepted this one on his terms. But P.K. continued working to pay the bills while he created different children's books. From 1973–1985, he worked for a company in San Diego as the Director of Marketing Communications, but lost his position when a large Chicago company bought the business. ("This after twelve long years of sort-of loyal service," he wrote later.) He had published five children's books by then, but still needed to have a day job; P.K. worked in corporate America for more than twenty years after he had sold his first children's book.

Then the time came. A publisher asked him to send one in, as it didn't have enough books for its spring catalog. *How Do I Love You?* was soon published and went on to become his best-selling book ever, now nearing the two-million-copies-sold mark. "It was simply a matter of preparation and opportunity crossing." In 1990 he and his family moved from San Diego to the Rogue Valley "for a change of scenery and to enjoy the seasons."

P.K. didn't feel successful two years later, even though he was: He questioned, "Is that all there is?" Feeling that there was a "spiritual hole" within himself and his marriage, he and his wife Jeanne began their spiritual search. After visiting different churches in the area, friends invited them to the Applegate Christian Fellowship in Ruch, where P.K. "found himself sitting with 5,000 Christians in the outdoor amphitheater." Liking that they played their guitars "well," he went back. "I went for the music, but I stayed for the Word," he often said.

His true conversion to Christianity did not happen until nearly one year later. It was November 4, 1993. Scheduled to do book sales and signings during school visits in Central California, he was concentrating on reading the bible in a Fresno hotel room. The readings crystalized his conversion that night. A few weeks later, Jon Courson asked him to start a men's morning Bible study.

P.K. became the assistant pastor in Green Springs in the mountains above Ashland; when the pastor left for a fellowship in the Salem area, Hallinan was asked in July 1995 to be the new pastor in Green Springs. He accepted. As strange as it may seem, "I was offered the position of pastor even though I had been a Christian for only eighteen months," he wrote in his book. After this and another pastor position out of town, he founded in 1999 and became the pastor for the tiny Joy Chapel Christian Fellowship in downtown Ashland. Held in the Community Center across from Lithia Park for some fifteen years, P.K. at the same time was creating more books.

All in all, P.K. has written and illustrated nearly 100 children's books, selling more than 9,000,000 copies worldwide. His children's books are filled with rhythm, rhyme, and life lessons about kindness and love—covering topics of inspiration, friendship, love, relationships, and life values. *Early Childhood News* recognized his book *For the Love of Our Earth* (1992) as one of America's "100 Best Product Picks for Children." *We're Very Good Friends, My Mother and I* (2015) and *We're Very Good Friends, My Father and I* (2015) made the "Top Five" of Waldenbooks National Bestsellers list. His favorite award was when Focus on the Family named his *Let's Be Kind* as "One of America's Top 10 Children's Books in 2008."

He lives with his wife, Jeanne, his dog Betty, and "a very annoying cat" in the mountains above Ashland, Oregon.

Sources: Amazon.com: "P.K. Hallinan"; Hallinan, *Medford Mail Tribune*, January 11, 2015; "Meet PK" at author's website; Decker, *Medford Mail Tribune*, April 8, 2015; P.K. Hallinan, *A Life That Matters*, Kregel Publications.

Ted Adams:
Comic Books (and More)

*T*ED ADAMS GREW UP IN GRANTS PASS, Oregon, and graduated in 1990 from Southern Oregon State College (now SOU). He worked at the SOU Bookstore to support his education and later received an MBA from Notre Dame. His father, Brady Adams, had moved the family to Grants Pass in 1972 to work as a loan officer and later became president of Evergreen Federal Bank in the mid-1980s. Brady—a Republican known for keeping a tight rein on budgets—served eight years in the Oregon Legislature and was president of the Oregon Senate for the 1997 and 1999 sessions. When he wasn't involved in politics, he was working to improve downtown Grants Pass and Josephine County, not to mention working on twenty local nonprofit boards over time. He died at age seventy in 2015.

Ted inherited his father's work ethic and also knew from an early age that he wanted to be a business owner. After his education, his passion for graphic design led to working for different comic book publishing companies. In 1999, Ted founded IDW (standing for "Idea+Design Works") with three others in San Diego. The company was envisioned originally as a creative services business and only tried comic book publishing as a "gamble" a couple of years later. Adams currently serves as the company's CEO and Publisher.

IDW began creating art and graphic design for entertainment companies, all on a work-for-hire basis. The four who started the business had all worked at WildStorm Productions. When DC Comics (i.e., Superman, Batman, Wonder Woman, and the Green Lantern) bought WildStorm, it didn't have interest in its creative service business and turned this over to them. Without the usual start-up hurdles, IDW was making money before it opened its first office.

IDW was making enough money that the group decided to gamble once a year on a new business. After trying a pilot for a failed TV show, producing an art book, and then *30 Days of Night* (a three-issue horror-vampire comic book miniseries, later made into a movie by Sony), they had their first hit comic book with *CSI*. This story is about an elite team of police forensic-evidence investigating experts who worked their cases in Las Vegas — and was the seventh longest running TV series. No one thought about this as a licensed comic book: that is, until IDW came along and published the serial comic books in 2003, after the TV series had been running for three years.

IDW Publishing now is one of the top four U.S. comic book publishers, and the #1 supplier of licensed comic books. Over eighty IDW titles have appeared on *The New York Times Best Sellers* list. In fiscal-year 2015 alone, IDW published over 500 unique comic book titles and over 250 graphic novel titles. (While a comic book tells a story over many issues, graphic novels have their storylines wrapped up in one or two books; graphic novels are much longer and tend to be more complex.)

IDW publishes some of the most popular titles in the industry, including: Hasbro's *Transformers, G.I. Joe, and My Little Pony;* Paramount/CBS's *Star Trek;* Nickelodeon's *Teenage Mutant Ninja Turtles;* Toho's *Godzilla;* Twentieth Century Fox's *The X-Files;* Sony's *Ghostbusters;* multiple monthly Disney titles; and many more. It also publishes classic comic reprints, but concentrates in taking existing entertainment brands and turning them into comic books — not competing with the likes of Marvel's superhero comics.

Ted's expertise is his ability to bring in the best talented artists and writers, and then work with them for success. His team's comic books have evolved into multiple Eisner awards (the Oscars for the comic world). In 2007, New Jersey-based telecommunications company IDT purchased a "major interest" in IDW. The large capital backing allowed IDW to reach out in different ways. (IDT is a global provider of domestic and international calling services, voice and data conferencing options, and prepaid calling cards).

In 2013, the company began to fund, develop, and produce television series based on IDW's books. Its projects include "Winterworld" (Earth turned into an "icy hell"), "V-Wars" (global vampire conflict), and "Dirk

Gently" (BBC's holistic detective series); its TV series "Wynonna Earp" currently airs on the SyFy (once named, "Sci-Fi") channel.

IDW is a very successful entertainment-oriented company with spin-offs not only in television series, but also in merchandise, tabletop games, and art books from its comics—and Ted Adams is a prime reason for its success.

Sources: CBR News (Ted Adams); IDW Website; Verrier, *LA Times*, October 17, 2013; *Raider News*, Spring 2016.

Kim Novak

MARILYN PAULINE "KIM" NOVAK WAS BORN in 1933. Her father was a Chicago railroad dispatcher and both parents were of Czech descent. As she grew up, she wanted an art career and won a scholarship to the Chicago Art Institute. Kim Novak's curvy figure, low voice, and natural beauty, however, led into working as a teen fashion model and a later national tour in 1953 promoting refrigerators as "Miss Deepfreeze." She came into films by accident. Kim was visiting a movie studio in Hollywood with a friend after being in San Francisco on a modeling job. She was asked to do a walk-on as a model in the Jane Russell movie, *The French Line*. Columbia soon put her under contract.

When domineering Columbia head Harry Cohn demanded that she change her name to "Kit Marlowe," she refused, saying that this was not a real person; she only compromised by changing her first name to "Kim." Her film debut was in *Pushover* in 1954 for which she received good performance reviews. In six years, she made fourteen films, including starring roles the following year. Novak's signature films of *Picnic* (1955), *Pal Joey* (1957), *Bell, Book and Candle* (1958), and *Vertigo* (1958) — her most famous film — were made during this time. With her meteoric rise to stardom, she was on the front cover of magazines such as *Time* and one of Hollywood's top box office stars in the late '50s and early '60s.

After playing the title role in the 1965's *The Amorous Adventures of Moll Flanders*," Novak left Hollywood to take time off. She didn't like the system, its underpayment of actors (especially actresses), and wanted time to herself. She would return to perform in other films, including for television, but the time between roles grew longer. Hollywood's demands were getting in the way of her personal life.

Kim Novak. (Image courtesy Robert Malloy)

She married Robert Malloy in 1976, an equine veterinarian who had been treating her animals, and they built a log home along the Williamson River near Chiloguin, which flows into Upper Klamath Lake. Kim's ties to Oregon dated back to her father's family, the Novaks, who settled in Scappoose, now a Portland bedroom community. They came from Czechoslovakia and settled there; her grandfather had been a logger. Even after her father moved to Chicago to take the railroad job, her parents and Kim headed back to Portland every year for a family reunion.

Her love of painting (oils, pastels, and watercolors), riding her horse, being outdoors, and living beside a river became her life. After using the Williamson River home as a weekend retreat, she and her husband eventually moved there fulltime to enjoy the outdoors of canoeing, hiking, and skiing. They came to the Rogue Valley in 1997 and settled along the Rogue River in what had once been a hunting and fishing lodge. When it burned down in 2000, the fire destroyed many of her souvenirs of the Hollywood days, including an autobiography that she had been writing. Although a new home was built to their specifications and design, the irreplaceable memorabilia couldn't be. She took this as a sign that "it wasn't supposed to be" and moved on.

A few years ago, the couple found themselves in a dispute with the Environmental Protection Agency (EPA) over their property. When two large trees pulled away by the roots and plunged into the Rogue River, the ensuing bank started to erode, a common problem on the river. To save the bank, the couple supported it with large rocks along a 345-foot stretch of frontage. Unfortunately, they didn't obtain the appropriate permits. Although the U.S. Army Corps of Engineers was agreeable to giving an after-the-fact permit, complications arose on the design approval for a new "rip-rap" wall owing to all of the involved agencies. The dispute was eventually settled on agency terms.

This didn't deter them, of course, from their enjoyment of the Rogue River and Southern Oregon. Her lifelong passion for art carries on, as she continues to work with other artists, including painting a poster for Jacksonville's Britt Music Festival. Although her films are classics, Kim Novak saw her acting career years ago as being a detour from living "life a lot." And that she has done.

Sources: Kristi Turnquist, *Oregonian,* July 31, 2010; Battistella, *Oregon Encyclopedia*: "Kim Novak"; Mann, *Medford Mail Tribune,* Sept. 1, 2009.

Jim Belushi
Comes to Town

*I*F YOU'VE EVER SEEN ACTOR JIM BELUSHI around town — whether at a restaurant, or even at the Pear Blossom Parade — then be ready for more. He's here, building community ties as well as a beautiful home on the banks of the Rogue River.

Jim was born in Chicago in 1954 — the third of four children — to Agnes Demetri (Samaras) and Adam Anastos Belushi, who ran a restaurant. His father was an Albanian immigrant and his mother was of Albanian descent. His brother, John, was born five years before and the family moved one year later to Wheaton, Illinois.

Both having strong interests in acting careers, the older John started off. He performed in summer stock, worked improv comedy, and became part of the famous ensemble, Second City in Chicago, where he perfected his "gonzo" comedic style. Moving later to New York City, he had his big break on the TV variety series, "Saturday Night Live" (1975), which made him a star.

During this time — and after Wheaton Central High School — Jim transferred from a small college to Southern Illinois University, where he earned a degree in Speech and Theater Arts. After graduating from college, he also joined in 1977 the Second City comedy troupe, which proved to be a major launching pad for his career.

In 1978, producer Gary Marshall saw one of his Second City performances and hired him for his first TV role: a part on the NBC sitcom, "Who's Watching the Kids?" One year later, Jim landed a part on a second sitcom, the CBS show "Working Stiffs."

That same year, brother John stole the spotlight with his role as the notorious, beer-swilling Bluto in the box-office hit *National Lampoon's Animal House* (1978). More fame came with Dan Aykroyd, in John Landis's *The Blue Brothers* (1980), with following films such as *Continental Divide* (1981) and *Neighbors* (1981). John tragically died from a drug overdose in 1982.

Still reeling in 1983 from his brother's death, Jim followed in John's footsteps and joined the cast of Saturday Night Live. Audiences roared with laughter at Jim's impersonations of popular celebrities like Hulk Hogan and Arnold Schwarzenegger. His popularity on SNL led to additional roles in films, such as *About Last Night* (1986), *Jumpin' Jack Flash* (1986), *K-9* (1989) and *Curly Sue* (1991). He continued on with more TV and film (now more than a dozen movies), including sequels to *K-9* that went directly to video.

Belushi was the star of "According to Jim" — a popular prime-time TV sitcom about a suburban father — that appeared on ABC from 2001 to 2009 and has been internationally syndicated. Since then, he has been quite active on Broadway, his blues band, and TV.

Trips to visit a friend and his love of fishing brought about the connection with this region. The construction of his house also became a feature, reality TV series, "Building Belushi" on the Do It Yourself Network. The six-episode series followed Jim and his team as they built on the thirteen acres he bought (with 1800 feet of river frontage), once the former 1930s-era Elks picnic ground off Agate road that was some two miles north of White City.

Belushi constructed a 1,200 sq. ft., two-level main house, 650 sq. ft. master suite and bathroom, and a 1,600 sq. ft. bunk house that by itself has three bedrooms and two baths — all with sweeping views of the river or surrounding countryside — not to mention 7,400 sq. ft. of raised decks with walkways. The grounds include a rebuilt stage, garage, barbeque pit, benches and tables that dated back to the Elks summer picnics. The foundation was designed to meet the "100-year flood requirements" and 600,000 pounds of concrete were poured into building one thick, continuous retaining wall and foundation.

Through subcontractor connections who were also working with the Holly Theatre restoration, Jim toured the facilities, became fascinated by it, and was named the honorary chairman of the renovation project. Built in 1930, the 1,000-seat Holly is being restored by Jefferson Live!, which also operates the Cascade Theatre in Redding.

Belushi and his blues band, "The Sacred Hearts," performed a benefit at EdenVale (Eden Valley) Winery for the Holly; one year later, in 2016, he performed another benefit concert to raise money to rebuild the historic Butte Creek Mill in Eagle Point after it burned down. Yes, we are glad that Jim Belushi has come here, joined our community, and continues to help it.

Sources: Mann, *Medford Mail Tribune*, April 7, 2015; Jim/John Belushi biographies.

PART XII

Tourist Attractions

The Jewel of Lithia Park

*T*HIS NINETY-THREE ACRE, EXQUISITE PARK IN THE HEART OF Ashland dates back to a Grants Pass minister, the Reverend J.B. Smith, who arranged for a summer series of lectures there in the 1890s named the "Chautauqua." The name came from the New York Chautauqua Assembly, which presented topics in art, politics, music, literature, and other subjects for several days in the mid-summer. William Jennings Bryan, Susan B. Anthony, and John Phillip Sousa were among the well-known personalities who came there to lecture or perform.

The Reverend Smith with others in September 1892 formed the Southern Oregon Chautauqua Association. Selling a bond issue of $2,500 to purchase eight acres above Ashland Creek, the association with countless volunteers built a large, domed wooden building that held up to 1,000 people for these lectures.

In 1904, the Ladies' Chautauqua Club formed and was a driving force in maintaining the Chautauqua property. Four years later, the Woman's Civic Improvement Club strongly supported an initiative to make this a city park and responsibility. Its residents in 1908 voted "yes" to dedicate all city-owned property on the creek for the park, authorized a tax levy, created a separate park commission, and included park maintenance in the city charter. Ashland tore down an abandoned 1850's flour mill on the plaza, and with landscaping, the town became known for its summer Chautauqua series and Lithia Park. The lower duck pond with its spilling waterfall was constructed in 1910.

Four years later, the owner and editor of the *Ashland Tidings*, Bert Greer, supported a health spa centered on the beneficial aspects of the park's lithium-concentrated water. Although this never came to being, the publicity helped the voters' passage of a $175,000 bond issue, $65,000 of which was earmarked to develop Lithia Park. This was a substantial

The early days in Lithia Park. (Terry Skibby photos)

amount of money then, as the total bond issue in today's terms would be over $4 million dollars—for a town with a population then of 3,000.

The Southern Pacific Railroad was promoting Ashland as a "mineral springs and spa" destination, and with others it also was behind the hiring of John McLaren, the designer and superintendent of San Francisco's Golden Gate Park, to be the landscape architect for the park. Given the available money and support, McLaren agreed, stating that the setting was "the most wonderful natural park" he had ever seen and with "little left to do except enhance nature's work." With more acreage acquired and the landscaping completed, the park's dedication was held over the July 4th holiday in 1916 with a three-day celebration that attracted more than 50,000 people (as estimated by the *Tidings*).

McLaren's landscape plan still forms the park's core and follows the natural canyon of Ashland Creek. Native alders, oaks, conifers, and madrones were planted on the canyon slopes, and other ornamental varieties, such as willows, maples, and sycamores were also brought in. Exotic varieties were mixed in, as well: ginkgo, maples, monkey puzzle, Chinese mulberry, and rhododendrons, to name a few.

Credit is also given to Chester "Chet" Corry, who from 1937 to 1969 was the parks superintendent. During his thirty-three-year career, he kept Lithia Park in excellent condition, no matter what money problems existed. When his budget didn't allow for a work crew, he gardened and fertilized plants by himself in his beat-up Ford dump truck. When the Oregon Shakespeare Festival began drawing more people, he worked to add a second recreation park, Hunter Park, with room for a ballfield and parking to keep Lithia Park from being overrun. He was successful. Corry retired in 1969, although he remained a consultant until he passed away in 1989.

Forty-two acres of the park were placed in 1982 on the National Register of Historic Places for its "outstanding example of distinctive American landscape architecture." Many of the trees are now a hundred years old and still in place. The curving parkway, an upper lake, Japanese garden, sycamore grove, hiking paths, and a formal terrace for the Italian marble fountain (purchased at the 1915 Pan American Exposition) still remain as seen years ago. Ashland is a town of some 20,000, but the park hosts one-million visitors every year. It is a jewel of a park within a small town's city limits.

Sources: Reynolds, *Oregon Encyclopedia*: "Lithia Park"; *Medford Mail Tribune,* April 22, 2007; Morgan, *Medford Mail Tribune*, April 14, 2013.

Lithia Water: In Bottles and Fountains

WITH OVER FORTY MINERAL SPRINGS bubbling in and around the City of Ashland, it was natural that people would commercialize this. Dating back to 1891, John Wagner (his family of Wagner Creek fame) built up a bottling business a few miles east of Ashland. Ordering crown-top bottles from a St. Louis concern, Wagner was the first to use these in Southern Oregon. He later purchased bottles made in Berkeley, California, with the words "Siskiyou Natural Mineral Water" stylized on them and delivered these by wagon throughout the region or by railroad to San Francisco and Portland.

This mineral water was drunk, soaked in, and its vapors even inhaled at baths, all due to the believed medicinal values. Lithia water is mineralized water with lithium salts, such as lithium carbonate or lithium chloride, and having these natural springs around Ashland was rare — although other locations such as Sarasota Springs (New York) and throughout Georgia were also then well known.

With Ashland's near equidistance between San Francisco and Portland, Southern Pacific Railroad championed the city's mineral springs and stated they were classified as "Lithia, Soda, and Sulphur Springs." The owner and editor of the *Ashland Tidings*, Bert Greer, is credited with bringing about the building of a system that brought the Lithia waters to town.

His support resulted in the residents passing a $175,000 bond issue (a large amount then) in 1914, of which $100,000 ultimately went to build a pipeline system from the "Lithia Springs" well house and pump — near Ashland's present airport and three miles east of the city — to a bottling station in Lithia Park; most of the remaining moneys went to develop the park. Wagner closed his bottling plant in 1913.

330

The original source of Lithia Water. (SOHS 2229)

Located roughly parallel to the "Mineral Water Pavilion" and upstream from the original bandshell, the spot fed Lithia fountains in the park and the railroad depot that greeted new arrivals. The mineral water was also mixed, carbonated, and bottled for sale. The Lithia water was highly concentrated in different minerals, including salt.

A 1915 plaque stated that the following was present in milligrams per liter: sodium chloride (4545), sodium melaborate (321), sodium sulphate (4), sodium bicarbonate (2456), potassium bicarborate (280), lithium bicarbonate (154), calcium bicarbonate (1404), magnesium bicarbonate (1153), iron and aluminum oxides (13), and silica (95). With this composition, one can see why drinking the water was not considered to be pleasant by most, either then or now.

The entire project proved unprofitable and a failure, as the mineral water business dried up during and after World War I due to changing tastes—and the depression ended what was left. The "Central Bottling Station" was abandoned; although used briefly as a Boy Scout headquarters, the building was ultimately demolished.

All that is left of the bottling center is a concrete slab after climbing a steep, staircase to the left when one is walking through the trees from Lithia Park's playground on Ashland Creek's east bank. After the slab, another staircase rises from there to South Pioneer Street. The remaining staircases were accepted for inclusion on the National Register of Historic Places and are part of the Lithia Park Historic District.

A two-inch iron pipe today still carries the mineral water to the fountains on Ashland's central plaza and nearby Lithia Park—although little else remains of these endeavors—with the visitors today carrying their drinking water in plastic bottles.

Sources: City of Ashland: "Lithia Springs Historic Photos"; Curler, JPR: "As It Was," May 26, 2005; *Medford Mail Tribune*, April 22, 2007; Mason, JPR: "As It Was," February 26, 2009.

Palmerton Park

ORIN PALMERTON WAS A VETERAN OF THE Spanish-American War, who came to the City of Rogue River in the 1920s and purchased five acres of land from the Skevington family. Located off West Evans Creek Road and a five-minute drive from the city's downtown, Evans Creek runs through the property before emptying into the Rogue River, west of the Depot Street Bridge.

Palmerton conducted a plant and tree nursery at the property for years; during this time he also planted many domestic and exotic trees that were from around the world. Orin sold the pristine acreage to Jackson County in 1960, and the City of Rogue River in 1994 acquired it from the County. It is part of the city's park system, which maintains the park and continues to expand the diversity of the different trees and shrubs.

Palmerton Park is an arboretum—defined as a place for the study and exhibit of trees—with ninety-six distinct tree specimens found around the world, including pines from Japan, cedars from the Mediterranean, and large coastal redwoods native to the Pacific Northwest. Numerous trees in Ashland's Lithia Park are also represented here: from different maples, monkey puzzle, and sassafras to the ginkgo, tulip tree, and mimosa.

A large black locust tree jutting into the parking lot first greets visitors. The most impressive gathering is just beyond the rest rooms: arborvitae, Arizona cypress, weeping hemlock and Deodar cedar. Exhibiting also azaleas, rhododendrons, and other plants and shrubs, the park has meandering paths throughout, a duck pond, playground, and picnic area. The paths are paved with looping walkways that lead to all of the trees, as well as to picnic tables, grills, and playground equipment.

Linking the arboretum to the Anna Classick Bicentennial Park, the bridge over Evans Creek washed away in the New Year's Day flood of 1997. In its place, an impressive suspension foot-bridge (like a miniature Golden Gate Bridge in one sense) was constructed in its place.

Born in 1924 on the property before Orin Palmerton's purchase, Dick Skevington not only designed the original crossing over Evans Creek in the late 1980s, he nailed in the last plank into the replacement bridge in 2001. Skevington had built bridges for the National Parks Service for twenty-eight years, before returning to Rogue River at retirement and being elected to the city council and then as its mayor. He died in 2008 at age eighty-four.

Palmerton Park and Arboretum is one of these jewels that tie us into the past with a presence today—and it is a beautiful setting. The little-known park is on five-acres and an easy drive for the experience.

Sources: John Darling, *Medford Mail Tribune*, November 20, 2005; Specht, *Medford Mail Tribune*, September 20, 2008.

The Ashland-Area
Mineral Springs

*D*URING THE LATE 1800s AND EARLY 1900s, the mineral springs percolating around the Ashland area were hailed for their medicinal and healing values. The bubbling carbon dioxide (CO_2) and presence of lithium salts (lithium carbonate and/or lithium chloride) were valued dating back to the Native American Indians. They soaked in the waters to ease sore muscles or skin rashes and believed in the healing properties. The natives called the mineral spring vapors "Hi-u-Skookum" medicine, or the "breath of the Great Spirit." Lying on pine boughs within a circle of stones, they breathed the CO_2 gases; they then would head to a skins-and-boughs enclosure for reviving, followed by chanting with a shaman in a sweat lodge.

Referring to the five mineral-springs-fed, public swimming pools, large colorful railroad posters in the early 1900s described Ashland as "The Venice of the West." These five pools were the Helman Baths, off Otis Street in Ashland; Twin Plunges at 1st and "A" Streets; Buckhorn Springs, off Green Springs Hwy./Hwy. 66; Colestin Springs, south of Ashland; and Jackson Hot Springs (now Jackson WellSprings) on Old Highway 99 North. Only Jackson WellSprings' reconstructed pool and drastically remodeled facilities remain open today to the public, although Buckhorn Springs is a destination resort with cabins, dining, lodging, and other facilities.

Throngs of tourists would get off at the Southern Pacific Railroad station at "A" Street. A 1915 Southern Pacific Railroad flyer heralded Ashland as a resort city on the Shasta route, midway between Portland and San Francisco, with eight trains arriving and leaving daily between these major cities. It read: "Ashland is noted for three things: beautiful environment, matchless climate, and wonderful mineral springs. There are over forty known mineral springs in and about the city."

The tourists apparently chose the Colestine Baths, whereas local families preferred the Helman Baths in town. The springs formed a marsh in the field in front of the Helman building, and its waters flowed between the rocks forming one end of the indoor pool. As with the Indians, older people soaked their aching joints and muscles in the heated spring waters to the building's front, as the water flowed from a holding tank through a pipe.

Even the City of Ashland tried to get into the act. The owner and editor of the *Ashland Tidings*, Bert Greer, strongly supported the creation of a health spa centered on the beneficial aspects of the lithium-concentrated water. Although this never came into being owing to acrimonious political and financial controversies, the publicity greatly helped the passage by voters in 1914 of a $175,000 bond issue, $65,000 of which was earmarked to develop Lithia Park.

Meanwhile, the mineral-spring pools continued to maintain their draw. During the Chautauqua series (summer-time, public lectures) in Lithia Park, exposition visitors camped in the maple and evergreen groves near the Helman Baths. Trains carried people to Colestin Springs — off Mt. Ashland Ski Road in the Siskiyou Mountains — for its medicinal properties. Passengers, baggage, and tents were offloaded onto a wooden platform. Since the small hotel could only house twenty-five guests, the rest (and as many as 100 families at a time) pitched their tents underneath the stars and conifers.

Buckhorn Mineral Springs was another prime destination, and this resort was adjacent to the current Cascade-Siskiyou National Monument and Pacific Crest Trail. A lodge with fir floors, high ceilings, and single-pane windows had been built on 120 acres deep in a canyon by Emigrant Creek. Health-seeking visitors flocked to its artesian well and drank the "sweet-tasting, bubbly waters rich in carbon dioxide." Among other facilities, a terra-cotta block hut housed six vapor-bath closets. With the water vapors containing carbon dioxide (valued for their effects on the body), users sat in a chamber with heads sticking out from the top. (It's now widely understood that breathing CO_2 in quantities is very dangerous.)

Over time, the attraction to these springs wore out, especially with the financial dislocations and hardships of the Great Depression. The public baths fell into disrepair and disuse. In 1989, the National Register of

Ashland Mineral Springs (lower middle) with structures. (SOHS 9521)

Historic Places placed the Buckhorn on its register. After extensive refurbishment, it has operated since as a resort, but not as a public pool. The Colestin Resort gradually disappeared. The "beautiful wood frame building" around the Helman pool burned down and later replaced by a plain metal structure with an inside private pool. Where the spring-fed Twin Plunges once existed, the Ashland Food Cooperative now stands.

Little remains of the time when mineral springs were considered to be more beneficial than good exercise, healthy foods, and vitamins — but those were heady times.

Sources: Reynolds, *Oregon Encyclopedia*: "Lithia Park"; Cowley, *Medford Mail Tribune*, April 29, 1979; Darling, *Medford Mail Tribune*, June 19, 2005; Darling, *Medford Mail Tribune*, July 26, 2011; City of Ashland: "Lithia Springs Historic Photos."

The Golden Ghost
Town of the Valley

NEAR FORGOTTEN AND DESOLATE, THE GHOST TOWN of Golden lies a few miles east of Wolf Creek in Josephine County. Its weathered-brown, old clapboard structures stand in mute testimony to a long-ago era. At its peak in the late Nineteenth Century, the town originally known as "Goldville" was home to 200 folks: Most of whom were earning their living from the gold taken out from Coyote Creek across from the town.

Although prospectors had worked the creek since the 1850s, the Reverend William Ruble and his wife Ruth established the town in 1890. Ruble had purchased nearly all of the mining claims east and west of Golden; his sons, Schuyler and William, mined the shallower ground and leased the creek's deeper portions to other miners.

The town sprung up with a general store, post office, homes, two churches, a school, orchards, and mills to pulverize the rock and extract gold. Owing to the activity, Oregon-California stagecoaches detoured there to deliver mail, passengers, and goods; the town was a center for miners who didn't live there but worked the surrounding area. With religion a major theme, no saloons were allowed; imbibers traveled to nearby Wolf Creek where they built a dance hall—followed by the church-minding folks who came to picket the rowdy place.

When the gold finally played out in the 1930s, the town rapidly declined. What's left now are a deserted residence, the church, general store, carriage shed, and other structures, but the old buildings still exude their charm, including the weathered church with its exquisite bell tower. The story, however, doesn't end here.

The Golden Community Church, Golden, OR.

A minister's son, Melvin Davis, built a 2,800-square-foot lodge in 1930 on four acres located one mile away; he moved an 1880s guesthouse and the historic school from Golden there, and mined the nearby wetlands. An African-American—Mr. Ivan St. John—purchased the holdings after the site had traded hands several times. St. John was a homeopathic doctor, a trance medium, and alchemist who had co-founded the Philosopher's Stone, an occult bookstore in San Francisco. (Alchemy is the "science" of turning base metals, such as lead, into gold or silver.)

When St. John in 1988 sold his bookstore interest, he bought the Davis property, known for its precious gold holdings. St. John died in 2005, but didn't leave any known heirs. The Oregon Department of Parks and Recreation owns and now manages the town as a Heritage site. The ghost town was placed in 2002 on the National Register of Historic Properties.

To see this nostalgic place, drive on Interstate 5 to Wolf Creek exit 76, twenty-five miles north of Grants Pass; wind back to the right and drive through the forests over Coyote Creek Road for three and one-half miles. The cluster of old buildings are on the left; the mined creek area and wetlands are to the right. The small cemetery next to the church was filmed in an episode on the TV series, "Gunsmoke," where grave marker props were added — but no one is buried there.

Golden is one of the best mining-era ghost towns in Southern Oregon that is easily accessible in a rural setting.

Sources: Swanson, ActiveRain.com: "Ghost Town of Golden, Oregon"; Kettler, *Medford Mail Tribune*, February 16, 2011.

The Old Wood House

SEEN TODAY FROM HIGHWAY 62 AND LOCATED roughly one and one-half miles north of Eagle Point, the "Old Wood House" is a testimonial to the hard, unsung efforts of historical preservationists. Owing to the continuing efforts of Skip and Charlotte Geear with other volunteers, this 1870's homestead has preserved what life was like then. Due to its old, weathered condition and Mt. McLoughlin's background, the Wood House easily is the most photographed and easel-painted pioneer house in the Pacific Northwest.

The story begins with Marvin S. Wood, who was a wounded Civil War veteran. With his brother Dennis, Marvin came to Southern Oregon in 1868 and established a homestead above Eagle Point. When Dennis Wood died in 1869, Marvin filed a land patent one year later and built the existing house. He married Susan Griffith in 1876, and the couple had three children: daughters Ora and Mayme with a son, Walter.

Walter Wood was born in the house in 1881; he lived there for his entire life and died in 1974. The Wood House was at risk of being demolished on different occasions. In 1946, Highway 62 was being worked on. Being in the way of the bulldozers, Walter Wood, one of the last surviving descendants, fought the State of Oregon to save his home. He caused the purchase of the thirty-eight acres across the highway and moved the house to its present location.

The house didn't have electricity or inside plumbing until it was moved. Three lights were installed inside with a sink and running water in the kitchen; an outhouse was still used. After Walter Wood died, the house was boarded up and abandoned. Although a California investor in 1983 bought the house and acreage, the home deteriorated as blackberry bushes and brush took over. Vandals removed nearly all of

Smoke billows out the chimney of the "Old Wood House" near Eagle Point, OR. (Photo courtesy of Gary Wilkinson, www.oldwoodhouse.org)

the doors and windows and set the house on fire several times; the house didn't burn down.

The owner in 2000 donated the structure to the Eagle Point Historical Society. Although retaining the land, he gave the society a one-acre lease underneath the house at $200 per month. With donations of money and time, the society with Skip Geear (the Wood House Project Chairman) restored the weather-beaten place. The roof was re-shingled with old cedar shakes, doors and windows added, and the structure made sound. No improvements were made inside, so that the house still looks as it did in the 1870s.

Judson Parsons and Diana Gardener from Salem bought the property in 2006 and greatly helped the volunteers. They gave a new lease on two acres, but at $1 per year. When Jackson County discontinued the funding to all of the local historical societies in 2007 (taking the proceeds from a state-wide levy), the Wood House was again at risk. The Eagle Point Historical Society didn't have the funds to continue.

The City of Eagle Point took title to all of its assets except for the Wood House and the historical society was dissolved. Skip and Charlotte formed a nonprofit organization, the Woodhouse Preservation Group, which received title to the Old Wood House. Working throughout all of these travails were these two, who deserve the credit for preserving, maintaining, and exhibiting the house — improved inside and out — as it is seen today.

Only donations and volunteer work maintain the property. There are no paid employees, nor any tax moneys used in this effort. Annual events to raise money are held, such as an October Harvest Festival and May Farm Festival show (complete with photographers and artists). Free tours of the Wood House are given during each event and otherwise by appointment.

As Skip Geear's website concludes: "Since the beginning in 1870, the Wood House has fought heavy rains, snow, the Columbus Day storm, hail, fire, vandalism and county politics, and through all of this, the house still remains to welcome you to come and visit." These volunteer efforts are to be congratulated.

Sources: Geear, "The Old Wood House," December 4, 2011.

The Hanleys and
Hanley Farm

MICHAEL HANLEY WAS RAISED IN OHIO, and the young twenty-five year old was lured to San Francisco by the Gold Rush of 1849. After trying his hand at mining, he and a partner decided to start a more lucrative business: selling beef to the miners. Michael then met Martha Burnett, who had arrived in Douglas County by the Oregon Trail. The two married and decided on Jackson County to settle; they purchased a 636-acre donation land claim near Jacksonville.

They had nine children and six survived into adulthood. As they raised their family, Michael Hanley continued to buy land and pursue various businesses, including creating a regional agricultural industry on what is now Hanley Road between Jacksonville and Central Point.

Despite Michael Hanley becoming an invalid and pronounced legally insane in his later years, his family had their own lives and prospered in different ways. Their eldest son, John, tried different businesses, such as a distillery in Jacksonville and ranching with his brothers. Son Bill left school when he was ten years old to become a cattleman like his father. By age seventeen, he had left home for wide-open Eastern Oregon, where he created a farming and cattle empire just like his dad. Bill Hanley not only owned different ranches, including the 16,000 acre "OO Ranch," he ran for Oregon Governor and the U.S. Senate. Although not successful, "Big Bill" was instrumental in the rail and highway development of Eastern Oregon.

The Yukon Gold Rush lured son Ed to Alaska, where he also decided that selling mining supplies (and running a toll road) made more sense. Ed later moved to Seattle and built a cannery operation, but also

The main house at Hanley Farm. (Courtesy Oregon State Historic Preservation Office, University of Oregon Libraries)

continued ranching on property north of the Hanley Farm and was known for his orchards. Daughter Ella also traveled away; she spent time in Alaska with brother Ed, and then married mining engineer Harry Bush in 1903. The couple lived in Chile, where her husband ran a large copper mine for sixteen years, and they returned to the Valley. Michael II inherited his father's Butte Creek Ranch property at age eighteen; in addition to running it, he also was involved with his brothers in other ranching endeavors. Over time, fortunes were made and lost.

Alice Hanley spent her life in the family home. Caring for her parents until their deaths (Martha in 1887 and her father two years later at age sixty-five), she inherited over 100 acres of the original farm and ran it for the rest of her life. In 1922 she ran for state representative but lost. Alice helped to establish the Oregon Home Extension Service (OSU's agricultural extension) and served on its board from 1919 until her death.

The extension service now is located on what was much of Alice's share of the original homestead. What was left was deeded to the Southern Oregon Historical Society in 1982 by Mary Hanley, the last descendant of Michael Hanley to live in the house and on the land. The thirty-seven-acre farm is open to the public and preserves the history of the early settlers and their contributions to this region.

Owing to Alice Hanley's long-ago purchase of auctioned pioneer furnishings, rooms have antiques dating back to those times. With a 1950 remodeling of the back (1860s) part of the house, there even is "modern" electricity, a furnace, TV, telephone, bathrooms, and a kitchen. Until then, this didn't exist.

The historical society has many public activities and presentations at the Hanley Farm—and is a must visit. For these activities, see http://www.sohs.org/hanley-events.

Source: Southern Oregon Historical Society website: "The Hanley Farm and Family."

The Applegate Trail
Interpretive Center

*L*OCATED IN SUNNY VALLEY FOURTEEN MILES north of Grants Pass on I-5, the Applegate Trail Interpretive Center was brought about by an ex-airline stewardess, Betty Gaustad. After college in California and working for United Airlines for eleven years, she and her family in 1974 bought a ranch in Sunny Valley that dated back to an 1851 land claim. Her mother, Irene, had a strong interest in history and was the one who discovered that the Applegate Trail—unmarked there and not known by anyone—cut directly across their property.

Betty was elated, as she remembered back to her elementary-school days in a tiny Minnesota town. The one-room brick schoolhouse had been filled with pioneer history books, and Betty first learned there about the trail cut by the Applegate brothers so many years ago. She never forgot the story of the hardy pioneers who had endured so much hardship.

The main Oregon Trail followed the Snake River across southern Idaho into Oregon, but forced settlers, their oxen, and wagons to make it down the dangerous Columbia River. When the Applegate bothers lost two young sons in 1843 owing to their raft overturning, they decided to find a safer route. Heading back to Idaho, they convinced other settlers to follow them on a different way.

They decided on a route that headed southward into present-day Nevada, worked through a desert and California, and then crossed the Klamath Basin into Southern Oregon; it followed the Rogue River into the Rogue Valley and then northward for the Willamette Valley, their ultimate destination. As the trail descended the Cascade Range into the Rogue River Valley, it cut across Emigrant Creek in Jackson County, now named for those pioneers; Highway 66 to Ashland and Interstate 5 heading to Sunny Valley basically follow the Applegate Trail.

The wagon train that first tried the new, uncertain route endured great hardships from disease, Indian attacks, flooded rivers, food shortages, and near impassible mountain passes, but they made the trek in three months, traveling 500 miles to reach the Willamette. A young woman (Martha Leland Crowley) died of typhoid in Sunny Valley in 1846, as the first wagon train rested there, and she was buried near the present old covered bridge; the stream was named Grave Creek six years later due to her death. Thousands of wagon trains over the years then followed this trail in settling Oregon.

Encouraged by her mother, Betty Gaustad was determined to build a center commemorating the Applegate Trail. With limited funds, she mortgaged her ranch, businesses (she owned a grocery store, gas station, and restaurant in town), and worked for donations and grants. Although she received regional economic grants, Betty financed 85 percent of the total project costs by herself. Her daughter, Jacquelana Ladd, worked in designing the center; Dennis Gaustad, her brother, built the 5,400 square-foot, rustic-looking museum, behind a two-story, fir-columned Western false front that was designed to look like the front of the 1860 Grave Creek Hotel.

The center portrays the history of Native Americans and trappers in the 1800s, as well as describing events after the Applegate Trail was blazed: the discovery of gold in 1851 in the area, ensuing Indian Wars, stagecoach era, coming of the railroad, and the life of early settlers. There is also a three-screen theater that shows a film depicting the struggles faced by the Applegate-Trail pioneers; dressed authentically, local residents show the challenges overcome in the film that was made in Sunny Valley.

The original 1929, log-constructed Sunny Valley grange hall is outside the center; seen from the museum, the Grave Creek covered bridge stands, one of the few ones still remaining in Southern Oregon. Although Betty's mother died one month before the museum opened in 1998, there is no question that she would have been impressed by it — and one woman's dedication.

Sources: Applegate Trail Interpretive Center at its website; LaLande, *Oregon Encyclopedia*: "The Applegate Trail"; *Seattle Times*, January 6, 1999; Fattig, *Medford Mail Tribune*, November 29, 1998.

The Wolf Creek Inn

*B*UILT IN 1883 AS A PRIME STOP ON THE sixteen-day stagecoach journey from San Francisco to Portland, the Wolf Creek Inn has continuously sheltered weary travelers longer than any other hotel in Oregon. The large wooden, two-story building with high-pitched roofs, a colonnaded front porch and upper deck, and wider back had nine guest rooms, complete with dining, reading, and lounging facilities. Located on the stagecoach run between Roseburg and Redding, it is located twenty-five miles north of Grants Pass.

Merchant Henry Smith contracted to have the premises built; the lodgings were advertised as a "first-class traveler's hotel" and it was first called the Wolf Creek Tavern, an old English term for a hotel that served food. Smith also accumulated large land holdings in the 1880s, and he planted orchards that are still in existence. The large apple and pear trees next to the Inn and north of the dining room date back to an orchard planted in 1885. The Wolf Creek Inn changed over time from a stagecoach stop and miners' lodging for a hot meal and a clean bed, to automobile travelers and celebrities.

Jack London stayed in 1911 for several weeks at the Inn, where he hiked through the forests behind it. During this time, he wrote a short story entitled "The End of the Story." He also completed his novel "Valley of the Moon" during another stay. Jack London's room is on the second floor at the front, and it shows now much as it would have then. A trail near Wolf Creek winds its way to a peak named for Jack London, owing to the time he spent in the area when writing. The summit overlooks Wolf Creek Valley and the tiny town of Wolf Creek.

During the 1920s and 1930s, numerous celebrities visited the Inn, including Clark Gable, Carole Lombard, Mary Pickford, Douglas

The Wolf Creek Inn.

Fairbanks Jr., and Orson Wells. Best known for his role as Rhett Butler in *Gone with the Wind*, Gable was a good friend of the innkeeper in the 1930s and several times stopped by. He enjoyed fishing in the Rogue River a few miles away—staying also with his wife, Carol Lombard. His "Clark Gable" room is available today.

When the Inn was in need of repairs, the State of Oregon in 1975 acquired it and property on Wolf Creek's north bank to preserve the historic hotel. With the Oregon State Historical Preservation Office reviewing original floor plans, wall coverings, and its history, carpenters and craftsmen were rebuilding the structure to bring back the look and feel of the mid 1920's. The process took four years and the restored Wolf Creek Inn is listed in the National Register of Historic Places. Although it has been closed for more renovations into 2017, the Inn offers dining, lodging, and special events, all located in the town of Wolf Creek, one-quarter mile from I-5 at Exit 76.

Sources: Oregon State Parks at its website; Kettler, *Medford Mail Tribune*, January 7, 2005; Dover, *Medford Mail Tribune*, July 6, 2014.

The Lady of the Woods

*D*URING THE WINTER OF 1917 AND LATER SPRING, reports of a discovered stone woman filtered into Crater Lake National Park headquarters. The naked figure sat against a large lava rock in near "full relief," legs bent, one arm placed over her head as if shielding away danger. Surrounded by trees, the figure was located on the lake's rim, 1.7 miles from the lodge. The media was incredulous at this find with story headlines such as "Mummy woman found in woods" and "Ancient figure of woman discovered."

The discovery of the "Lady of the Woods" brought about remarkable theories as to how she had come about. Park workers speculated in 1919 that this was a petrification that could be older than the Egyptian mummies. Some thought this to be a natural formation. The curator of archaeology at the Oakland Museum believed the lady was the cast of an actual woman, engulfed by a volcanic mud flow that had poured down Mt. Mazama.

It turns out, Dr. Earl Russell Bush—the official surgeon for the U. S. Engineers in 1917 and stationed at Crater Lake that summer—was the creator. He had time on his hands with "diminished responsibilities" toward the end of the 1917 season. Dr. Bush had persuaded the park blacksmith, William Ivy, to make a set of rock-sculpting tools. With some stonemason experience, he began his work. From Oct. 4th to Oct. 19th, the metallic sounds of *Clink! Clink! Clink!* penetrated the usually quiet hemlock forests on Mt. Mazama's slopes.

Dr. Bush didn't tell anyone about his work or visits into the woodlands. Curiosity and the persistent tapping of hammer and chisel against volcanic rock, however, eventually led a few to seek out the site. Although he was reassured by their praise, Dr. Bush pledged all to secrecy. The good doctor left for the East and his secret was well guarded. Park Superintendent Alex Sparrow was alone granted

351

The Lady of the Woods at Crater Lake National Park.

permission to let William Steel, the U. S. Park Commissioner, know the truth the following summer. Thus, in 1918, Sparrow covered the stone chips with pine needles and took Steel out to see it. Told the truth later, Steel joined the others in keeping the secret—that is, until four years later, when someone gave up the story and Bush later verified it.

The truth concerning "The Stone Lady of Crater Lake" didn't gain traction after that first revelation in 1921. The *Fresno Bee* broke the story on October 24, 1923. The interest in the "lady" had increased so greatly afterwards that it became necessary in 1930 to construct a trail there. Marked by simple signs, the trail passes the south end of the Ranger Dormitory, over the creek crossed by a small bridge, and westward a few hundred feet to the actual site. (Ask park rangers for the directions.)

Over the years, the story has inspired poems, articles, and feature stories: Even now, she sleeps in the woods for those who will seek her.

Sources: *Fresno Bee*, October 23, 1923; Brown, *Nature Notes From Crater Lake:* Volume 21, 1955.

The Oregon Vortex

AN UNUSUAL PLACE EXISTS FIVE MILES UP Sardine Creek Road from Highway 99/234 (which turns two miles later into Second Avenue in Gold Hill). Calling it the "Forbidden Ground," Native Americans avoided the area, as apparently did their horses, wild birds, and other wildlife. Despite this, in the 1890s the Grey Eagle Mining Company built a gold assay office on the site and near their mine. The structure was plumbed level when constructed.

During a heavy rainy season in 1910, a mudslide carried the slanted-wood building down the hill where it slid against a maple tree. No longer plumb or level, the house is still there but rests at a weird angle. Now named the "House of Mystery," balls inside roll uphill, people stand weirdly, and brooms angle on end. Outside the twisted house, people appear dramatically taller when they shift positions.

John Lister was a geologist, mining engineer, and physicist. Visiting the area in 1913, the Scottish scientist became intrigued by what he saw. Named the "Vortex"—defined as a fluid or gas circulating around a core with its inside pressure being lower than its outside—Lister later bought the property. He developed it in the early 1920s, conducted thousands of experiments, and in 1930 opened it to the public.

Lister claimed that the property was at the intersection of strange forces he named terralines, or energy that causes a repelling (anti-gravitational) electromagnetic field. The story goes that Lister became so frightened by his discoveries that before he died, he burned all of his notes. After his death, Maria Cooper's family in 1961 left their Gold Hill service station and motel to buy the Vortex. Then in high school, Maria twenty years later quit her job as a social worker to run it when her father became ill. She continued on for years.

People enjoying a visit to the "House of Mystery" near Gold Hill, Oregon. Is it an optical illusion or a magnetic vortex? (Gold Hill Historical Society, GHHS)

The controversy also continues. Balls seeming to run uphill and a pendulum hanging at an angle can be possibly explained by the crazy, skewed building. It's argued that this effect is caused by the distorted perspective of not seeing the horizon, but one against the background of converging lines. When visual references are skewed sufficiently, people can actually feel dizzy—which they do. Outside, however, is another story. Photographs of people changing places (one taller than the other) evidence their changing heights, based solely on the new position. Trees grow in weird shapes; people shrink or grow as they walk, one way or the other.

Is this an optical illusion, caused by terralines, or due to a deep metallic core with different influences? As the questions continue today, however, there is little doubt that the Oregon Vortex is a special place and considered by experts to be one of the best — if not the best — of the dozen such mystery spots around the country. And it's an easy drive to visit.

Sources: Oregon Vortex at its website; Barnard, Associated Press: *Salt Lake Tribune*, March 14, 2004.

The Creation of ScienceWorks

SHARON AND JOHN JAVNA MOVED TO ASHLAND from Berkeley, so their son, Jesse, could be in a good public school system and start kindergarten in 1995. John was a successful writer and publisher: His self-published book, *50 Simple Things You Can Do to Save the Earth,* had sold five million copies, was printed in twenty-three languages, and was number one on a number of 1990 national best-seller lists. Sharon Javna had been a public defender in Oakland, who quit her job to stay at home when Jesse was born, joined three years later by their daughter, Sophie.

They loved being in the Rogue Valley and Ashland, but missed taking their children to the interactive museums found in the Bay area. Although lacking in experience, they started a small science museum (700 square feet) at Ashland Middle School, so that children could have hands-on experiences such as dissecting fish. They built the exhibits, a lab for experiments, and even showed a giant python. The tiny museum—named the Ashland Middle School Science Institute—was a success.

Sharon later was looking at the old natural history museum building, the once Pacific Northwest Museum of Natural History, above East Main and off Walker Avenue in Ashland. Although it was empty, she thought that this would make a perfect museum, even if it was 26,000 square feet. The couple visited large science museums throughout the country, talking to administrators and understanding the operations.

Afterwards they met with joint founders, Marge and Dave Bernard, known for community activities and his connection with Ashland-based Darex Corporation (the family-owned, industrial sharpening firm with

Children and adults enjoying the various exhibits at ScienceWorks in Ashland.

its Drill Doctor handyman tool). They also met with a good friend, Dan Kranzler, in Seattle who was president of his family's Kirlin Charitable Foundation.

In 2001, through a cooperative arrangement with Kirlin (that purchased the building) and SOU (that leased back the underlying land), ScienceWorks leased the structure. Sharon's legal background came in handy in taking over the administrative duties; John had been a toymaker before becoming an author and managed the exhibits. In the following year, a small museum staff with over 100 volunteers retrofitted the structure and built the exhibits. With such volunteering, opening the facilities cost $300,000, far below the $3 million price tag that consultants had predicted.

It opened in December 2002. Called one of the country's best small science museums, it has some 100 interactive exhibits. From its highly popular "Bubble-ology Room" — where people blow bubbles and learn about bubble-surface tension — to "Pedal Power" (a stationary bicycle that powers an electric train) and a nano-technology exhibit, adults and children alike learn while being entertained. Hands-on exhibits range from "Da Vinci's Garage" and "Discovery Island" to the outside "Black Bear Garden."

Arguably the second largest tourist destination in Ashland outside of the Oregon Shakespeare Festival, it also conducts on-site school programs and an outreach program for teacher development. ScienceWorks relies on admission charges, contributions, and membership fees to operate. Currently utilizing about half of an available 20,000 square feet of exhibit space, future expansion awaits — and all for the benefit of this region and beyond. See its website for the latest exhibits.

Sources: Fattig, *Ashland Daily Tidings*, December 1, 2012; ScienceWorks: "History" and latest exhibits at its website; Specht, *Medford Mail Tribune*, April 14, 2013.

Hellgate Jetboat Excursions

*I*N 1980, ROBERT HAMLYN AND HIS WIFE TRAVELED throughout the Pacific Northwest in their motorhome. After spending several days in Grants Pass, they sold their Southern California home and moved there. First owning and operating an equipment rental business in Grants Pass, they sold it when Robert was managing Rogue Jet Boat Excursions. In 1988, he purchased Hellgate Jetboat Excursions and merged the two operations together. The business has prospered over the years to where it now employs over 100 staff members during its peak season.

Hellgate Jetboat Excursions started in 1961 when Grant Garcia began using a flat-bottomed, thirty-two passenger wooden boat on the thirty-five mile round-trip from the Bridge Motel in Grants Pass to the Hellgate Recreational Area. His boat could operate in as little as six inches of water owing to its water-jet propulsion system. The ticket price then was $4 for adults and $2 for children under twelve on the three-times-a-day trips. The Hellgate is a narrow, deep canyon with sheer rock walls that rise over 250 feet above the river and its boiling rapids.

Thirteen years later, Gary and Julie Woolsey bought the business and greatly expanded its operations. In the ten years to 1987, they built seven boats (from smaller ones with a sixteen-passenger capacity to ones that carried eighty-two people), all being propeller-less with a hydro-jet system. The Grants Pass departure point moved from the Riverside Inn to Riverside Park, and they introduced brunch and dinner stops on different trips. The Woolseys brought in the OK Corral as the dining facility and added a five and one-half hour, seventy-five-mile round-trip to Grave Creek with a lunch stop at Galice.

A day on the Rogue River with Hellgate Jet Boat Excursions.

In 1985, the owners of the Riverside Inn started Rogue Whitewater Excursions, a competitor to Hellgate. One year later, they hired Hamlyn to manage its problematic operations, and he soon changed the rival's name to Rogue Jetboat Excursions. Robert Hamlyn then bought both and merged the competing operations into the present company.

Hellgate designs and manufactures its jet boats in Grants Pass. It has added numerous new vessels since then with improvements on each one. A windshield with wipers, for example, was added so that pilots could see the river more clearly. More efficient pumps improved fuel efficiency, and internal speakers were added so that passengers could always hear the pilot.

After the boat cruises through Hellgate Canyon, it turns around, heads back upstream, and docks at the OK Corral. The OK Corral was renovated in 2005, and the 12,000 square-foot, open-air facility by the Rogue River — where osprey, bald eagle, and deer sightings are common — is reserved exclusively for Hellgate guests. Located eighteen miles west of Grants Pass, up to 350 people can dine at a time after traveling past rocky beaches and sheer cliffs.

Its ShopRiverRock gift store is located within the reservation facilities, open year-round, and contains more than 6,000 square feet. The season is from May to mid-September, depending on the trip, and over 70,000 people take a Hellgate excursion every year.

Sources: See generally Hellgate Jetboat Excursions website; Stumbo, *Grants Pass Daily Courier*, February 21, 2013.

Eden Valley Orchards

L OCATED IN SOUTHWEST MEDFORD, THE Eden Valley Orchards date back to a former donation land claim and use since 1853; its location was chosen due to it being between two of the few settlements that then existed, one known as Ashland Mills (Ashland) and the other being Jacksonville. Addison and Martha Ball constructed the original house on a 160-acre parcel in the 1860s.

Joseph H. Stewart in 1885 bought the land and house for $5,400 — a large sum in those days — and paid it to the pioneer photographer and horticulturalist Peter Britt, who held the note on the property (and who also introduced the first pear root stock to the Valley three decades before). Steward was an Illinois legislator, nurseryman, and Chicago fruit broker who understood the growing, marketing, packing, and shipping of fruit.

Stewart over time established his Eden Valley Orchards and planted pears, apples, prunes, and almonds. Completed before 1898, he moved his family into a larger home on the property. (The smaller Ball home existed until destroyed many decades later in a fire.) In 1890, Stewart sold the area's first commercial pears by shipping railroad cars of fruit to the outside markets.

His trees yielded later the stems and branches for grafting and propagating many of the large orchards throughout the Valley. By six years, his annual output was ninety-five carloads of pears and apples. Recognized as the "father of the fruit industry" in Southern Oregon, Joseph Stewart became wealthy and started construction of a mansion. He was a founder of Medford Bank (later part of U.S. Bank) and the Medford Commercial Club (which later became the Chamber of Commerce).

The sixty-five-year-old Stewart sold his property in 1898 to Colonel Gordon Voorhies, who had graduated from West Point and was a

Pear picking in Eden Valley Orchards, circa late 1800s. (SOHS 00052)

Spanish-American War veteran. Although born and raised in Kentucky, Voorhies was then in Portland, Oregon, having married in 1893 Helen Burrell, daughter of a prominent Portland merchant family.

When the Orchard Boom in Southern Oregon began around 1906, Colonel Voorhies with his partner and brother-in-law, Walter Burrell, began acquiring more land. Over time, he increased his acreage to 770 acres and financed this by selling orchard lands to his wealthy friends during the boom.

The Colonel hired builders at times to extensively remodel the estate home first built by Joseph Stewart. The last prominent remodeling was in 1920 with his son, Charles Voorhies—a Harvard-educated, architecture student—who headed the project. The 8,000 square-foot, four-columned mansion had seven bedrooms, seven bathrooms, and six fireplaces with manicured gardens and wide-sweeping lawns. Dating back to the original 1898 structure, the mansion showed lath-and-plaster walls, high ceilings, maple flooring, a library, sunroom, numerous rooms, and gables.

Colonel Voorhies' success led to his creating in 1913 with others the Fruit Growers League of Southern Oregon (FGL), so that orchardists could meet about their mutual concerns, including that year about their fight against fire blight, a bacteria disease that kills pear and apple trees. He was also a founding member of Southern Oregon Sales (SOS), the regional fruit cooperative in 1926. (Although these organizations were successful for decades, the SOS closed in 2008 due to the economy and industry consolidations; the FGL disbanded one year later owing to similar considerations.)

Despite the wealth and financial successes, the orchard industry began its decline, especially as World War I intervened and stopped export markets. Overproduction and lower prices contributed to the falling off. (Voorhies also served in World War I as a Lieutenant Colonel in the Army.) Although the area's fruit and agricultural production made a comeback, the Great Depression of the 1930s ended that.

Throughout the economic cycles, the property remained in the Voorhies family for three generations until 1986 when a Medford orchardist bought it. The Voorhies mansion and its twenty-seven acres were sold in 1999 to the long-time Jackson County pear family of the Roots (founders of Sabroso Company) — Tim Root and his wife, Anne, are owner/managers.

Although the mansion again was extensively refurbished inside, the huge home remained designed as first built. The grounds were lushly recreated and the property was accepted in 2000 for inclusion on the National Register of Historic Places. At South Stage Road and Voorhies in southwest Medford, the Eden Valley Orchards is now more than an estate with orchards. The property today has extensive vineyards, a winery, tasting room, tours, and puts on numerous events.

The beautiful surrounding hillsides and scenery from different directions have not changed greatly since the first shipment of pears was made over 125 year ago. Grapes and fine wines have greatly replaced the apples and pears, however, and the sound of jazz and salsa now fills the air.

Sources: Eden Valley Orchards: "A Living Monument" and "History" at its website; Darling, *Medford Mail Tribune*, September 28, 2002; Burke, *Medford Mail Tribune*, March 13, 2009.

Del Rio Vineyards

THE DEL RIO VINEYARDS AND WINERY outside of Gold Hill began as the small community of Rock Point, founded by John B. White in the early 1850s. In exchange for his services in the Rogue Indian Wars (1855-1856), White received land and later established the Rock Point post office. In 1863, John decided to open a general store and sold his homestead to L.J. White (who was not related) for $2,000. Soon after, L.J. decided to build his own hotel as a regular stagecoach stop, and the Rock Point Hotel opened to the public in 1865 with a grand ball.

The town flourished with the addition of homes, church, a blacksmith shop, saloon, school, and other structures. But when the railroad passed it by, the town dwindled, buildings vanished, and the hotel eventually closed. In the early 1900s, the property grew from a one-acre family orchard to the 800-acre Del Rio Orchards, which primarily grew pears, along with apples, cherries, peaches, walnuts, and apricots.

In 1997, Lee and Margaret Traynham purchased the land and began transforming the third-generation pear orchard into a premium wine grape vineyard. Since the Traynhams ran a trucking and almond business in California, they asked fourth-generation farmer Rob Wallace—who had spent years farming in the Sacramento Valley—to run the daily operations. Rob and his wife, Jolee, sold their large tomato and vegetable farm in 1999 (which ran twenty-five truckloads of tomatoes every day) to be the managing owners of the Del Rio vineyard and winery. The Wallaces renovated the hotel.

Today, Del Rio Vineyards grows fifteen varietals on 300 acres in neatly manicured rows over the surrounding hills (which includes 100 acres planted in 2015). Del Rio sells its premium wine grapes to Willamette Valley wineries (and over twenty vintners in Oregon and California),

Del Rio Vineyards. (Photo courtesy GHHS)

produces its own labeled wines, and sells bulk wine. Pinot noir, merlot, syrah and pinot gris are the primary grapes that are grown.

In March 2016, Del Rio acquired two parcels encompassing 215 acres from the descendants of David and Clarissa Birdseye, who purchased a donation land claim and settled on the property in the 1850s (while also operating a trading post in Jacksonville), several years before Oregon joined the Union. Sixth-generation Ted Birdseye was raising cattle on the sloping, boot-shaped property, when Rob and Jolee approached him to buy the property. It's bounded by the Rogue River Highway, Birdseye Creek Road, and Birdseye Creek with a purchase price of $2 million. (Ted Birdseye planned to continue in the cattle business at another location.)

Del Rio expects to plant 175 acres of wine grapes on the property in 2017. Crews now are clearing the parcels of stumps and rocks, tilling the hillside, building new irrigation, and will be planting different varietals at this new location—across the Rogue River from the Valley of the Rogue State Park.

It presently is the largest vineyard in Southern Oregon (Quail Run Vineyards, off Wagner Creek by Talent, has 300 acres planted in twelve different sites.) The refurbished Rock Point Hotel is now the wine tasting facility; the rebuilt postmaster's house is adjacent to the tasting room; and the winery is located inside the historic red barn, once the original packing house. And where bartenders once served up shots of whiskey to dusty stage-coach pioneers, Del Rio now offers up premium wine tasting to tourists who arrive in upscale cars.

Sources: Stiles, *Medford Mail Tribune*, April 21, 2016; "Del Rio—Our Story" at its website; Powers, JPR, June 29, 2009.

Angus Bowmer and the Oregon Shakespeare Festival

*A*FTER ACCEPTING A POSITION IN THE English Department at Southern Oregon Normal School (now Southern Oregon University), twenty-seven-year-old Angus Bowmer came to Ashland in 1931 during the dark days of the Great Depression. While gazing at the old Chautauqua ruins in Ashland's Lithia Park, Bowmer had an inspiration. The Chautauqua for years had been a summer series that presented programs in art, politics, music, and other subjects for several days in the mid-summer — but by the time he arrived was no more. The building had been torn down, leaving only its curving lower walls. "It gave me the impression of a 16th-century sketch of the Globe Theater [the site in England where Shakespeare's plays were originally performed]," he said later. "I began to do some research and got excited about the possibility of producing a Shakespearean work there."

Owing to Governor Julius Meier's interest in supporting the arts and Bowmer's talents, Angus received the commission to write, produce, and direct the historical pageant for Oregon's 1934 Diamond Jubilee. By 1935, Bowmer's idea caught on with other residents, and he asked the city to start its Fourth of July celebrations again, but by producing plays at the Chautauqua site. Pageant volunteers agreed to help, the city granted up to $400 as seed money, and the State Emergency Relief Administration chipped in, allowing a stage to be built within the old concrete Chautauqua shell.

The festival began as a two-play production on July 2, 1935, performing William Shakespeare's *Twelfth Night* and *The Merchant of Venice*. Ashland's grant was with the stipulation, however, that

Photo of the Elisabethan Stage at the Oregon Shakespeare Festival. (Photo by T. Charles Erickson)

afternoon boxing matches would also be held to help cover costs. The festival succeeded so well that the theatre ticket revenues covered the losses from the boxing matches. In 1937, the Oregon Shakespeare Festival was incorporated as a nonprofit, membership organization.

Although operations ceased from 1941 to 1946 owing to World War II, performances started up again in 1947 with four productions and a new stage. The first Green Show was performed in the 1950s; these free shows are put on before the evening plays, originally featuring musicians playing Elizabethan-era music, and then changing over time to mixtures of dance, music, and rhyme. Bowmer continued teaching as he built OSF, and a greatly expanded Elizabethan stage opened in 1959.

As the OSF added non-Shakespearean plays to its schedule, additional venues became vital. With Duke Ellington's orchestra as the kick-off for fundraising for an indoor theatre, the contributions mounted as residents and non-residents joined together. The Angus Bowmer Theatre opened in 1970, and the following year Angus retired from being the OSF's artistic director.

Over time, the OSF received numerous awards and achieved national status. OSF and Angus Bowmer were the recipients of the Oregon Governor's Award for the Arts in 1977; six years later, a National Governor's Association Award for "distinguished service to the arts" was received, along with winning the Tony Award for Regional Theatre; and since 1977, four others with OSF have received the Oregon Governor's Award. Angus Bowmer passed away in 1979, but he had seen the wondrous development from what years ago had only been an idea.

In 1984, the OSF instituted a play-reading service, expanded into Portland for six seasons, and increased the size of the company and its coverage. It added a pavilion to the Elizabethan theatre, reconfigured seating, and improved the acoustics. In 1995, the OSF began fundraising for the moneys to replace the Black Swan Theatre (which opened in 1977) with the modern New Theatre (opened in 2002).

The three OSF stages are: the Elizabethan Stage/Allen Pavilion (1,190 seat capacity), the August Bowmer Theatre (601 seats) and the New Theatre (up to 360). It presents in a typical season some eleven different plays (four of Shakespeare and seven in the classics or modern works) with over 700 performances to a yearly attendance of some 400,000. The Oregon Shakespeare Festival performed all of Shakespeare's thirty-seven works during the 1958, 1978, and 1997 seasons.

Well-known actors and actresses perform each year: George Peppard (e.g., *Breakfast at Tiffany's*), Gretchen Corbett, Harry Anderson (e.g., TV's "Night Court"), Dick Cavett, Jean Smart (e.g., "Designing Women" and "Fraser"), and many more. William Hurt with Emmy-winner Jean Smart, for example, was in the 1975 production of *Long Day's Journey into Night*; he won an Oscar for his role in *Kiss of the Spider Woman*, among nominations for other films. Stacy Keach was in the title role in *Henry V* in 1963; later he had the lead in the 1990s TV series, "Mike Hammer; Private Eye," and various other roles on Broadway, movies, and television.

Others include Kyle MacLachlan (*Blue Velvet, Dune*, and *The Doors*); Tony-nominated Anthony Held (*The Silence of the Lambs*, "Boston Public," "Boston Legal," and many others); Joel David Moore (SOU graduate, who was in *Avatar*, "House, M.D.," and "Hawaii Five-O"); Peter Frechette (*The First Wives Club*, "Thirtysomething," "Hill Street Blues," "Cagney & Lacey," "L.A. Law" and "Matlock"). We could go on and on.

The icing on the cake, however, was announced in April 2017: Playwright Lynn Nottage's play *Sweat* was awarded the Pulitzer Prize for drama. The play premiered in 2015 as part of the OSF series, "American Revolutions," which analyzed important moments in U.S. history. Nottage became the first female playwright to win this award twice, her first award being for the play *Ruined* (2009).

This region has been so enhanced by the Oregon Shakespeare Festival and its continuing excellence — thanks to the vision of Angus Bowmer.

Sources: Leary, *The Oregon Encyclopedia*: "Oregon Shakespeare Festival"; see "About OSF," at OSF website; Darling, *Medford Mail Tribune*, April 17, 2011; *Medford Mail Tribune*, April 14, 2013.

PART XIII

Towns and Valleys

Ashland

URING THE 1850S, GOLD-SEEKING MINERS didn't find much gold in what's now Ashland; the best sites were located in the Gold Hill, Jacksonville, and other areas. Abel Helman and Eber Emery were the smart ones: They decided as other bright ex-miners did (i.e., C.C. Beekman and his Jacksonville bank; Michael Hanley and Hanley Farm) that it was easier and more profitable to supply the miners with what they needed. With Helman staking a donation land claim on a creek, they started a water-powered saw mill and later flour and woolen mills by 1854, near today's Lithia Park. Calling the stream, Mill Creek, the site began as Ashland Mills, later renamed as Ashland Creek and Ashland respectively. According to the story, Helman chose "Ashland" as he was originally from Ashland (the county), Ohio.

One year later, Helman donated twelve building sites around the mill to create a central business district. Merchants soon built wooden buildings to house their businesses, ranging from a blacksmith and livery to a meat market and cabinet shop. The place became a gathering spot for residents and became known as the "Plaza," which is the name that continues today. The settlement had an advantage as the main wagon-trail to Jacksonville passed through, as did the stagecoach line, the Oregon-California wagon trail over the nearby Siskiyou Mountains, and the later district headquarters in the mid-1880s for the Oregon & California Railroad.

In addition to Abel Helman, leaders appeared who greatly supported the town, such as John McCall. In 1852, the twenty-seven-year-old McCall settled in Jackson County on a mining claim along Jackson Creek. After spending two rough winters, "subsisting a good portion of his time on venison alone," he bought an interest in the Ashland Flour

Ashland Plaza and Mill, circa 1890. (SOHS 00061)

Mills. After the Civil War, he became Ashland's mayor in 1886, after also being elected as a state legislator. His business interests flourished to include owning the Ashland Flour Mill, Ashland Woolen Mill, and the McCall Mercantile on the Ashland Plaza. McCall ran the newspaper, the *Ashland Tidings*, and helped found the Ashland College and Normal School in 1872, which later became Southern Oregon University.

With its hosting of Southern Oregon's annual Chautauqua festival, the town in the 1890s became the area's cultural center. Presenting programs in what is now Lithia Park in politics, art, literature, music, and different subjects for several days during the mid-summer, this nationwide program of lectures, seminars, and entertainment had started in New York as the New York Chautauqua Assembly. Well-known personalities such as Susan B. Anthony, William Jennings Bryan, and John Phillip Sousa were among those over the next two decades who came to Ashland to lecture or perform.

Despite this, Medford's orchard boom in the early 1900s (and the downtown building spree that it started) brought Medford to prominence in the Valley; Jacksonville had greatly tapered off when the railroad in the mid-1880s bypassed it in favor of Medford. Ashland continued, however, with its development of what would become the ninety-three acre, exquisite Lithia Park in the heart of Ashland in the 1900s. Its mineral springs and promoted medicinal properties also attracted tourists.

Despite its cultural and location significance, Ashland suffered economically over the years. The Southern Pacific Railroad's opening of its "Natron Cut-off" from California to Eugene, by-passed the town and passenger rail traffic dropped. After the Great Depression's financial woes, other parts of the country began to recover somewhat due to the economic impact of World War II. But here in the Rogue Valley, cities stagnated—even Ashland with its mills continued to struggle.

During the late 1940s and even into the early 1970s, Ashland was primarily a blue-collar, working class town, owing to its dozen or so saw and lumber mills (including several operating on Dead Indian Plateau, east of the city). These, however, started closing as the timber industry began winding down.

Ashland's transition to a prime tourist and vacation resort was greatly assisted by the growth of two local institutions: the Oregon Shakespeare Festival and what is now known as Southern Oregon University. In 1946, Elmo Stevenson was hired to actually close the local college campus (then named the "Southern Oregon State Normal School") if he couldn't increase enrollment. After arriving, he thought that the setting was unique and started a passionate goal to save the institution. He was successful. Southern Oregon University now has over 6,000 students, 750 faculty and staff/administrators, and its numerous buildings are spread over 175 acres.

While staring at the old Chautauqua ruins in Ashland's Lithia Park, Angus Bowmer conceived the idea of producing Shakespearean works there. By 1935, his idea caught on with other residents and with volunteers, city, and state help, the Oregon Shakespeare Festival began with a two-play production on July 2, 1935. From there, the festival has grown to an annual attendance of 400,000-plus.

Today, Ashland is home to 20,000 residents. Although it isn't the county seat, it has become a destination tourist and retirement town. With additional cultural activities — from the Ashland Independent Film Festival to the Oregon Cabaret — the former mill town on Mill Creek has come a long way.

Sources: LaLande, *Oregon Encyclopedia*: "Ashland"; Pfeil, *Medford Mail Tribune*, April 14, 2013 (McCall); Asnicar, *Medford Mail Tribune*, April 24, 2016.

Talent

*T*HE FIRST SETTLER CREDITED WITH MOVING into the Talent area was Jacob Wagner, who in 1852 filed a 160-acre donation claim along the creek that bears his name, "Wagner Creek." The land was some five miles north of Ashland and near the present city. Wagner was successful in farming and raising stock; one year later, he built a log stockade known as "Fort Wagner."

He constructed the fort with the help of Yreka's Captain Alden and his men, and this was a place of safety during the Rogue River Indian Wars of 1853 and 1855. The surrounding walls covered an acre, were two-feet thick and twelve-feet high, with portholes for rifles. A large "blockhouse" was built inside for the Wagner family, but this was a place of refuge during attacks. Once the conflicts ended, the settlements of Ashland and Jacksonville developed quicker than smaller places as Talent. Jacob Wagner later sold most of his town-site area to Horace Root for $3,500 and moved to Ashland, where among other pursuits, started up a bottling enterprise with water from Wagner Soda Springs, east of the city.

A Tennessee carpenter by the name of Aaron P. (A.P.) Talent moved into the area in 1875 and in few years had purchased part of the original Wagner claim with adjoining lands that totaled 106 acres. He began to subdivide this into lots and blocks. Having foreseen the coming growth from the railroad's approach, Talent by the early 1880s had opened a general store north of the old fort site (which was disintegrating from lack of use).

As the region was quite suitable for growing fruits and vegetables, different structures and enterprises began to rise around his store, which in 1883 became the site of a new post office. After a short-term political

Children enjoying the "Splash Pad" in one of Talent's fine community parks.

appointment, A.P. Talent became the new postmaster, which position he held for seven years. When residents headed there for their mail and general goods, it was commonplace to say they were going to "Talent's" and the name stuck.

Although the railroad came by Talent, it didn't establish a station as in Medford, Phoenix, and then Ashland. Talent was a stopover, but its leaders were never able to secure a depot. Despite this, landowners such as Horace Root, A.P. Talent, the Wagner Creek Baptist Church, and E.K. Anderson (for whom Anderson Creek is named) created the town of Talent by subdividing their lands, selling off lots, deeding streets, and recording a plat map in 1889.

Talent was a beneficiary of the early 1900's Orchard Boom and incorporated in 1910. Its growth was somewhat set back by a destructive fire one year later, but it continued expanding, although experiencing the downturn of the Orchard Bust. With the growth and selection of Medford as the county seat, coupled with the depression years, Talent lost employers and employment.

After World War II and over the years, however, it has transformed into a quaint residential community with boutique restaurants, antique shops and even a popular community theatre, the Camelot.

Sources: Talent Historical Society at its website; Asnicar, *Medford Mail Tribune*, April 24, 2016.

Phoenix

*I*N 1850, SAM COLVER AND HIS BROTHER HIRAM moved with their families over the Oregon Trail to Oregon. Sam had studied law at Plymouth College in Indiana, served as a Texas Ranger, was involved at the Battle of San Jacinto with General Sam Houston, and later served as an Indian scout. Called the first resident of what is now Phoenix, Oregon, Sam Colver took up a donation land claim in 1851 where the city is now located.

Following the Jacksonville gold strikes, miners and settlers began arriving in the Rogue Valley. In 1852, Colver built a cabin on his claim that was located on what is now Highway 99 in Phoenix. As it grew in size with the arriving newcomers, a hamlet began developing around the Colver settlement, as it served as a fort during the Rogue Indian Wars of 1853 and 1855. Colver not only became an Indian Agent in the Valley, he was also a signer of the Table Rock Treaty in September 1853 and a U.S. Marshall. He laid out the town in 1854 and one year later built his permanent home.

The town was a stage stop and first known as "Gasburg." As the time-accepted story goes, the numbers of single men far outweighed whatever eligible women were around. During the 1850s, a Mrs. Waite had hired Kate Clayton to help her cook for the men working at her husband's local flour mill. Miss Kate was "about twenty" and a very "fluent" talker. She had a number of admirers, as she not only could cook and carry on different conversations with the men, but she could "put any of them in their place with fast and fiery repartee." Due to this talent, Clayton was given the nickname of "Gassy Kate." When the topic of the town's name came up for discussion, the decision was to call it "Gasburg" for her chatty ways.

Phoenix main street, circa 1914. (SOHS 00994)

After several years of being called Gasburg, Sylvester M. Waite was not only the owner of the grist mill, but also an insurance agent for the Phoenix Insurance Co. of Harford, Connecticut. When a post office was set up at the mill, he attached the large Phoenix insurance company metal plate to the building for the name of the post office. Despite this, it took time before the residents began calling the town Phoenix, instead of its former name.

Although Phoenix was a railroad stop, nearby Medford eventually became the county seat and largest city in Jackson County. Like its neighboring town of Talent, Phoenix grew with the early 1900's Orchard

Boom and consequently incorporated in 1910. The downturn of the Orchard Bust crimped its growth, and it followed the general regional economics of the Great Depression, World War II, and the swings of the timber industries. Over the years, however, its proximity to Bear Creek Corporation/Harry & David cushioned this. Also following Talent, it transformed into a residential community, including mobile home parks, owing to its location and less-expensive housing as compared to Medford and Ashland.

With its population nearing 5,000, Phoenix also opens up westerly beyond its city limits to fields, orchards, and vineyards—a fine combination.

Sources: *Wikipedia*: "Samuel Colver"; Asnicar, *Medford Mail Tribune*, April 24, 2016.

Central Point

*T*HIS TOWN WAS SO NAMED BECAUSE two pioneer wagon trails crossed at where it now exists. One of the roads ran north and south, linking the Willamette Valley with Southern Oregon, and the other led from Butte Falls and Sams Valley to Jacksonville, which was then the county seat. Until the railroad came through in the 1880s, the wagon trains and stagecoaches made their slow way over muddy paths during the rains, but that were as hard as cement under a hot summer's sun.

Isaac Constant was a pioneer who settled there in 1852, and he is credited with naming the hub "Central Point," an appropriate observation. The Magruder brothers followed in building a store there, and when the post office was established in the spring of 1872, the town became officially known as Central Point. The coming of the railroad cemented its permanence.

When the townsfolks heard that the California & Oregon Railroad would bypass it, enterprising landowners made a deal. They agreed to give a right-of-way with the railroad to build its tracks over their land. In return, these owners relocated Central Point there, and the township flourished with the station depot in the middle on its main street.

Sharing its southern border with Medford, it incorporated as a city in 1889. Over time, Central Point followed the regional ups-and-downs as Southern Oregon did: part of the 1900's boom and bust of orchards, followed by the "Roaring Twenties" and then the Great Depression.

In an enterprising move, farmers in the Valley invested $10 each in 1934 to form a cooperative. By joining together, they could pool their produce for better prices, secure a lower price for livestock feed, and purchase needed equipment, supplies, and feed at bulk prices. Today, some eighty years later, the Grange Co-op has grown into a multi-

Central Point Looking West, circa 1915. (SOHS 01985)

million dollar business in different locations. Rising 135 feet above Central Point, its grain elevator is an imposing landmark that is the tallest manmade structure in Southern Oregon.

The Jackson County Expo also moved to its present 200-acre location in Central Point. It offers a wide range of activities: from the annual Jackson County Fair, rodeos, music events, and Harvest Fair to the Hot Air Balloon Festival, Christmas fairs, and other activities throughout the year.

As streets and highways replaced the old wagon roads, the town of 18,000 still retained its central location—and it's now a hub for tourists and residents alike, both here and over the busy I-5 corridor.

Sources: *Medford Mail Tribune*, August 12, 2009; Asnicar, *Medford Mail Tribune*, April 24, 2016; "The Grange Co-op" in this book.

Medford

*F*OUR MEN OWNING EQUAL SHARES, INCLUDING C.C. Beekman, in October 1883 conveyed land to the Oregon & California Railroad Co. for its depot, right-of-way, and facilities. This conveyance also granted the railroad every other block of the 160-acre site, in addition to the initial railroad reservation. Mr. J.S. Howard, the railroad surveyor, with his son surveyed the new townsite, and Medford was founded on December 20th of that year when the plat was recorded. David Loring, the civil engineer and right-of-way agent for the railroad, named the beginning town for his home town of Medford, Massachusetts

The railroad tracks reached Medford in mid-January 1884. As one wrote, "Medford was a typical little Western railroad town in those days, with a few wooden store buildings and a great many saloons (actually four), some of them occupying tents. Frequently one could hear some of the more hilarious men riding up and down Main and Front streets, shooting their revolvers into the air."

Within three months, the sparse settlement on the unbroken land covered by high brush had grown to thirty-six structures. As quickly as supplies of lumber from Grants Pass and brick manufactured locally became available, houses and commercial buildings rose; by early spring two hotels, saloons, a livery stable, and a dozen businesses "already dotted the muddy streets of this rapidly growing railroad town." By December, Medford had 110 businesses and residences with a population of 400; the businesses ranged from dry goods, meat markets, and furniture to livery stables, drugstores, and general stores.

Medford incorporated in early 1885, and its first city ordinance was to prevent and punish disorderly conduct, riots, and disturbances. The second one was "to prevent minors from loitering about the depot," and

Downtown Medford, circa 1909. (Image courtesy Ben Truwe)

another banned hogs from running wild. After the boom of its first two years, Medford settled into a steady growth—that is, until the Orchard Boom began.

With access by railroad to faraway markets, the orchard industry flourished; hundreds of thousands of apple and pear trees were planted in the early 1900s, and the Valley's major export was that of commercial fruit, especially apples. The Medford Commercial Club (presently the Chamber of Commerce) promoted a very successful, extensive advertising campaign in the early 1900s about the great advantages of the area's orchard industry: Easy money was to be had. This, Southern Pacific's advertising, and real estate agents pushed the boom. For example, real estate agents met the out-of-towners—arriving in numbers—at the train station to promote this "easy business."

By 1909, numerous Medford buildings were under construction or in the planning stages. Buildings with the names of Sparta, the Carnegie library, Woolworth building, and four-story Liberty brick building had been built or underway. The newcomers wanted also the new "horseless buggies" to travel from their country homes to the city. A *Medford Mail Tribune* article on November 28th reported that the city led the world in the number of automobiles per capita in 1909: It had one automobile for every thirty people when nationally there was only one car for every 500.

One year later, more people were there than could be housed. Since the town couldn't handle the incoming swell, the city erected a tent city and the railroad even put up new arrivals overnight in its train station. By 1912, Medford had a high school, four banks, three elementary schools, a city park, new passenger depot, Carnegie library, indoor swimming pool, several movie theatres, and an opera house. Mountain water came by way of twenty-one miles of wooden pipe; electricity and telephone service was reaching to the outskirts. The streets were paved and with fruit packing sheds with warehouses built by the train yard, Medford was Jackson County's transportation and commercial center.

The boom turned to bust, however, owing to the real estate speculation, property overvaluation, and fruit oversupply. By the mid-teens, Medford's population had declined with World War I blockades having ended its international markets; insect blight, frost, and drought didn't help either. Medford's population by 1920 had dropped by 28 percent, all due to the orchard bust, and it took years to recover.

Despite the economic setbacks that came and left, Medford during the Roaring Twenties opened its fairgrounds with five exhibition buildings and racetracks for car, motorcycle, and horse racing. Inside the racetrack was a dirt landing strip that was part of Oregon's first municipal airport. With the winning of a post-office delivery contract in 1926, Medford's airport became the first and only airmail stop in Oregon. One year later, Medford's campaign won and the city was selected to be the county seat.

World War II finally overcame the last remnants of the Great Depression and its effects. The round-the-clock building of nearby Camp White brought about such heavy traffic over Crater Lake Highway, it became one-way out of Medford with Table Rock Road heading back in the other. More than 10,000 workers were involved, and many lived in tent or trailer cities. Completed in some six months, the camp was officially dedicated on August 15, 1942, and nearly 40,000 soldiers at a time trained there, greatly helping to bring prosperity back when on leave.

After the war, the pent-up, regional demand for housing sparked a boom for the area's timber industry. However, the consistent economic cycles of boom and bust continued into the 1980s, the lumber industry falling into long-term stagnation. The services of healthcare, computerization, selling of cars, shopping centers (with Californians avoiding their sales taxes), and real estate construction took over, only to be followed by the Great Recession of 2008.

With this continuing recovery, another boom starts, followed by another ending. Throughout it all, Medford continues to flourish as the center of Jackson County and for those close enough in Northern California.

Sources: Truwe, "Southern Oregon History, Revised"; Fattig, *Medford Mail Tribune*, November 1, 2009; Asnicar, *Medford Mail Tribune*, April 24, 2016.

Jacksonville

*T*WO MULE PACKERS—JOHN R. POOLE and James Cluggage—were hauling supplies in January 1852 from the Willamette Valley to Sacramento. They camped by a foothill and began digging a hole to find water for their mules. As they dug, they noticed a gold color in the hole: They had accidentally discovered a rich gold deposit. The two men quickly filed claims on the land on Daisy Creek and named it "Rich Gulch." The two also filed claims along Jackson Creek, where large quantities of course placer gold were discovered. Once the news shot out, hundreds of men flocked there to find their share of the precious gold. Cluggage and Poole filed donation land claims, named their town "Table Rock City," which was soon renamed as "Jacksonville."

Oregon was still a territory, Indian conflicts were commonplace, food was scarce, and all of the supplies came by mule train from faraway Crescent City. The gold-driven town grew by the winter of 1852, however, from a mining camp to over 2,000 people in the area, complete with a bank, shops, businesses, saloons, and gambling halls. A few months later in January 1853, it became the county seat for the newly created, Jackson County. That same year, a destructive fire destroyed most of the wooden structures, but these were quickly rebuilt although mainly in brick.

Jacksonville's fortunes seemed assured, but by the late 1870s much of the easy ore deposits had been taken. The railroad in 1884 then decided not to connect with Jacksonville, but to head directly to Medford. The expense of building the track did not justify sweeping down to it, but to angle on a straight line through Bear Creek Valley. Once this happened, Jacksonville began to lose residents and businesses.

Agriculture supplanted mining in the 1890s, and a privately-owned railroad spur connected Jacksonville with the main line. In 1927,

View of Jacksonville, circa 1858. (SOHS 00738)

however, the county seat moved to Medford with its airport, previous building expansion from the orchard boom, and location. Jacksonville's economic decline continued into the 1960s.

In 1962, the proposal to re-route a new four-lane Highway 238 directly through the town's middle brought its residents together to fight the project. Robby Collins had moved that year into Jacksonville and with others led the successful opposition against the highway project. This movement galvanized these people into their efforts to preserve the historic, remarkable 19th century buildings and residences.

Their efforts met with success when the town's core in 1966 was designated a National Historic Landmark, the first time a town was so honored by the U.S. Department of the Interior. Approximately 326 acres in size and including nearly 890 structures, the Landmark District is large, but not the same size as the city limits. More than 100 individual buildings are on the National Register of Historic Places. In 1977, the

National Landmark Advisory Board adopted a larger formal boundary, which included the supporting residential neighborhoods.

Located some five miles from Medford, residents and tourists alike now flock to Jacksonville and have given it a real vitality. Its historic vintage is now its gold, not to mention the Britt Festival and other attractions.

Sources: Asnicar, *Medford Mail Tribune*, April 24, 2016; U.S. National Park Service: "Jacksonville National History District."

Eagle Point

*A*S SETTLERS MADE THEIR WAY TOWARDS THE Willamette Valley over the Applegate Trail, numbers stopped in Southern Oregon and decided to start their new lives here. With the Jacksonville gold rush as a magnet, pioneers settled in the Eagle Point area in the 1850s to sell their produce to the miners. The Englishman, James J. Fryer, acquired his property on Little Butte Creek in 1852; he established a general store and planted a fruit orchard. Considered to be the "Father of Eagle Point," Fryer caused the settlement to grow around his operations.

The area became another center for agricultural production and supplied food—along with Sams Valley to one side and the Medford-Talent area further south—to the Valley. In 1872, the Snowy Butte Mill (now named the Butte Creek Mill) was constructed along the banks of Little Butte Creek. It drew farmers from around the region, as wagons lined the dirt road to the mill to have their grain ground into flour.

Constructed of local pine trees, the four-story, 5,500-square-foot structure had two, four-foot diameter, 1,400-pound millstones that ground the grain. Water was diverted from the creek into the mill's basement where the water's weight turned a turbine that powers the equipment. Although the Butte Creek Mill unfortunately was basically destroyed by fire in 2015, the owner (Bob Russell) is working to rebuild the grist mill (once the only commercially-operating one west of the Mississippi).

As the fertile land drew farmers and ranchers, eagles soared overhead and nested high up on a bluff that overlooked the town. In 1877, John Mathews named the town Eagle Point, after the butte with its eagles. The advent of the railroad along the Rogue River limited Eagle Point, as the line passed through Gold Hill, Central Point, and Medford, on its way to Ashland. Farmers had to bring their products to these stations for shipment.

Eagle Point, circa 1909. (SOHS 03792)

The town accordingly didn't have a commercial center until the early 1900s, when the Pacific and Eastern Railroad arrived in the early 1900s. The city then incorporated in 1911 with three hotels to go along with its livery stable, blacksmith shop, a few saloons, and rowdy dance halls. Dependent on the fortunes of the timber industry, the town ebbed and flowed with this industry, as the railroad spur served the Medford mills.

Although the construction and operation of Camp White during World War II at what's now White City was an economic shot-in-the-arm, afterwards this stimulus ended when the camp was torn down. The large available blocks of land brought about a rebirth, however, as seen in the 18-hole championship golf course — designed by Robert Trent Jones Jr. — that came into being in 1995 with housing developments clustered about. A city of some 8,750 people, Eagle Point today is a retirees' destination and a commuting center that has grown over the decades.

Sources: Eagle Point: "History"; LaPlante, *Eagle Point: Images of America*; Asnicar, *Medford Mail Tribune*, April 24, 2016.

Gold Hill

ORN IN 1814 IN IRELAND, Thomas Chavner came to the United States when he was six-years-old. He was a cabin boy on riverboats, a trapper with Kit Carson, a Comanche interpreter, and fought in the Mexican War (1846-1847). Chavner arrived in the Rogue Valley in 1856. He next bought land near Dardanelles, directly across the Rogue River from where Gold Hill is now. Buying another 160 acres for $750, he built a farm near what would become Gold Hill on the other side of the river.

Two of his ranch hands were looking for stray horses four years later in the hills above Chavner's property on the Gold Hill side. Sitting down on a large rock, one of the men looked around and stared at a "dull, yellowish something" that was embedded in the boulder. He brought a piece of the brilliant white rock to his boss, Thomas Chavner, who immediately recognized this as being houndstooth quartz and heavily laced with gold.

Five men—Chavner, the two "finders," and the property owners— immediately filed mining claims. By the following night, however, 150 men had staked claims around the mountain top, as one of the owners had a "strong liking" for liquor and blurted out the news. Known as the Gold Hill Pocket that stood above the town-to-be, this rich discovery was one of the better ones. The pocket was above ground, heavy with gold, and pieces were so knit together with gold threads, a sledgehammer's blow couldn't separate them.

Although the find played out in eight months, some $700,000 (or nearly $40 million in today's dollars) of fine "jewelry like" gold was taken out. Chavner had bought out his other partners before then, and he was a wealthy man. As miners flooded the area and region searching

Fourth avenue, Gold Hill, circa 1890. Note the free-grazing cattle. (GHHS)

for gold, Chavner used his proceeds to acquire more real estate — and more real estate.

When nearby farmers and ranchers came to him for loans, he would grant them, naturally expecting repayment. When they didn't or couldn't pay him back, Thomas Chavner foreclosed. By this and outright acquisitions, he had accumulated 2,000-plus acres by 1880 that stretched three miles up the valley along the Rogue River to Central Point. He also owned ranches, orchards, farms, and assorted businesses from hotels and bars to toll bridges and blacksmith shops.

When the Oregon & California Railroad was approaching the area, Thomas Chavner was ready. In late 1883, he sold seventeen acres to the railroad for its Gold Hill depot, right-of-way, freight office, and stockyard. On January 7, 1884, he and his second wife, Rosa, recorded a plat map encompassing eighty acres that surrounded the railroad's center; he donated the intended streets and alleys to the public and sold the individual lots to the people.

When he died in 1888, the seventy-two-year-old Chavner had four adult children to continue the family's businesses. Gold Hill was incorporated in 1895, and the town at its core is basically as he had recorded. Thomas Chavner was one man who had created an entire town by himself.

Sources: Powers, *Oregon Encyclopedia*: "Gold Hill"; Asnicar, *Medford Mail Tribune*, April 24, 2016.

The City of Rogue River

*T*HE TOWN OWES ITS START TO A CARD SHARK named Davis "Coyote" Evans, who built cabins and a ferry in 1851 to cross the Rogue River near where Evans Creek poured into it. A swinging footbridge was later built for prospectors who wanted to cross and look for the gold on Evans Creek.

As the story goes, if miners didn't want to pay the toll to cross the river, they crossed by pulling their horse into the river, and then grabbing its tail to hold on as it swam across. The name given to the tiny settlement then was Tailholt. Some feel that the name meant more than crossing the Rogue. "Tailholt" could also mean, according to some, that the settlers had found a tough life, but that it was more dangerous to let go, if they had made a "tail-hold" there: "A tailholt was better than no holt at all."

Building a home and store of broad boards milled on Evans Creek in the early 1870s, John Woods picked an excellent location at Tailholt. It was not only where mail and people were dropped off for the prospectors working Evans Creek, but this was where folks crossed the Rogue headed for the other side. Although it wasn't an official stage stop, Woods kept an extra team of horses for the stage line.

While Woods ran his general store, the population also grew. When the post office was established in 1876 in his home owing to his efforts, and he became the town's first postmaster, it non-surprisingly took on the name of Woodville. When the Oregon & California Railroad ran through it to Gold Hill and set up a station stop, Woodville in 1884 gained in importance. In 1909, the first bridge to allow wagons, buggies, and teams to cross to the other side was constructed. The town's residents then decided three years later that a new name would be better for the times and voted for its incorporation as the City of Rogue River.

Aerial view of the City of Rogue River. (Courtesy City of Rogue River)

As sawmills and farming gave way to tourism and commuting to outlying areas, the Rogue River Rooster Crow was first put on in 1953 to publicize the city. Since that time, its National Rooster Crow Championship has been held on the last Saturday in June. A five-minute drive from the downtown, Orin Palmerton during this time had operated a plant and tree nursery with many domestic and exotic trees that eventually became the city's property. The city maintains the exquisite Palmerton Park that has a suspension footbridge over Evans Creek.

Over time, the Rogue River bridge was replaced, first in 1950 and then again in 2006. This project attracted national attention, as the designers employed a "slow slide" to move the 550-ton, 300-foot long bridge into its final position. Located some twenty miles northwest of Medford on I-5, the City of Rogue River — and its population of 2,000 being about what it was when the town incorporated — is still well known for its fishing, rafting, small size, and beautiful scenery along the river.

Sources: Twitchell, *Medford Mail Tribune,* February 10, 1991; Bill Miller, *Medford Mail Tribune,* January 17, 2010.

Shady Cove

*D*ATING BACK TO THE MID-1800s, passersby described the shady cove — from which the town derived its name — as a shelter where weary travelers could rest from the hot sun. This river bend is located 300 yards upstream from the present Highway 62 bridge in town, and the name then was descriptive, not an official name. It isn't known precisely when folks started referring to the bend as the "cove" or "shady cove."

The place was also where people stayed while waiting for the ferry at a nearby river crossing. Before bridges were built, folks crossed the Rogue this way, whether it was to commute between the gold camps at Jacksonville and John Day in Eastern Oregon, or to travel between Trail and Eagle Point.

In the early 1900s, two developers built a home and vacation cabins at the cove, and they were the first to officially use the name in their recorded map. Area residents came to spend their summertime while enjoying the river and away from the summer heat. Over time, however, the cabins were abandoned, pathways washed away, and vegetation overtook the beach.

As with most Rogue Valley communities, the economy depended on the timber industry. With it being on a main access to Crater Lake — some sixty miles away — tourists naturally passed by or stayed in the town. As timbering moneys diminished, the town became more of a tourist and retiree destination. The town grew as newcomers replaced the loggers and industry suppliers.

The disastrous Rogue River flood in 1964 nearly destroyed it. After five days of heavy rains and snowmelt, the swollen river rose over its banks at night on December 22nd. The raging waters hit Shady Cove almost the

Ferry, Shady Cove, circa 1891-1895. (SOHS 21147)

hardest. The flood and mudslides destroyed homes, stately pine trees, the original bridge crossing, the saw mill next to the bridge, and other structures, as tons of heavy mill-logs and rooftops surged past to crush downstream houses. The town was totally dark as power was out, but everyone could hear the river's roar. The town rebuilt—but it took time.

Shady Cove incorporated in 1972; led by Faye Thompson, the city embarked on a beautification project to make the town "shady with trees." The U.S. Forest Service donated Evergreen seedlings that were planted throughout in returning the place to its pre-1964 flood days. Owing to this, people now see forty-year-old-plus Pine trees that stand tall.

For flood control, the U.S. Army Corps of Engineers in 1977 completed construction of the William Jess Dam and Lost Creek Lake, a reservoir nine miles north of Shady Cove. With the recreational draws of the lake and adjacent parks, the town had another added attraction.

With RV parks, close-by camping facilities, motels, and different parks, Shady Cove, a town of 3,000, has found its niche as a tourist and retiree destination. With the magnificent Rogue River running through the city limits, it has found its place.

Sources: *Medford Mail Tribune*, April 22, 2007; see "Christmas Flood of 1964" and "Lost Creek Lake (and Jess Dam)" in this book.

Grants Pass

*T*HE GROWTH OF JOSEPHINE COUNTY AND Grants Pass was based on gold mining and the railroad. Learning about the newly discovered gold finds in Jacksonville in 1852, sailors deserted their ship near Crescent City and found rich gold deposits in the Illinois Valley, twenty-five miles south of present-day Grants Pass. Known as "Sailor Diggings" (then in Jackson County), its population of several thousands made it an important mining center. Although later named Waldo, numbers of the miners left six years later for British Columbia's Frazier River with the news of its gold discoveries. Gold mining centers in the Illinois Valley as Sailor Diggings, Althouse, and others vanished over time with little remains left behind.

With its importance as a gold mining region, however, Josephine County was carved out in 1856 from a portion of Jackson County; it was named for Josephine Rollins, the first non-Native American woman to settle in Southern Oregon. Before the easy-to-find gold was exhausted, Sailor Diggings became the first county seat, and later when named as Waldo. The settlement was naturally rustic and remote; for example, the courthouse was a log house bought from a local settler. By 1857, however, the population center had shifted to Kerbyville in the Illinois Valley, a town settled earlier by James Kerby — and the county seat again moved.

The county's population by 1873 was said to be 1,500 and there were only seven towns listed: Althouse, Kerbyville, Leland, Slate Creek, Waldo, Williamsburg, and Wolf Creek. Most commercial activity centered on gold mining and supplying the miners with their needs. There were a few hotels but more saloons as tent cities were a basic part of every town, while the miners came and left based on where the gold was.

Orson Gilbert had settled on a donation claim in 1854 that later became Grants Pass. The small village was first named Perkinsville, and

Early Grants Pass, circa 1890. (SOHS 1960355)

it was little more than a stagecoach stop in the 1860s; however, the coming of the Oregon & California Railroad (O&C) changed everything. The stop was located centrally on the railroad's path, on the Rogue River, and since building track was very expensive, the surveyed line lined up with the settlement of Rogue River, the next station stop.

The O&C line was completed to Grants Pass on Christmas Eve, 1883. With the railroad in place, businesses sprang up to serve the train passengers and those who decided to make it their new home. Hotels, stores, saloons, and churches appeared in wood structures along Front Street, or what is now "G" Street. Within five years of the railroad's coming, the population doubled from 2,500 residents to nearly 5,000.

A leading citizen, Henry Miller, soon built an extensive sawmill that covered nearly ten acres in the town's middle; this operation became its largest employer with an estimated 300 employees. Miller then spearheaded the move to make Grants Pass the county seat in 1896 and was successful. He also lobbied the state for an appropriation of $7,000 to build the first bridge that spanned the Rogue River, downstream from the current Caveman Bridge.

Tradesmen, farmers, lumbermen, and orchardists over time settled around the city and replaced the transient miners who moved on. With its location and transportation network, Grants Pass became the county's trading center. By the 1890s the city had its own opera house, the first of several bridges crossing the Rogue, a water company, and light and power, generated from a dam a few hundred feet west of Caveman Bridge.

The town was named in honor of General U.S. Grant's capture of Vicksburg in 1863. When this news reached the area, the nearby stagecoach station was so named. Once Ulysses S. Grant became the 18th President of the United States (1869 to 1877), the name was a fixture. With the railroad's coming, the post office moved to near the depot, taking the name with it. Even into the 1900s, the town retained the original spelling of "Grant's Pass," using the apostrophe — before finally dropping the punctuation.

When gold mining played out, Grants Pass's fortunes fluctuated with the economics of the timber industry. With the opening of the Oregon Caves to the public after a 1920's road completion, Grants Pass was on the route to the Pacific Ocean and became more tourist-centered. After the Great Depression, World War II, and into the 1980s, the timber industry had its ups and down but then stagnated. With the fabled Rogue River fishing, river explorations (such as the growth of Hellgate Jet Boats), and outdoors becoming popular, the city became more retiree and tourist-oriented, joining farming, dairying, and even planting vineyards as economic activities.

The population of Grants Pass is presently 35,000, or roughly 40% of Josephine County's 85,000, and a vast improvement from the mining camps that had once been the county seat — and it still is the center for Josephine County.

Sources: Stumbo, *Grants Pass Daily Courier*, March 11, 2010; Richter, *Grants Pass Daily Courier*, March 11, 2010.

Sams Valley

*E*LEVEN MILES NORTH OF MEDFORD, AT HIGHWAY 234 and Antioch Road, lies the unincorporated community of Sams Valley. The first settlers in the area who owned large ranches were Enoch Pelton and Jose Sizemore, who arrived in the early 1850s. The James Pankey family from Tennessee also settled there, had numerous children, and were part of the large landholding families.

The community was first named "Moonville," when Andrew Moon settled there in the late 1850s and established a general store; the wooden structure also housed Arad Stanley's drugstore, the local doctor in the area. A tin shop and blacksmith shop were part of the hamlet. The boundaries of Sams Valley were generally considered to be now Ramsey Road to the west and Table Rock Road or Meadows Road to the east.

Sams Valley was named in honor of Chief Sam of the Rogue River tribe. He signed the peace treaty in the mid-1850s that ended the hostilities between the settlers and Indians, lived on the Table Rock reservation, and subsequently was removed with the tribe in 1856 to southeastern Oregon.

Located five miles from Gold Hill (now on Highway 234), the rich valley produced grains, livestock, dairy products, vegetables, and other products that were wagoned to Gold Hill and outlying areas over that basic trail. It was as an important provider of food for the many miners and settlers that had flooded into the Gold Hill and Rogue River area.

When the railroad chose Gold Hill, Central Point, and then Medford for its stations and right-of-ways in 1884, these towns surpassed Sams Valley in importance. Nearby Gold Hill became the trading center for the vicinity, and even a few prominent families left Sams Valley for that town. The Ray brother's construction of Gold Ray Dam in 1903 with its

Sams Valley. (GHHS)

ensuing supply of hydroelectric power furthered solidified Gold Hill's then prominence. The important agricultural base continued, however, as most families stayed in an endeavor that they knew and enjoyed, dating back for years.

Although the precise boundaries of Sams Valley can depend on the resident, it is still dominated by farms, large ranches, orchards, acreage, and now vineyards. The number of working farms has extensively decreased, as commuting to nearby Central Point and Medford replaced farming as the area's main livelihood. Its peaceful nature, however, and the generations of families who live there still stand out.

Sources: Jackson County: "Rural and Suburban Lands Element: Sams Valley Rural Service Center"; Fattig, *Medford Mail Tribune*, September 19, 1999.

Applegate Valley

NAMED FOR ONE OF THE PIONEERING Applegate brothers, the Applegate River winds its way northward from its forested headwaters in Siskiyou County, California, into Jackson County and then into Josephine County where it spills into the Rogue River downstream from Grants Pass. Southern Oregon's Applegate Valley (named for the river) extends from Wonder and Wilderville to the north, the Rogue River National Forest to the south, Ruch to the east, and Williams to the west. The small unincorporated town of Applegate is fifteen miles from Jacksonville along Highway 238 in this valley.

The 1850's area discovery of gold brought a rush of miners into the Applegate River and its watershed, followed by merchants and settlers. With a strong market for supplying the miners and settlers, the completed Crescent City to Jacksonville wagon road in 1858 allowed wagon trains to bring needed goods from the port. The town of Applegate was originally named Bridge Point, as those on this trail—heading to and from the Pacific Ocean—crossed the Applegate River there over an 1860-built wood bridge.

Close to this crossing was a dance and events hall built by a local farmer by the name of Orlando Rose. The Pernoll family built a store at the crossing later that housed the post office and other structures followed. As mining declined, other economic activities took its place, including logging, farming, and ranching.

In the decades after World War II, farming and ranching declined, and folks moved there in their search for a simpler, rural life. Land once used for farming was subdivided into small lots and houses constructed. More residents commuted to work and larger, expensive homes were built on acres, especially in the Upper Applegate Valley.

Applegate Lake in the Applegate Valley.

To protect the region from flooding, the Army Corps of Engineers began construction in 1976 on the Applegate Dam and completed this four years later. The dam created Applegate Lake — a 988-acre reservoir located twenty-five miles from Jacksonville along Upper Applegate Road. The fishing, boating, camping, and recreational activities added to the region's allure.

In 1977, a few recent converts to Christianity asked the Reverend Jon Courson to come to the Applegate. The charismatic Courson built the bible-study group in Ruch over time into Southern Oregon's largest church, the Applegate Christian Fellowship. Under his leadership, the Ruch campus grew from nothing to now covering several acres with a large church, an open-air amphitheater, and different structures. The Applegate Fellowship draws large crowds on Sundays that pack the roads and parking in its rural setting.

Wineries and vineyards also sprouted up and the Applegate Valley was designated as an American Viticultural area in 2000, joining the Napa and Rogue Valleys. One of the state's first wineries began here and reopened as the Valley View Winery with some twenty vineyards and wineries now in operation in this area. This bucolic area is now a place where retirees live with younger, working people, one that successfully changed with the times.

Sources: Jackson County: "Rural and Suburban Lands Element: Applegate Rural Service Center."

PART XIV

Potpourri

Beaver Money

*I*N THE MID-NINETEENTH CENTURY WHEN Oregon was still a territory, U.S. currency was scarce and seldom used. Oregonians used Mexican pesos, beaver pelts, wheat, otter pelts, and even traded blankets as the currency for their transactions. To solve their need for standardized money that was easy to hold and use, the Oregon Provisional Legislature authorized in 1849 the Oregon Exchange Company in Oregon City to mint gold coins.

One side was hand-stamped with a large beaver crouching over a log, hence the name "beaver money"; the other side of these coins had the name of the Oregon Exchange Company and the year, 1849, stamped on it. The exchange melted down gold dust into molten strips and struck 6,000 coins with a five-dollar ($5) domination, and then produced nearly 3,000 with a ten-dollar ($10) value.

Despite being the size of a minted U.S. Half-Eagle, beaver money actually held more gold. In fact, 8% more than the $5 and $10 coins being struck by the U.S. Mint in Philadelphia. In months, however, the private firm stopped its work when a key investor left in late 1849 to try and strike it rich in the California gold fields. Although it was illegal federally for a private entity to have minted these coins, settlers used them—even after the U.S. San Francisco Mint was established five years later and ordered all of the illegal coins to be brought in and smelted down.

With U.S. gold coins now available from the U.S. Mint—along with gold dust, nuggets, and U.S. currency—nearly all of the beaver coins disappeared over time. For their historical value and rarity, these coins are now very valuable. With no more than fifty of the $5 and $10 coins believed to be in existence today, one $5 coin sold in 2014 for more than

Front and back of an 1849 "Beaver Money" coin.

$257,000 and the $10 coin is valued substantially higher. Reproductions of these coins are abundant and not nearly worth as much.

As the price of buying and selling beaver money is typically kept confidential, these coins become even more highly valued as collectibles over time.

Sources: Willamette Heritage: Beaver Money; Russo, the *Eugene Register Guard*, March 4, 2015.

Camp White

EDFORD PROMOTED ITS "AGATE DESERT" — a flat area seven miles east — in 1941 as the best place for military training with a topography perfect for needed buildings, parade grounds, and training. In May, the War Department decided the area would be one of nine new training camps throughout the U.S. A large-staffed architect office was established in Medford to design the camp, including its roads, power, and utilities.

The camp became a high priority when the Japanese bombed Pearl Harbor on December 7, 1941, and war was declared against Japan and Germany. Five firms combined to submit the low bid of $27.5 million dollars, construction soon began, and work went around the clock under huge lights. Traffic over Crater Lake Highway became so heavy that it became one-way out of Medford with Table Rock Road heading back in the other direction. More than 10,000 workers were involved and many lived in tent cities.

Completed in six months, the camp was officially dedicated on August 15, 1942, as "Camp George A. White," after the Adjutant General of the Oregon National Guard who had recently died. It encompassed seventy-seven square miles, trained 40,000 troops at a time, a building core that was a one-mile rectangle, 1,300 buildings, and the second largest city in Oregon. Camp White trained the 91st and 96th Divisions — as well as engineering, medical, and artillery units — that then headed off to different war fronts.

After the troops departed, the former barracks and quarters held German POWs; over 1,600 German prisoners were detained there. The facilities included barracks, mess hall, storage, and offices with the area guarded. Owing to the war effort, the Rogue Valley was experiencing a

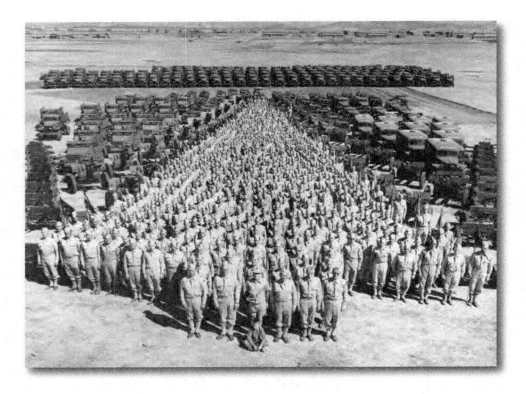

Soldiers and materiel pose for this WWII era photo at Camp White.
(SOHS 13408)

shortage of farm laborers; the U.S. Government decided that the POWs at Camp White would work in the orchards and be paid eighty-eight cents with a bottle of beer each day — a far cry from what U.S. POWs were suffering thru.

Even though repatriated after World War II, some POWs returned to the U.S. and even to Medford to live. In fact, one POW was so happy with his life in the valley, even as a prisoner of war, that he returned twenty-one years after being sent back to his native country and for years afterwards ran a Medford upholstery shop.

After the war, most of Camp White's buildings were torn down and salvaged for their materials. Structures also were moved intact to the

University of Oregon; the bricked camp hospital became the Veteran's Administration Domiciliary (now operated by the V.A. as the Southern Oregon Rehabilitation Center and Clinics), known locally as the "Dom." Camp White's building core became the basis for the White City Industrial Park; the unincorporated area surrounding the industrial part became the residential side, renamed White City in 1960.

Sources: Kramer, George, *Oregon Encyclopedia*: "Camp White"; Kramer, *Camp White: City in the Agate Desert*, 1992.

Ghosts, Spirits, and Other Apparitions

G HOST STORIES AND SPIRITUAL ADVENTURES have been part of mankind dating back to the caves. This belief — or concept — is based on the ancient idea that a person's spirit exists separately from ones body with a continued existence after death. Haunted locations typically connect with a happening in the ghost's past, often where one died or a former home. Aside from actual sightings, signs of their presence range from strange noises, lights, odors or breezes to objects that move, windows that slam, and doors that open.

The Roman author and statesman Pliny the Younger recorded in the first century A.D. one of the first notable ghost stories in his letters, which became famous for their vivid account of life during the height of the Roman Empire. Pliny wrote that an old man's ghost with a long beard and rattling chains was haunting his Athens home. Southern Oregon is no different.

A few of the memorable ones — and you will have yours as well — start with the Plunkett Center in Ashland. Southern Oregon University acquired the old structure in 1966 and uses it for alumni and development functions. It is also known as the Swedenburg House for the doctor who lived there from 1919 until his death in 1937. Several believe that a ghost resides there, including a professor, group of students, their teacher, and the head of campus security.

From the beginning, the campus security guard in the 1980s had a strong sense that he was being watched when inside and decided to announce himself before entering. Later driving by the house, he and another guard spotted a woman that the porch light illuminated. She was sitting beside a window in a first floor office, but the apparition suddenly vanished. The men searched for her inside but found nothing. The building was empty and all of its doors locked.

The Oregon Caves is the setting for another famous presence. Couples who have stayed in or beside the Chateau's infamous Room 310 report being awakened at night by the sounds of someone walking in the hall — or from actually inside the room. The tale goes that a young couple in 1937 was spending their wedding night at the hotel. After the bride caught her husband in an embrace with a hotel employee, the bride (named Elizabeth) took her life. Employees tell of strange occurrences in room 310: the room's furniture will be rearranged, or on rare occasions, even placed out in the hallway. Guests have reported unpacking — and on returning from dinner — find that their bags have been repacked. On occasion, the baby grand piano in the lobby plays by itself.

The Oregon Vortex is another site for continued paranormal investigations. John Lister arrived in the early 1900s to conduct mining surveys, only to discover the strange anomalies in the magnetic fields at this Sardine Creek location. Famous for its strange effects — for example, two people can change place, and then become taller or shorter simply by that — Lister became obsessed with the place. Brooms stood upright at an angle and balls rolled uphill inside an old assay shed. After Lister's death in 1959, people discovered that he had burned all of his notes, saying that the world wasn't ready for them yet. Visitors told about spotting him standing at the top of the sloping floor of the assay shed. Tour guides reported the same sightings, but no one was physically around.

Gold Hill's Beeman-Martin house is another ghost center. The wealthy Josiah Beeman built this fine home in 1901, and it still is standing, now as the museum for the Gold Hill Historical Society. Volunteers insist that the sounds they hear in an upstairs attic, the cupboards that slam, or furniture that change locations is owing to the apparition of a friendly ghost that they named "Willie." The spirit is either that of Bill Hay, who spent time there, or a handyman of the same name who died in the house.

From the green mists of the nearby Rock Point Cemetery to old structures in Grants Pass and the mining ghost towns of the present, the stories are abundant.

Sources: History.com: "History of Ghost Stories"; Davis, "Ghosts and Critters"; Swanson, "Ghosts in Southern Oregon's National Monument"; Powers, *Images of America: Gold Hill*, pp. 56.

Southern Oregon's Bigfoot

ROM GRANTS PASS AND ASHLAND TO Cave Junction and Prospect, the sightings of Bigfoot, otherwise known as Sasquatch, have been numerous over the years; state and federal parks are also noteworthy as to these encounters, such as around Crater Lake or the Oregon Caves. Given the widespread, thick forests and remote areas in Southern Oregon, it isn't too much of a stretch to see that our area has more than its share of these sightings.

Bigfoot is defined in most dictionaries, as a "very large, hairy, humanoid creature reputed to inhabit wilderness areas of the U.S. and Canada, especially in the Pacific Northwest." These human-like beings are believed to be eight-foot-plus in height, primate-like, and the surviving descendants of a species named Gigantopithecus, a tall, ape-like creature from the Pleistocene epoch (a long period that ended 11,700 years ago.)

With the numerous sightings in Jackson and Josephine counties, it is difficult to pick the best ones, as all are interesting and certainly important to whoever's making the report. Crater Lake and the Oregon Caves are the site of well-evidenced ones. In 1976, the Chief Park Naturalist observed a Sasquatch-like creature, for example, that was crossing the South Road at dusk. Two years later, two park rangers reported seeing "something large in the forest with a foul odor" that threw a pinecone at them.

If having reports from rangers is doubtful, then the experiences of a Grants Pass clinical psychologist in 2000 at the Oregon Caves is noteworthy. Matthew Johnson was on a summer walk on the Big Tree Loop Trail, when he left his wife and children to "answer nature's call." He previously had heard strange "whoaa, whoaa, whoaa" sounds and smelled a skunk-like stench.

While off the trail, the 6'9", 300-pound man had the scare of his life. Seeing movement to one side, Johnson turned to watch a Bigfoot—nine feet tall, hairy, huge, and quite real to him—who then disappeared back into the brush. The psychologist ran to his family and quickly herded them back to the caves. A long-time park ranger at the Oregon Caves accompanied Johnson the next day to investigate the site. Although he didn't believe then in Sasquatch, he said that without any question, Johnson had not made up the story. Finding a large footprint by the area of the sighting, the ranger became a believer.

Matthew Johnson was so taken by his experience, he told about this on television and through newspapers around the country. He established the Southern Oregon Bigfoot Society (SOBS) so that others could join him in finding the creature. This organization put together different expeditions into the forests near Grants Pass. The SOBS has reported discovering hair samples, handprints, footprints, and teeth imprints with a three and one-half inch gap between them. The group states they have come across boulders tossed in a road's middle that were too heavy for a man to lift, along with trees broken off ten-feet high with limbs that were six inches in diameter.

These searches are not isolated occurrences. In the 1970s, three men built a Bigfoot trap west of Applegate Lake. Led by reports that an old miner had found eighteen-inch human-like tracks (indicating a six-foot stride) in his garden near the upper reaches of the Applegate River, Ron Olson and two others decided to build a trap near the location. The constructed wooden box was 10-feet x 10-feet and built of two-inch thick planks. A metal grate was the trap door and to be triggered by a Bigfoot reaching for a deer or rabbit carcass hung at the rear.

Built by special forestry permit, this cage is most likely the only official Bigfoot trap in the world. Located one-half mile west of Applegate Lake on the Collings Mountain Trail, telephone poles anchor it to the ground. Although the structure is in disrepair owing to the elements, it is a testimonial to the belief that such creatures do exist.

Although the arguments continue as to whether Sasquatch is a fact or only a myth, even some academics and anthropologists have written books and articles supporting its reality. Even so, your belief might depend on whether you are reading this article in a home study or camping out in the wilderness at night.

Sources: Oregonbigfoot.com; Duewel, *Grants Pass Daily Courier*, August 5, 2006; Fattig, *Medford Mail Tribune*, September 3, 2006.

The Ballot Stealing Caper

*T*HE CHARISMATIC ORCHARDIST AND PUBLISHER of the *Medford Daily News*, Llewellyn Banks, became sharply critical during the Great Depression over the depressed conditions in Southern Oregon. He and Earl Fehl — a Medford contractor and businessman — joined forces to create a power base that took form as the Good Government Congress (GGC).

Banks had a powerful forum in his daily column, "Once in a While," throughout 1931-1932 that blamed the region's economic problems on different factors, ranging from the Federal Reserve Bank to the "local corrupt Courthouse Gang." The battle raged between the GGC/*Daily News* and the *Medford Mail Tribune* with its editor, Robert Ruhl, who wrote editorials urging people to uphold "rationality and fairness."

In the November 1932 elections, Earl Fehl won election as a county judge and another GGC supporter, Gordon Schermerhorn, won the sheriff's office. Tensions continued to mount between the two forces and the newspapers; the *Medford Mail Tribune* was threatened with sabotage, and Robert Ruhl ordered his printers armed with shotguns. Named the "Green Springs Mountain Boys," a group of young roughnecks guarded Banks and Fehl.

Reports of ballot irregularities led to a state-ordered recount, when state politicians became concerned over this. Acting upon orders from Banks and Fehl, men at night broke into the county courthouse on February 20th, 1933, in Medford through a rear, ground-floor window. They stole thousands of ballots from the vault with the next day set for the vote recount; GGC's gamble was that it could stop any later investigations when its sheriff hired his deputies.

Oregon State Police investigated after officials discovered the missing

A portrait of Llewellyn A. Banks in the mid-1920s. (Courtesy *Oregon Historical Quarterly*)

ballots. The state police found burned ballot pouches in the courthouse furnace with more floating in the Rogue River. After two young GGC members confessed, the police began to arrest the culprits. In mid-March, Constable George Prescott headed to arrest Llewellyn Banks at his home.

Answering the door, Banks's wife opened the door, but began to close it upon seeing Prescott. As the policeman put his foot on the door, Banks stepped over and fired a rifle at Prescott's chest. He died on the spot, although three supporting officers there tried to revive him.

Once word of the murder came out with the bad publicity, the GGC movement stopped in its tracks, as hundreds of its members said that they weren't part of it or ever active. The trials of the involved conspirators lasted into late 1933. For the murder, Banks was convicted and sentenced to life in prison. Fehl also was convicted and sentenced to jail for his role in the ballot stealing, as was the incumbent sheriff, county jailer, a Rogue River mayor, the ballot stealers, and others.

Although *The New York Times* and *San Francisco Chronicle* won Pulitzer Prizes in 1934 for their reporters, the jury also selected the *Medford Mail Tribune* for its "meritorious public service" gold medal in its reporting against the "unscrupulous politicians in Jackson County, Oregon." The award acknowledged the role of Ruhl for his part in resisting the GGC (also called the "Jackson County Rebellion"). Banks died in the penitentiary in 1945 at age seventy-three; however, Fehl was paroled, returned to Medford, and lived until 1962.

Sources: LaLande, *Oregon Encyclopedia*: "Good Government Congress (Jackson County Rebellion)"; Twitchell, *Medford Mail Tribune*, November 2, 2009.

The State of Jefferson

ATING BACK TO THE 1850s, THE RESIDENTS of the bordering mountain counties in Southern Oregon and Northern California felt neglected by their respective Salem and Sacramento legislatures. Especially burdensome years ago was that this region needed roads and bridges for access to their great supplies of timber, gold, copper, and other resources; their state capitals, however, didn't seem to be interested in repairing or building such access, but instead were funding campgrounds and infrastructure in the more heavily populated regions with more voters. The solution: To seek separation from their respective states and form a new one that stood on its own.

The attempt that drew by far the greatest national attention was the 1941 "secession" campaign to form a 49th state, the State of Jefferson. Although the U.S. Constitution provides that no new state can be formed from an existing one without the consent of both state legislatures and Congress, the Siskiyou County Board of Supervisors started this off with a grant of $100. In contrast to such efforts in the 1850s, the State of Jefferson was mainly a publicity gimmick (although treated seriously by others); but it was one with a serious purpose: To finally secure federal aid for the repair and building of needed infrastructures such as roads and bridges.

The Yreka newspaper held a contest to name the new state, and the winner entered the name "Jefferson" — after the third United States President, Thomas Jefferson — for which the author received $2. Delegates from the border counties met in Yreka on November 17, 1941, to discuss their approach and Yreka was agreed upon to be the temporary state capital.

Members of the Yreka 20-30 Club set up a roadblock as "State of Jefferson Border Patrol" officers during the first Secession Thursday. This staged photograph shows a motorist accepting a copy of the "Proclamation of Independence" from one of the men. (Photo: *San Francisco Chronicle*)

Outside of Yreka, the State of Jefferson Citizens' Committee erected every Thursday roadblocks on Highway 99 and handed out their "Proclamation of Independence." These efforts made national headlines, including that of the *San Francisco Chronicle* which ran stories that competed with Germany's war on Europe. A young reporter, Stanton Delaplane, traveled to the proclaimed State of Jefferson, and his articles on the movement earned the Pulitzer Prize for this newspaper. (Moreover, experts maintain that Delaplane was part of the publicity-garnering events in order to build reader interest.)

The committee elected Judge John Childs of Crescent City in Del Norte County on December 4th as the new state's governor with a torchlight parade in Yreka, followed by his inauguration on the courthouse lawn. National media and newsreel companies were on hand to record this, as well as picturing the highway barricades.

Before the newsreels could run nationally, however, Japan bombed Pearl Harbor on December 7th, 1941, and war was declared. Everyone went to work for the war effort and the secession movement came to an end. Owing to the World War II mobilization, roads and bridges were finally built to retrieve the area's valuable minerals and timber—but at times residents in this area still see the need to create a State of Jefferson.

Sources: LaLande, *Oregon Encyclopedia*: "State of Jefferson"; Jefferson Public Radio: "State of Jefferson."

Two-Bits:
The World War II Hero

A DETERMINED FOX TERRIER BY THE NAME OF "Two-Bits" became a canine war hero during World War II. This wasn't due to his feats in combat under fire, but instead due to surviving his station on Whiskey Peak Lookout in Josephine County during the home-front defense efforts. The term "Two-Bits" then meant twenty-five cents, or a quarter, and usually described something that wasn't expensive.

Whiskey Peak Lookout was an isolated U.S. Forest Service fire-spotting point used during World War II to spot and warn about incoming Japanese aircraft. This was before radar could be developed or even installed at such places. A 14 x 14-foot, sparse structure with a pitched roof had been constructed on top of 6,497-foot-high Whiskey Peak, located in the remote wilderness of the Rogue River National Forest in southeastern Josephine County. It overlooked a 600-foot plunge to the valley below.

During the winter of 1942-1943, Bill Ziegler — the terrier's owner — and a partner worked for the Army Air Corps and used a cranked telephone to report every aircraft that they spotted. Forest Service men skied to the lookout each two weeks to bring in food and supplies. The men watched for enemy planes in twelve-hour shifts during the tough winter conditions due to the lookout's high elevation.

Scampering around the heavy snows and winter ice that surrounded the nearby cliff, Two-Bits loved to chase the chipmunks that begged for food. In January 1943, he ran after one with too much enthusiasm and slid across the ice, disappearing over the cliff. Bill Zeigler watched in

Top: Lookout on Whiskey Peak.

Left: Two-Bits, the War Hero.

(Rogue River National Forest Historic Photograph Collection, courtesy Jeff LaLande)

horror and assumed his dog couldn't have survived the plunge. He sadly went about his duties.

One week later, Bill headed down the trail to cut a pole. He had navigated around the first snowed-in curve when—to his amazement—he saw Two-Bits climbing slowly up towards him, head down and tongue out, but with a happily wagging tail. It turned out that the terrier had fallen into a deep snowdrift that had cushioned his fall; after digging himself out, he then worked his way back up the snow-covered, two-and-one-half mile trail to his master.

After a meal and some rest, Two-Bits returned to his normal routine. A few weeks later, the fox terrier again slid over the cliff and disappeared once more from view. If that wasn't enough, the little dog again reappeared later at the top of Whiskey Peak to the men's amazement.

Once their duties were completed, Two-Bits and Bill Zeigler left the mountain in the summer of 1943 and returned to their Jacksonville home. The news of the canine surviving not only one great plunge, but two, and "without physical impairment or loss of morale," came to the attention of the *Medford Mail Tribune* that broke the story. This news went national and became a symbol of the homefront efforts' dedication and "winning ways," as newspapers across the country and even *Life* magazine ran it.

Two-Bits lived a good life and died a few years after the war ended. The Whisky Peak Lookout was abandoned in the mid-1970s, fell into disrepair, but was later dismantled to be rebuilt on Sand Mountain in the Willamette National Forest. The story of Two-Bits, however, lives on.

Sources: LaLande, *Oregon Encyclopedia*: "Two-Bits."

The Grants Pass Cavemen

*T*HE GRANTS PASS CAVEMEN DATE BACK TO the initial development of the Oregon Caves. In 1922, the completion of the road there (now Highway 46) from the Redwood Highway (Hwy. 199) allowed the general public to visit. With this access established, the Forest Service (later the National Park Service) granted a concession to the Oregon Caves Company for accommodations and guide services that's still in effect. Grants Pass businessmen financed the lodging and staff to run the resort, while the Forest Service provided oversight and infrastructure (i.e., interior cave lighting, trails inside and out, and a water system).

That summer a few Chamber of Commerce members showed up at a luncheon meeting wearing animal skins and long straggly wigs. Fellow members laughed as the group proclaimed their dominion over the country — and their home, the Oregon Caves. The group agreed that this would be a fine way to promote tourism in Josephine County. In October 1922, "Oregon Cavemen, Inc. of Grants Pass, Oregon" was officially incorporated.

Wearing their caveman furs, wielding burly clubs, and scowling as Neanderthals, the list of their impromptu event interruptions became legendary–with national recognition. Accompanied by their Cave Queen and Princesses, the cavemen performed "uncivilized" acts, such as capturing female crowd members and politicians, and then imprisoning them in a rustic cage towed by a pickup truck. The Cave Queen and Princesses would appease any upset women by giving them polished stones as mementos or just freeing them with smiles. The group became braver and even stormed the stage during one local Broadway musical performance (*Hellzapoppin'*) to the onlookers' surprise.

Shirley Temple posing with one of the Cavemen. (SOHS 14067)

With this promotion, organizers typically didn't care if their event was interrupted, especially given Josephine County's promotion. As often, this seemed at the time to improve the event. In 1948, Governor Dewey of New York was running for president against Harry Truman. At a scheduled Grants Pass campaign speech, the bus carrying Dewey arrived downtown — but with numerous Cavemen who then "arranged" for the governor's release after the pre-arranged hijacking. Even the Soviet newspaper *Pravda* ran the story of Dewey's cavemen capture, but wrote that this was a protest against the Wall Street "Moneygogs."

One-thousand folks in 1960 lined for one mile along Highway 199, as they awaited the formal ground-breaking for the Oregon Mountain Tunnel. When state officials headed to the platform to give their dedications, a pack of ape-men suddenly appeared with clubs, guttural sounds, and fierce glares. After some "discussions," the ape-leader drew a large "X" on the wooden platform where the speaker's stand stood. Once the Grants Pass Cavemen had given their needed approval, the tunnel dedication could be finalized — and construction was then able to begin.

Cavemen events ranged from blocking traffic to bidding on constructing the San Francisco–Oakland Bay Bridge (at a cost of 23, 756,000 deer hides) and initiating politicians into their club, including Mark Hatfield, Dewey, and other notables from Shirley Temple to Dennis Day. During their most active years, the Oregon–Grants Pass Cavemen name (by survey) was known by one of every ten people in the United States.

To honor the group, an eighteen-foot, fiberglass Caveman statue was built and dedicated in 1971. When exiting I-5 to downtown Grants Pass, it's the first thing seen in front of the Chamber of Commerce building. The Caveman is not only the mascot for Grants Pass High School, but businesses from towing companies and bowling alleys to auto parts, the bridge, and municipal swimming pool use "Caveman" in their name.

Although the group still meets regularly for lunch, it has been inactive in their public exploits for over fifteen years — a victim of potential liability, aging members, and a society that puts more premium on Facebook, computer websites, and political correctness. But don't be surprised if you see them one day at a Josephine County event. Or if you are lucky enough to be captured.

Sources: Oaks, "Historical Society of Josephine County"; Miller, *Medford Mail Tribune*, November 21, 2010.

Susie Jessel: The
Spiritual Healer

$\mathcal{P}$EOPLE TRAVEL TO OR LIVE IN ASHLAND for different reasons, and for some it is as a place for different ways of healing. From the earliest days, Native Americans believed in the spiritual powers of the area's mineral springs; Ashland's Lithia water and different mineral-spring spas were an attraction from the early 1900s. Although the mineral water demand and springs over time diminished in importance, the town continued to attract those who wanted non-traditional ways of healing.

Susie Jessel was unknown when she and her family moved to Ashland in 1931 to begin her healing practice. Area residents had no idea that she would become a magnet for people searching for help from different conditions ranging from bad colds to arthritis and cancer. Over thirty years, countless thousands of patients filled the local hotels and restaurants — greatly helping the town's economy — as they waited to see the thin woman who became a nationally-recognized healer.

Born in 1891 in North Carolina, Susie was the last of nine children, her mother then being fifty-two years old. She was born with a caul — or a membrane covering her face — that in the local lore meant that she had been born with a gift. When her mother put the baby in the arms of others, she noticed that the infant seemed to have a healing effect. Susie's earliest memory was that of her mother carrying her at night as an infant through the cornfields to be placed into the arms of someone who was ill.

When Susie Jessel was older, the afflicted constantly called upon her to heal their various sicknesses. Susie tried to avoid this by becoming a schoolroom teacher, then as a seamstress, but left this when she met and married Charles H. Jessel. She was busy afterwards raising their six children. Prior to her marriage, however, Susie had a vision of Jesus that called on her to be a healer of the sick, but she couldn't do it now with her new family responsibilities and the hard work required.

Leaving North Carolina, the family first moved to South Dakota before heading to Ashland, where she opened her clinic in 1933. Susie did not advertise or ask money for her services, and told her patients that she wasn't a healer: She said she was only a vehicle for God's work, but also said her ability was given to her by "My Creator." More and more people came to her clinic, as the word spread, and her overriding goal was to heal "suffering humanity."

A sign in the clinic read, "With God All Things Are Possible." Susie Jessel came to her clinic every afternoon and stayed until the last patient was seen, which could be very late at night and turn into sixteen-hour sessions. Bandaged or holding their heads in their hands, the sick and afflicted sat patiently in her waiting room. Once inside a private room, Susie asked the patient not to tell her about their particular ailment. Letting her hands find the location, she passed them over the torso of the sitting patient, stroking the arms from shoulder to hands, as well as the legs if the trouble could be there.

Often times, the veins on the back of her hands would harden and stand up when over the location. She wouldn't make a diagnosis, although perhaps commenting on the condition, and then said when the person could return home. A treatment took from one to three minutes with different sessions before the patient's condition was considered to be improved. No forcing, poking, or manipulation was done. The treatment ended when Susie walked over to a stand, wiped her hands on a wet towel, and her veins returned to normal.

After *True* magazine profiled her nationally in 1943, she was soon seeing up to 600 people a week. Numerous patients traveled thousands of miles to see the healing woman who had the touch. *Time* brought even more recognition with a 1953 article that began: "In a white frame building in Ashland (pop. 8,000), Ore. one afternoon last week, some 140 people packed into seats in a low-ceiling, fetid room, 30 ft. square. Many wore bandages or held to canes and crutches. Some bore the grimace of chronic pain. But all stood up when a thin, wrinkled woman in white nurse's uniform and fancy-print apron with prominent pockets came in. Faith-Healer Susie Jessel raised her arms toward a picture of Christ on the wall and said: 'I dedicate my hands to the Lord…'"

She accepted very little money, a dollar or less per patient tucked inside her apron. Larger gifts were either discouraged or returned; many seemed to give nothing but a word of thanks. Much of the money received was used to house and care for patients who didn't have the resources to stay in Ashland for the longer periods needed for their treatment.

One writer reported, "A count of autos, lined up on the street in front of the healing room, added up to 20 from states from Texas to Maine plus a number with Oregon licenses." Charles Mayo of the Mayo Brothers Clinic in Rochester, New York, was the most famous visitor to the clinic, and physicians in town shared or referred patients to her. A girl came from San Francisco to see the famous healer and benefit from Jessel's treatment for her juvenile rheumatoid arthritis. She became better. When her family moved to Ashland, she set up a coffee shop next to the treatment room to serve Susie's patients and stayed in town for the rest of her life.

Susie died in 1966, but two of her children inherited her gift. Her son, Joe, carried on with her work until he passed away in 1975; her daughter, Alma, then took over. In Ashland alone, there are numerous non-traditional medical practitioners: from massage therapists, chiropractors, and nutritionists to herbalists, psychic healers, and reflexologists. Practitioners work with acupuncture, energy fields, crystals, past-life therapies, deep-tissue work, and other ways.

Susie Jessel's life and work stand out, however, and meet the passage of time.

Sources: *Time*, September 7, 1953; Taylor, *Ashland Daily Tidings*, July 29, 1990; *Ashland Daily Tidings*, August 13, 2005.

Partial Bibliography

Adams, Susan. "The Coffee Cult: How Dutch Bros. Is Turning Its 'Bro-istas' into Wealthy Franchisees," *Forbes*, June 29, 2016.

Aleccia, Jonel. "Harsh Financial Realities Swallowed up Natural History Museum Founders' Vision," *Medford Mail Tribune**, August 3, 1997 (Ralph Wehinger).

Amazon.com: "P.K. Hallinan (Books)" at http://www.amazon.com/.

Anderson, Wing. "Spirit Healer Lauded by Thrice-Aided Writer for Lifetime of Service," *The Complete Aberree*, Vol. 10, No. 3, June 12, 1963 (Susie Jessel).

Applegate Trail Interpretive Center at http://www.rogueweb.com/interpretive/.

Asante Rogue Regional Medical Center website at http://www.asante.org/.

Ashland Daily Tidings*, "Susie Jessel: Village Healer," August 13, 2005.

Ashland Independent Film Festival website at http://www.ashlandfilm.org/.

Asnicar, Tammy: "How Rogue Valley Towns Came to Be," *Mail Tribune*, April 24, 2016.
—"Mercy Flights Earns Its Wings," *Mail Tribune*, April 24, 2016.

Atwood, Kay: *Oregon Encyclopedia*: "Frank Clark (1872-1957)."
—Kay Atwood and Dennis J. Gray: *Oregon History Project*: "Orchard Boom and Bust."

Augusta State University/Reese Library Special Collections: "Edison Marshall" at http://www.augusta.edu/library/reese.

Bane, Vicki. "Lottery Winners, One Year Later!" *People* magazine, March 26, 2007, Vol. 67, No. 12 (The Record Powerball Win).

Barnard, Jeff. "Woman Seeks Good Family to Take Over Mysterious Vortex," *Associated Press: Salt Lake Tribune*, March 14, 2004 (Oregon Vortex).

Battistella, Edwin: *Oregon Encyclopedia*: "Ashland Independent Film Festival."
—"Ebbert T. (Bert) Webber (1921-2006)."
—"Kim Novak."
—"Lithia Motors."
—"Tucker Snow-Cat."

Becker, Hattie B. *The History of the Rogue Valley International-Medford Airport*. Gandee Printing Company: Medford, Oregon, 1995 (Rogue Valley International-Medford Airport).

Biography. "Lisa Rinna" at http://www.biography.com/.

---

* The following newspaper names have been shortened: *Medford Mail Tribune* (*Mail Tribune*), *Ashland Daily Tidings* (*Daily Tidings*), *Grants Pass Daily Courier* (*Daily Courier*) and the *Eugene Register Guard* (*Register Guard*).

Bishop, Greg. "For 41 Years, Town Cheers Danny's Boys," *New York Times*, February 22, 2012 (Danny Miles).

Blackstone Audio at http://www.blackstoneaudio.com/.

Blanchard, G.M. "Lincoln Savage: Josephine County's Man of the Century," *Grants Pass Daily Courier*, September 11, 1995 (Lincoln Savage).

Boom, Tony: "Pieces of the Past," *Mail Tribune*, April 17, 2011 (Beekman House).
—"Restaurant Opening Marks Return of the Nunan Estate," *Mail Tribune*, April 11, 2016 (Neuman Hotel Group).
—"Abundant Snow Puts Mt. Ashland in the Black," *Mail Tribune*, April 20, 2016 (Mt. Ashland Ski Park).

Britt Festival. Generally and "Our History" at http://www.brittfest.org/.

Brown, Richard M. "The 'Lady of the Woods' Revisited," *Nature Notes From Crater Lake*: Volume 21, 1955 at http://www.craterlakeinstitute.com/.

Bryden, Vicki. *Oregon Encyclopedia*: "Edison Marshall (1894-1967)."

Buford, Bill. "Extreme Chocolate," *The New Yorker*, October 29, 2007 (Frederick Schilling/Dagoba Chocolate).

Burke, Anita. "Fruit Growers League Disbands After 96 years," *Mail Tribune*, March 13, 2009 (Eden Valley Orchards).

CBR News. "IDW Founder Ted Adams Discusses the 'Unexpected' Past 15 Years" at www.comicbookresources.com.

Camelot Theatre Company at https://www.camelottheatre.org/.

Chris Korbulic at http://chriskorbulic.com/.

City of Ashland. "Lithia Springs Historic Photos" at http://www.ashland.or.us/.

Climbing.About.Com. "Facts About Mount Shasta" at http://climbing.about.com/.

Colburn, Don. *Oregon Encyclopedia*: "Ben Hur Lampman (1886-1954)."

Conrad, Chris: "Role Call," *Mail Tribune*, April 17, 2011 (Hollywood Lives in Southern Oregon).
—"Continuing Mission," *Mail Tribune*, April 14, 2013 (Jon Courson).
—"Healthy Environment," *Mail Tribune*, April 14, 2013 (Asante).

Cook, Dan. "Will Medford Ever Be Cool?" *Oregon Business*, February 2015 (Lithia; Neuman Hotel Group; Rebuilding of Medford's Downtown).

Cowley, Joe. "Bathing Ghosts," *Mail Tribune*, April 29, 1979 (Ashland-Area Mineral Springs).

Craft Business. "Meet the Maker: Chris and Stuart Freedman, Founders of Fire Mountain Gems and Beads," at http://www.craftbusiness.com/ (or Google search).

Crater Lake Institute: "John Wesley Hillman" at http://www.craterlakeinstitute.com/ (Crater Lake).
—*Fresno Bee*. "Stone Woman of Crater Lake No Longer Mystery," October 23, 1923, at http://www.craterlakeinstitute.com/ (under "Crater Lake National Park News").

Craterian Theatre. "History" at http://www.craterian.org/.

Curler, Dawna: "Bottled Water," JPR: "As It Was," May 26, 2005 (Lithia Water: In Bottles and Fountains).

—*Oregon Encyclopedia*: "Robinson, Regina Dorland (1891-1917)."

—*Oregon Encyclopedia*: "Vance DeBar (Pinto) Colvig (1892-1967)."

Darling, John: "Applegate Fellowship Pastor Takes New Post," *Mail Tribune*, July 19, 2002.

—"A Refuge for Oiled Birds," *Mail Tribune*, September 6, 2002 (Ralph Wehinger).

—"A Vintage Eden," *Mail Tribune*, September 28, 2002 (Eden Valley Orchards).

—"Restorative Property: Buckhorn Mineral Springs," *Mail Tribune*, June 19, 2005 (Ashland-Area Mineral Springs).

—"Shhh! One of the County's Best-kept Secrets," *Mail Tribune*, November 20, 2005 (Palmerton Park).

—"The Fire of 1959," *Daily Tidings*, August 6, 2009 (Ashland Wild Fire of 1959).

—"Seeing Stars," *Mail Tribune*, April 17, 2011 (Oregon Shakespeare Theatre).

—"Ashland Housing Project Targets Helman Area," *Mail Tribune*, July 26, 2011 (Ashland-Area Mineral Springs).

—"Ashland's Blackstone Audio Adds Print Publishing," *Daily Tidings*, February 15, 2016 (Blackstone Audio).

—"From Vision to Reality," *Mail Tribune*, April 13, 2016 (Neuman Hotel Group: Circle of Teran)

—"The Engine That is Southern Oregon University," *Mail Tribune*, April 24, 2016.

—"Going Live," *Mail Tribune*, April 24, 2016 (Bill Smullin).

Davis, Jefferson. "Ghosts and Critters" at http://www.ghostsandcritters.com/ (Ghosts, Spirits, and other Apparitions).

Davis, Jim. "Sabroso: Enjoying the Fruits of Success," *Mail Tribune*, May 9, 1999.

Dear, Tony. "Favorite Designers: H. Chandler Egan" at Cybergolf (http://www.cybergolf.com/).

Decker, Angela. "Children's Author P.K. Hallinan Upbeat amid Adversity," *Mail Tribune*, April 8, 2015.

Del Rio Vineyards. "Our Story" at http://www.delriovineyards.com/.

Denson, Bryan. "Bad Guys Who Hurt Animals? Ashland Forensics Lab Is on the Hunt," the *Oregonian*, June 7, 2009 (U.S. Fish and Forensics Wildlife Laboratory; Ralph Wehinger).

Dick Fosbury. "Dick's Bio" at http://www.dickfosbury.com/.

Dogs for the Deaf. "History" at http://www.dogsforthedeaf.org/.

Dover, Peggy. "Wolf Creek Inn is the I-5 Corridor's Original Rest Area," *Mail Tribune*, July 6, 2014.

Drake University. "Drake Honors Outstanding Alumni Achievements, Loyalty," May 31, 2006 at http://news.drake.edu/ (James Collier).

Duewel, Jeff: "Encounter at the Caves," *Daily Courier*, August 5, 2006 (Southern   Oregon's Bigfoot).

—"Paddling the Globe," *Daily Courier*, May 3, 2015 (Chris Korbulic).

Dunn, Joy B., editor. *Land in Common: An Illustrated History of Jackson County, Oregon*, Medford, Oregon: Southern Oregon Historical Society, 1993, pp. 53-69 (Orchard Boom and Bust).

Dutch Bros. "About Us" at http://dutchbros.com/AboutUs/.

Eagle Point. "History" at http://www.cityofeaglepoint.org/.

Eden Valley Orchards. "A Living Monument" and "History" at http://www.edenvalleyorchards.com/.

Fattig, Paul: "Trail Takes a Historic Turn," *Mail Tribune*, November 29, 1998 (Applegate Trail Interpretive Center).
   —"Speaking up for Sams Valley," *Mail Tribune*, September 19, 1999.
   —"The '64 flood," *Mail Tribune*, December, 19, 2004.
   —"I've Always Believed There is a Bigfoot," *Mail Tribune*, September 3, 2006.
   —"Historians Publish Dorland Robinson Book," *Mail Tribune*, November 29, 2007.
   —"$5 Million Made Available for Taking Out Gold Ray Dam," *Mail Tribune*, July 1, 2009.
   —"1909: The Year That Changed Medford," *Mail Tribune*, November 1, 2009 (Orchard Boom and Bust).
   —"Ski Area Wins Latest Round in Legal Battle," *Mail Tribune*, August 18, 2012 (Mt. Ashland Ski Area).
   —"The (Not So) Great Train Robbery," *Mail Tribune*, October 11, 2012 (D'Autremont Brothers and the Old West's Last Train Robbery).
   —"All Hell Broke Loose," *Mail Tribune*, October 12, 2012 (Columbus Day Storm).
   —"Happy Birthday, ScienceWorks," *Daily Tidings*, December 1, 2012.
   —"A Visionary is Derailed," *Mail Tribune*, December 23, 2012 (Railroads—Joseph Gaston).
   —"The Birth of Medford," *Mail Tribune*, December 25, 2012 (Railroads).

Fire Mountain. "The History of Fire Mountain Gems and Beads" at http://www.firemountaingems.com/.

Fowlkes, Caitlin. "Camp Low Echo Funding Gets a Boost," *Mail Tribune*, June 21, 2016 (Sid DeBoer and Lithia Motors).

Freeman, Mark. "Kayak Krazy," *Mail Tribune*, August 7, 2009 (Chris Korbulic).
   —"Hook, Line & Drifter," *Mail Tribune*, April 14, 2013 (Willie Illingworth).
   —"River Man," *Mail Tribune*, April 14, 2013 (Glen Wooldridge).
   —"Another Reminder of River's Dangers," *Mail Tribune*, July 19, 2013 (Rogue River).

Fundinguniverse.com. "Bear Creek Corp. History" at http://www.fundinguniverse.com/.

Geear, Skip. "The Old Wood House," December 4, 2011 at http://oldwoodhouse.org/.

Gold Hill Historical Society. *Nuggets of News*, September 1992, pp. 1-5 (Ben Hur Lampman).
   —*Nuggets of News*, December 1992, pp. 1-4 (Rhoten Brothers).

Grange Co-op. "About Grange Co-op" at http://www.grangecoop.com/.

Hallinan, P.K: *A Life That Matters: Five Steps to Making a Difference*. Kregel Publications: Grand Rapids, Michigan, 2012.
   —"It's About What We Give Out," *Mail Tribune*, January 11, 2015 (P.K. Hallinan).
   —"Meet PK" at http://www.pkhallinan.com/.

Hellgate Jetboat Excursions (generally) at http://hellgate.com/.

Henry, Kris. "Ex-grid Star, Challengers Coach Maurer Dies," *Mail Tribune*, January 5, 2016 (Andy Maurer).

Historic Jacksonville. "Beekman Bank/Beekman House" at http://www.historicjacksonville.org/.

History.com. "History of Ghost Stories" at http://www.history.com (Ghosts, Spirits, and other Apparitions).

Hoffer, Richard. "The Revolutionary," *Sports Illustrated*, September 14, 2009 (Dick Fosbury).

Hoffman, Marilyn. "Delhi, Macao: Retiree Travels Globe to Help Restore Heritage Sites," *Christian Science Monitor*, July 22, 1988 (Robby Collins).

Holly Theatre at http://www.hollytheatre.org/.

Horn, Huston. "Steps to the Stars," *Sports Illustrated*, February 3, 1964 (John Day).

Hsuan, Amy. "Dutch Bros. Coffee Co-founder Dies," the *Oregonian*, October 15, 2009.

Hughley, Marty. "Camelot's Cinderella Story: Talent Theater Company Gets a $2.4 Million New Home," the *Oregonian*, July 23, 2011 (Camelot).

Iowa State University. "Raymond F. Baker Center for Plant Breeding" at http://www.plantbreeding.iastate.edu/ (James Collier).

Jackson, Kerby: "Finding Gold in Oregon" at http://www.oregongold.net/.
—Oregongold.net: "Great Gobs of Gold Abound in Southern Oregon" (Mattie's Nugget).

Jackson County: "Emergency Management" (1997 Ashland Flood).
—"Rural and Suburban Lands Element: Applegate Rural Service Center" at http://www.co.jackson.or.us/(Applegate Valley).
—"Rural and Suburban Lands Element: Sams Valley Rural Service Center" (Sams Valley).

Jay, Susan. "Pace of Growth Challenges RCC," *Mail Tribune*, April 22, 1999 (Rogue Valley Community College).

Jefferson Public Radio. "State of Jefferson" at http://ijpr.org/.

Jim/John Belushi Biographies at http://www.biography.com/.

Jones, Dan. "The Last Mile(s)," *Mail Tribune*, February 6, 2016 (Danny Miles).

Jones, Greg. Email to the author, August 19, 2016 (The Vintners and Their Wine).

Kids Unlimited of Oregon at http://kuoregon.org/.

Kettler, Bill: "Enjoy the Views and Some History at London Peak," *Mail Tribune*, January 7, 2005 (Wolf Creek Inn).
—"Snapshot: The Church at Golden," *Mail Tribune*, February 16 2011 (The Golden Ghost Town of the Valley).

Kingsnorth, Carolyn. "Father of Southern Oregon's Orchard, Wine & Horticulture Industries," *Jacksonville Review*, July 2014 (The Vintners and their Wine).

Kramer, George: *Camp White: City in the Agate Desert*; White City, Oregon: Camp White 50th Anniversary Committee, 1992.
—*Topsides: The A.S.V. and Helen Bundy Carpenter House*, National Register of Historic Places Nomination Form, 2004 (Carpenter Foundation).
—"The Interstate Highway System in Oregon: A Historic Overview," Heritage Research Associates: Eugene (Oregon), May 2004.
—*Oregon Encyclopedia*: "Camp White."
—"Carpenter Foundation and Alfred (1881-1974) & Helen Bundy (1886-1961)."
—"Interstate 5 in Oregon."

Kramer, Ron: *Pioneer Mikes: A History of Radio and Television in Oregon*, Western States Museum of Broadcasting and JPR Foundation, Oct 15, 2009 (KMED/Bill Virgin; William B. Smullin).
—Western States Museum of Broadcasting: "Bill Virgin: Southern Oregon's Radio Pioneer" at http://wsmb.org.
—Western States Museum of Broadcasting: "History of Radio in Southern Oregon" at http://wsmb.org (KMED/Bill Virgin; William B. Smullin).

LaLande, Jeff: *Oregon Encyclopedia*: "The Applegate Trail" (Applegate Trail Interpretive Center).
—"Ashland."
—"Good Government Congress (Jackson County Rebellion)."
—"Biscuit Fire of 2002."
—"Columbus Day Storm (1962)."
—"Harry & David/Bear Creek Orchards."
—"Mt. Ashland."
—"Mt. McLoughlin."
—"Siskiyou Pass."
—"State of Jefferson."
—"The Council of Table Rock."
—"Two-Bits, the World War II Lookout Dog."
—"Chipmunk-Chasing Dog Becomes War Hero," JPR: "As It Was," January 22, 2015.

LaPlante, Margaret. *Eagle Point: Images of America*, Arcadia Publishing: Charleston, South Carolina, 2012 (Eagle Point).

Landers, Meg. "Higher Education Center on Track for Fall 2008 classes," *Mail Tribune*, November 9, 2007 (Rogue Community College).

Lang, Frank A. *Oregon Encyclopedia*: "Abraham Lincoln Savage (1864-1950)" at https://oregonencyclopedia.org/.

Leary, Kathleen F. *Oregon Encyclopedia*: "Oregon Shakespeare Festival" at https://oregonencyclopedia.org/.

Lemon, Sarah. "Giving Back," *Mail Tribune*, May 31, 2007 (The Record Powerball Win).
—"The High Point," *Mail Tribune*, April 17, 2011 (Grange Co-op).
—"A Century of Divine Providence," *Mail Tribune*, May 22, 2011 (Providence Hospital).

Los Angeles Times. "Animal Trainer Roy Kabat Dies," November 7, 1986 (Dogs for the Deaf).

Macomber, Paul. "Dip Stick Dream Dries up in Fight Over Bankruptcy," *Mail Tribune*, July 2, 1994 (Mean, Stream Machine).

Mahoney, Barbara. *Oregon Encyclopedia*: "Glenn Jackson (1902-1980)."

Mail Tribune: "Enos M. Rhoten, Pioneer Miner of Rogue, Dies," December 13, 1931 (The Golden Rhoten Family of Giants).
—"Since You Asked: Old Dairy Holds Fond Memories," February 16, 1999 (Snider Dairy).
—"Florence Schneider Left Indelible Mark," December 30, 1999 (Bill and Florence Schneider).
—"Robertson E. Collins," May 28, 2003 (Robby Collins).
—"Obituary: Ebbert True (Bert) Webber," April 23, 2006 (Bert Weber).

—"Where Can You Find 'Old' Highway 99?" April 22, 2007 (I-5; Cars in the Valley; Siskiyou Summit).

—"Why a Viaduct?" April 22, 2007 (I-5, Medford, and Glen Jackson).

—"How Does Medford Get its Water?" April 22, 2007 (Water Systems of Medford).

—"Glenn Jackson King of the Roads," April 22, 2007 (Glen Jackson).

—"When Did Electricity First Arrive in the Rogue Valley?" April 22, 2007 (When Electricity First Came).

—"When Was Lithia Park Built?" April 22, 2007 (Lithia Park).

—"Where Did These Stairs Lead?" April 22, 2007 (Lithia Water: In Bottles and Fountains).

—"Where is the 'Shady Cove' in Shady Cove?" April 22, 2007 (Shady Cove).

—"Why Are They Called the Black Tornado?" April 22, 2007 (Medford football).

—"Central Point was Wagon Roads Hub," August 12, 2009 (Central Point).

—"Celebrities in Southern Oregon—Sure," October 17, 2010 (Hollywood Lives in Southern Oregon).

—"Oregon Rails to California—a Timeline," December 23, 2012 (Railroads).

—"Our Legacy in Brief: Angus Bowmer," April 14, 2013 (Oregon Shakespeare Festival).

—"James Collier Funds Elevator at the Holly Theatre," February 24, 2016 (James Collier).

Mann, Danielle L. *Oregon Encyclopedia*: "Blackstone Audio, Inc."

Mann, Damian: "Actor, Husband Resolve River Permit Issue," *Mail Tribune*, Sept. 1, 2009 (Kim Novak).

—"Pouring It On," *Mail Tribune*, March 12, 2013 (Medford's Water System).

—"Building the 'Barneburg Hilton'," *Mail Tribune*, April 14, 2013 (Rogue Valley Manor).

—"Ashlanders Plan Major Upgrade for Red Lion." *Mail Tribune*, August 22, 2013 (Building of Medford's Downtown).

—"Good to the Last Drop," *Mail Tribune*, April 14, 2013 (Medford's Water System).

—"Actor Jim Belushi Joins in Holly Theatre Drive in Medford, Will Appear in Parade," *Mail Tribune*, April 7, 2015.

—"$20 Million to Upgrade 3 Facilities," *Mail Tribune*, April 15, 2016 (Asante).

—"Sam Jennings Cited by City," *Mail Tribune*, May 11, 2016 (Rebuilding of Medford's Downtown).

Mark, Steven R: *Oregon Encyclopedia*: "Crater Lake National Park."

—*Oregon Encyclopedia*: "Oregon Caves National Monument."

Mason, Maryann: "Lithia Mineral Water Has Long History," JPR: "As It Was," February 26, 2009.

—*Oregon Encyclopedia*: "Britt Music Festival."

McLoughlin Memorial Association at http://www.mcloughlinhouse.org/ (Mt. McLoughlin).

Mercy Flights at http://www.mercyflights.com/.

Miller, Bill: "From Worst to First: The History of the City's Water System," *Mail Tribune*, May 31, 2009 (The Water Systems of Medford).

—"Hellgate Canyon Rogue River Landmark is a Hollywood Favorite," *Mail Tribune*, June 21, 2009 (Films Made in Southern Oregon).

—"The 'Wizard of Berkeley' & the D'Autremont Brothers," *Mail Tribune*, August 30, 2009.

—"Keeping a 'Tailholt' Attitude," *Mail Tribune*, January 17, 2010 (City of Rogue River).

—"The Whispering Walls of Fort Lane," *Mail Tribune*, March 28, 2010 (Table Rocks).

—"Collier's Impossible Hole in the Mountain," *Mail Tribune*, November 21, 2010 (Early Days of Cars in the Valley; Grants Pass Cavemen; Redwood Highway).

—"Betrayal? Railroad Misses Jacksonville," *Mail Tribune*, December 25, 2012 (Railroads).

—"New Way to Ship Goods or Travel Eases Isolation in Rogue Valley," *Mail Tribune*, December 27, 2012 (Railroads).

—"A River Runs into It," *Mail Tribune*, April 14, 2013 (Lost Creek Lake/Jess Dam).

—"Jump-Start for an Industry," *Mail Tribune*, April 14, 2013 (Early Days of Cars in the Valley).

—"Something to Draw On," *Mail Tribune*, April 14, 2013 (Architects Who Changed the Towns).

Mims, Steve. "Ex-Duck Andy Maurer Dies at Age 67," *Register Guard*, January 5, 2016.

Monroe, Bill. "Where's Willie? Everywhere, and Always with Us," the *Oregonian*, May 29, 2010 (Willie Illingworth's Driftboats).

Montgomery, Teresa. *Oregon Encyclopedia*: "Southern Oregon University."

Moore, Kim. "Preserving the Legacy," *Oregon Business*, July/August 2015 (Harry & David/Bear Creek).

Morgan, Nick: "Creating a Gem," *Mail Tribune*, April 14, 2013 (Lithia Park).
—"Redwood Highway," *Mail Tribune*, May 23, 2014 (Films Made in Southern Oregon).
—"Lisa Rinna Remembers her Father," *Mail Tribune*, January 22, 2016.

Mt. Ashland Ski Area. "A Historical Perspective" at http://mtashland.com/.

Mullaly, Alice. "Rock Point House Provides Stagecoach Break," JPR: "As It Was," September 14, 2011 (Del Rio Vineyards).

New York Times: "Obituary: Bill Bowerman, 88, Nike Co-Founder, Dies," December 27, 1999.
—"Obituary: Schneider, Florence Hemley," December 31, 1999.

Newberry, Daniel. "Nordic Skiers Race in the Tracks of John Day," *Mail Tribune*, February 22, 2013 (John Day).

Oaks, Michael. "Historical Society of Josephine County: Oregon Cavemen" at http://roguerivervalley.com/historical_society/oregon_cavemen.htm (Grants Pass Cavemen).

Oregon Bigfoot at http://www.oregonbigfoot.com/ (Southern Oregon's Bigfoot).

Oregon Dept. of Fish and Wildlife. "Cole Rivers Hatchery" at http://www.dfw.state.or.us/ (Lost Creek Lake/Jess Dam).

Oregon Encyclopedia at https://oregonencyclopedia.org/:
Kay Atwood. "Frank Clark (1872-1957)."
Ed Battistella: "Kim Novak."
—"Ebbert T. (Bert) Webber (1921-2006)."
—"Lithia Motors."
—"Tucker Snow-Cat."

Vicki Bryden. "Edison Marshall (1894-1967)."

Don Colburn. "Ben Hur Lampman (1886-1954)."

Dawna Curler: "Regina Dorland Robinson (1891-1917)."
  —"Vance DeBar (Pinto) Colvig (1892-1967)."

George Kramer: "Camp White."
  —"Carpenter Foundation and Alfred (1881-1974) & Helen Bundy (1886-1961)."
  —"Interstate 5 in Oregon".

Jeff LaLande: "The Applegate Trail (Applegate Trail Interpretive Center)."
  —"Ashland."
  —"Good Government Congress (Jackson County Rebellion). "
  —"Biscuit Fire of 2002."
  —"Columbus Day Storm (1962)."
  —"Harry & David/Bear Creek Orchards."
  —"Mt. Ashland."
  —"Mt. McLoughlin."
  —"Siskiyou Pass."
  —"State of Jefferson."
  —"The Council of Table Rock."
  —"Two-Bits, the World War II Lookout Dog."

Kathleen F. Leary:"Oregon Shakespeare Festival."

Barbara Mahoney. Glenn Jackson (1902-1980)."

Danielle L. Mann. "Blackstone Audio, Inc."

Steven R. Mark: "Crater Lake National Park."
  —"Oregon Caves National Monument."

Maryann Mason. "Britt Festival."

Teresa Montgomery. "Southern Oregon University."

Joe Peterson. "Chautauqua in Oregon."

Dennis Powers: "City of Gold Hill."
  —"Gold Ray Dam."

Phyliss Reynolds. "Lithia Park."

Oregon History Project at http//oregonhistoryproject.org:
  —Cain Allen. "Ashland Chautauqua, 1895" (Chautauqua in Ashland).
  —Kay Atwood and Dennis Gray. "Orchard Boom and Bust."

Oregon Shakespeare Festival ("about") at http://www.osfashland.org/about/.

Oregon State Parks. "Wolf Creek State Heritage Site" at http://www.oregonstateparks.org/.

Oregon Vortex at http://www.orenvortex.com/.

Pacific Northwest Books at http:ww.pnwbooks.com.

Pahl, Michelle. "U.S. 'Animal Detives' Fight Crime in Forensics Lab." *National Geographic Today*, April 2, 3 (U.S. Fish and Forensics Wildlife Laboratory).

Paulson, Dash. "The End of the Oon University System," *Eugene Weekly.com*, July 9, 2015 (SOU).

Pet Meds Blog: "Interview with Van Maurice, General Manager, Dogs for the Deaf," October 17, 2012.

Peterson, Joe. *Oregon Encyclopedia*: "Chautauqua in Oregon" (Chautauqua in Ashland).

Pfeil, Ryan: "The Stars Were Out," *Mail Tribune*, October 23, 2012 (Films Made in Southern Oregon).
—"A Most Useful Citizen," *Mail Tribune*, April 14, 2013 (Ashland: McCall).

Plain, Robert. "Memories of Major Flood Remain Clear in Ashland," *Mail Tribune*, January 1, 2007 (Ashland 1997 Flood).

Powers, Dennis M: *Images of America: Gold Hill*. Arcadia Publishing: Charleston, South Carolina, 2010, pgs. 7-8, 21, et al (Mattie's Nugget); pp. 56 (Ghosts); pgs. 79-84 (Sams Valley).
—"Neuman Hotel Group: The Neuman Family and How it All Began…" at http://neumanhotelgroup.com/about/.
—*Oregon Encyclopedia*: "Gold Hill."
—"Gold Ray Dam."
—"Vineyard Traces Roots to Early Town of Rock Point, Oregon," JPR: "As It Was," June 29, 2009 (Del Rio Vineyards).
—"Wealthy Easterners Flock to the Valley," JPR: "As It Was," September 7, 2009 (Orchard Boom and Bust).
—"Norton Eddings Gains Recognition as Outstanding Stage Driver" JPR: "As It Was," August 16, 2011 (Stagecoaches and their Drivers).
—"Pioneer Woman Runs Stagecoach Station after Husband's Death," JPR: "As It Was," August 22, 2011 (Stagecoaches and their Drivers).
—"Automobile Brings Striking Changes to Region." JPR: "As It Was," August 24, 2011 (Early Days of Cars in the Valley; Redwood Highway).
—"Electricity Arrives in Grants Pass in 1889," JPR: "As It Was," October 11, 2011.
—"Rhoten Brothers Follow Gold Trails to Source," JPR: At Was, May 10, 2012.
—"California-Oregon Power Co. Dominates Region," JP: "As It Was," July 6, 2012 (When Electricity first came to the Region).

Raider News. "Comic Genus: Ted Adams Puts his Comic Gus to Work," Spring 2016.

Reynolds, Phyllis. *Oregon Encyclopedia*: "Lithia Park."

Richter, Patti. "In this Section: Indians, Gold and a Newspaper's Birth," *Daily Courier*, March 11, 2010 (Grants Pass).

Ristow, Teresa: "The Big Push," *Mail Tribune*, April 14, 23 (Mt. Ashland Ski Area).
—"School of Hard Knocks," *Mail Tribune*, April 14, 20 (Elmo Stevenson, SOU).

Rogue Creamery. "An Historical Overview" at http://www.roguecreamery.com/.

Rogue Credit Union. "The History of Rogue Credit Union" at https://www.roguecu.org/.

Rogue Valley County Club. "History" at http://rvcc.com

Rogue Valley Manor at http://www.retirement.org/rvm/.

Root, Jim and Company. "About" at http://www.jimroocompany.com/ (Roots, Sabroso, and Tree Top).

Russo, Edward. "Eugene Dealer Snares 165-year-old Con 'Beaver Coin,'" *Register Guard*, March 4, 2015 (Beaver Money).

Savage, Sam. RedOrbit: "Monster in the Woods: the Biscuire" at http://www.redorbit.com/.

Scafani, David. "Snider's Dairy." *Southern Oregon Heritage*, February 2003, vol. 5, no.

ScienceWorks. "History" and latest exhibits at http://www.scienceworksmuseum.org/.

Seattle Times. "Oregon's Other Trail," January 6, 1999 (Applegate Trail Interpretive Center).

Silow, Frank. "A Splash in the Market," *Mail Tribune*, April 14, 2010 (Mean, Stream
　　Machine).

Southern Oregon Historical Society: "The Hanley Farm and the Family" at http://www.sohs.org/.
　　—"Colvig, Pinto."

Specht, Sanne: "Rogue River Mayor Dick Skevington Dies at 84," *Mail Tribune*, September
　　20, 2008 (Palmerton Park).
　　—"Jacksonville Honors Artist Eugene Bennett," *Mail Tribune*, September 23, 2010.
　　—"Artist Eugene Bennett Leaves Legacy of Talent, Community," *Mail Tribune*,
　　November 5, 2010.
　　—"Cheesemaker Vella Dies at 83," *Mail Tribune*, June 14, 2011 (Rogue Creamery).
　　—"The Power of Community," *Mail Tribune*, April 14, 2013 (ScienceWorks).

Spokesman-Review. "WSU Graduate, Prominent Oregon High School Coach Spiegelberg
　　Dies At 76," March 24, 1996 (The Heyday of Medford Football).

Squires, Jennifer. "Dagoba Chocolate Founder Frederick Schilling," *Daily Tidings*,
　　October 18, 2005 (Frederick Shilling/Dagoba Chocolate).

Stiles, Greg: "Top Arts Patron," *Mail Tribune*, January 19, 2000 (Sabroso).
　　—"Channel 5 Celebrates 50 Years," *Mail Tribune*, August 3, 2003 (William B. Smullin).
　　—"Adroit t Adapting," *Mail Tribune*, May 2, 2007 (Adroit Construction).
　　—"Tree Top Buys Medford-based Sabroso," *Mail Tribune*, October 27, 2008.
　　—"A Cat with Teeth," *Mail Tribune*, April 14, 2010 (Tucker Sno-Cat).
　　—"Bowerman Among Medford's Greats," *Mail Tribune*, December 17, 2010
　　（Medford's Nike Connection: Bill Bowerman).
　　—"Commercial Projects Create Rogue Valley Construction Mini Boom," *Mail Tribune*,
　　November 20, 2011 (Adroit Construction).
　　—"Inside Lithia's Glass Walls." *Mail Tribune*, August 9, 2012 (Building Medford's
　　Downtown).
　　—"Southern Oregon Wine Industry Growing Like a Vine," *Mail Tribune*, August 20, 2015.
　　—"Providence to Be First Tenant at Stewart Meadows Village," *Mail Tribune*,
　　March 8, 2016 (Providence Medford Medical Center).
　　—"Del Rio Vineyards Buys Historic Birdseye Property for $2 million," *Mail Tribune*,
　　April 21, 2016.
　　—"Lithia Revenue Hits $2.1 Billion in Second Quarter," *Mail Tribune*, July 28, 2016.
　　—"Dagoba Founder Frederick Schilling Now Global Player," *Mail Tribune*,
　　December 28, 2016.

Stumbo, Stacy. "OK Coral an Open-air Dining Experience Close to Nature." *Grants Pass
　　Daily Courier*, Febnary 21, 2013 (Hellgate Jetboat).

Stumbo, Stacy and Patti Richter. "First County Seat was Sailor Diggins, Later Called Waldo,"
　　Daily Courier, March 11, 2010 (Grants Pass).

Swanson, Gary: ActiveRain.com: "Ghost Town of Golden, Oregon" at http://activerain.com/.
　　—"Ghosts in Southern Oregon's National Monument" at http://bigfoothikes.blogspot.com.

Talent Historical Society at http://www.talenthistory.org/.

Taylor, Ted. "Heal: Ashland A Hotbed of Offbeat Medical Practices," *Daily Tidings*, July 29, 1990 (Susie Jessel).

Thomas, Teresa. "Demolition of Blighted Houses Paves Way for Kids Unlimited Expansion," *Mail Tribune*, March 23, 2016.

Time. "Medicine: Straw for the Drowning," September 7, 1953 (Susie Jessel).

Truwe, Ben: "Southern Oregon History, Revised," among other links at
   http://id.mind.net/~truwe/tina/s.o.history.html.
   —"Holly Theatre."
   —"The Orchard Boom and Bust."
   —"Who Was W. J. Bennet?" (Architects Who Changed Towns).
   —"William Mackey: Althouse Creek in the Early Days." (Ghost Towns of the Illinois Valley).
   —"Wm. Mackey: Sailor Diggings Pioneer Town of Gold Production."

Tucker Sno-Cat at http://www.sno-cat.com/.

Turnquist, Kristi. "Interview with Actress Kim Novak, Who Lives in Oregon and Is Revisiting Her Cinematic Past," the *Oregonian*, July 31, 2010.

Twitchell, Cleve: "A Woodville, A Rogue River or a Tailholt by Any Other Name," *Mail Tribune*, February 10, 1991 (The City of Rogue River).
   —"Historic Dwelling Housed Writer, Practitioner," *Mail Tribune*, December 13, 1997 (Edison Marshall).
   —"MT's Pulitzer-winning Editorials Tackled Corruption, Violence," *Mail Tribune*, November 2, 2009 (Ballot Stealing Caper).

Ulmer, Jerry. "Class 6A Girls Basketball: South Medford Ready to Make Its Mark," the *Oregonian*, March 6, 2012 (Kids Unlimited).

U.S. Bureau of Land Management. "How Did the Table Rocks Form?" at http://www.blm.gov/.

U.S. Fish and Wildlife Service. "Our Lab's History" at https://www.fws.gov/lab/ (Forensics Lab).

U.S. Forest Service. "Lower Rogue River" at http://www.fs.usda.gov/ (Rogue River).

U.S. National Park Service: "Crater Lake: Frequently Asked Questions" at http://www.nps.gov.
   —"Jacksonville National History District."
   —"Redwood National Park/History Basic Data." Chapter 9B: Roads, Sept. 1, 1969 (Redwood Highway).
   —"The Underworld of Oregon Caves: Human Story."

Varble, Bill: "Doctoring Differed in RVMC's Early Days," *Mail Tribune*, May 3, 1998 (Asante).
   —"'Sweeney' Brings Life to Camelot's New Stage," *Mail Tribune*, June 26, 2011 (James Collier).
   —"Craterian Renamed for Donor," *Mail Tribune*, August 31, 2012 (Craterian; James Collier).
   —"A Man with a Plan," *Mail Tribune*, April 14, 2013.
   —"Medford's Lisa Rinna Joins 'Real Housewives of Beverly Hill,'" *Mail Tribune*, November 28, 2014.

Vella Cheese Company. "The History of Vella Cheese" at http://www.vellacheese.com.

Verrier, Richard, "Comic Book Firm IDW Publishing to Expand into TV," *LA Times*, October 17, 2013 (Ted Adams).

Waymarking.com/Hospitals. "Providence Medford Medical Center" at www.waymarking.com.

Webber, Bert and Margie. *Railroading in Southern Oregon and the Founding of Medford*. Ye Galleon Press: First edition, June 1985 (The Story and History of the Railroads).

Weisman, Jonathan. "Harmonic Convergence at Mt. Shasta: New Age Dawning on Fewer Than Expected," *Los Angeles Times*, August 16, 1987 (Mt. Shasta).

Wheeler, Sam. "Southern Oregon University's Building Boom Adds up to $130 million," *Mail Tribune*, March 17, 2015 (SOU).

Wikipedia: "Chandler Egan" at https://www.wikipedia.org/.
—"Christmas Flood of 1964."
—"Harry Hamlin" (Lisa Rinna).
—"Kyle Singler."
—"Rogue River" (Oregon).
—"Samuel Colver" (Phoenix).

Wildlife Images. "About Us" and "Wildlife Images: Message from Dave Siddon, Director" at http://www.wildlifeimages.org/.

Willamette Heritage Center. "Beaver Money" at https://willametteheritage.org.

Wines Northwest. "Rogue Valley and Applegate Valley" at http://www.winesnw.com/rogue.html (The Vintners and Their Wine).

Acknowledgments

*T*HIS IS TO ACKNOWLEDGE THE STAFF of the Southern Oregon Historical Society's (SOHS) Research Library, who worked so politely and professionally in providing many of the images in this book. The ones who spent the most time—and I thank specifically—were Billie Taylor, Vicki Bryden, Pat Harper, and Rick Black. Rick was a master with image technology, while Billie helped with our reviewing boxes of files. Showing their commitment to documenting history, SOHS and its research library did not charge for these images. In this regard, I thank specifically Pat Harper, Vicki Bryden, and the governing board of the SOHS. This historical society deserves so much credit for what it does with volunteers.

I thank Janet Sessions of the Gold Hill Historical Society (GHHS) for its permission in running images that are so credited. Where also indicated, images are credited to other sources, of which I appreciate their assistance.

Jeff LaLande, George Kramer, Larry Mullaly, Alice Mullaly, Greg Jones (SOU Professor), Sylvia Leatherman, Ben Truwe, and Vicki Bryden—for starters—deserve special mention for their editing of important articles. Jeff, George, and Ben also shared images that helped make this book; and Jeff LaLande stands out on his manuscript review with fine edits and observations.

Further, Dawna Curler, Steve Mark, Phyliss Reynolds, Paul Fattig, Bill Miller, Ron Kramer, and Ed Battistella also reviewed different articles with helpful comments. I hope that I haven't missed anyone. Individual entities additionally reviewed specific works involving their activities, but they are too numerous to mention—but also with my thanks.

I also thank Bill Meyer (KMED) and Bill Ashenden (Bi-Coastal Media) for their support of this project, including the many hours I have enjoyed with Bill Meyer on our "Past and Present" show on KMED that is into its fifth year and has been so fun—plus still going strong! And to "As It Was" with Kernan Turner on Jefferson Public Radio.

Last but not least, I thank Harley Patrick who is the owner and publisher of Hellgate Press, this book's angel. He worked closely in reviewing every page of the manuscript, arranged for many of the images that are shown without an SOHS or GHHS credit, and kept to our schedule. We were friends before this project, but are close friends now—thanks Harley!

About the Author

Dennis Powers was a full-time attorney specializing in business law before turning his concentration to writing nearly three decades ago. He is the author of fifteen published nonfiction books, among other publications, along with numerous fictional, poetry, magazine, and newspaper works. Dennis's maritime series—*The Raging Sea, Treasure Ship, Sentinel of the Seas, Taking the Sea,* and *Tales of the Seven Seas*—placed him on national and regional book tours. See www.dennispowersbooks.com for all his works.

A graduate of the Harvard Business School, he is the Professor Emeritus of Business Law at Southern Oregon University in Ashland, Oregon, where he resides with his wife (Judy), one cat, and libraries of books.

He has written over 200 scripts for Jefferson Public Radio's "As It Was" historical radio program, as well as over 200 historical treatises for his weekly radio program, "Past and Present," on radio station KMED (1440-AM, 106.7-FM, 99.3 FM--Grants Pass). Dennis authored the *Images of America: Gold Hill* book and assigned all of the royalties to the Gold Hill Historical Society. His ventures into the digital world include the CD (2013) entitled: "Past and Present: What You Might Not Know (But Want To) About Southern Oregon History" (see http://southernoregonpastandpresent.com).

About the Publisher

*F*OUNDED IN 1997, HELLGATE PRESS IS NAMED after the historic Hellgate Canyon on the Rogue River, which was the first river in the United States to be designated as "wild and scenic." So, we like to think that the books we publish reflect the rugged yet subtle nature of this incredible river canyon. While our primary niche is military history and veteran memoirs, we also specialize in non-fiction travel adventure and historical and adventure fiction. Recently, we have begun adding local and regional history to our list of genres, as is evident with this book.

In addition to Hellgate Press, its parent company, L&R Publishing, LLC, also publishes books under the imprints Grid Press (covering family issues, relationships, political humor, and others) and Paloma Books (books for children, tweens and young adults).

After working for the original owners of Hellgate Press, current owner-publisher Harley Patrick purchased the company in 2007. Prior to that, he earned an MA in Literary Nonfiction from the University of Oregon and served as the Marketing Director for the Southern Oregon Historical Society (SOHS) from 2005-2007. He and his wife currently reside in Ashland.

To see a full listing of our books, visit us online at:

www.hellgatepress.com and *www.palomabooks.com.*